THEOLOGY
FOR A
LIBERATING CHURCH

THEOLOGY
FOR A
LIBERATING CHURCH

The New Praxis of Freedom

Alfred Hennelly, S.J.

Georgetown University Press
WASHINGTON, D.C.

Library of Congress Cataloging-in-Publication Data

Hennelly, Alfred T.
   Theology for a liberating church : the new praxis of freedom /
Alfred Hennelly.
      p.   cm.
   Includes bibliographical references.
   ISBN 0-87840-473-2.   ISBN 0-87840-474-0 (pbk.)
   1. Freedom (Theology)   2. Liberation theology.   I. Title.
BT810.2.H46 1989
230--dc19   88-24701
                                                 CIP

For my mother, Nora Curran Hennelly,
my first teacher in the life of the Spirit
and still the best.

Contents

Acknowledgements

To begin with, my sincerest thanks are owed to a number of institutions that were of invaluable help to me in the research for this book. These include the staff and facilities of the Woodstock Theological Center Library at Georgetown University, the libraries of the Catholic University of America, the Maryknoll Missionaries in Maryknoll, N.Y., and the Library of Congress, especially its Latin American department. I am also very grateful to Fordham University for a research grant that contributed greatly to the completion of the manuscript, as well as to the Woodstock Theological Center community for its gracious hospitality and encouragement during my trips to Washington.

On a personal level, the contributions to my thought from various conferences, discussions, and even arguments are too numerous to record. Of singular importance were the suggestions and criticisms of the manuscript by Joseph Fitzpatrick, S.J., and Peter Schineller, S.J. My greatest debt, however, is to my editor, John Breslin, S.J., who displayed great patience and skill in helping to shape a manuscript into a book. But I, of course, take full responsibility for its contents.

I am also indebted to *Theological Studies* for permission to use material from an earlier version of Chapter Three that appeared in that periodical's December, 1977, issue as "Theological Method: The Southern Exposure," as well as to *Thought* for permission to use material from a version of Chapter Two that appeared in its June, 1988, issue as "Liberation Theology: Origins, Content, Impact."

Prologue
The Precious Tincture of Rage

In what has been a rather extensive experience of reading and commenting on theological literature, I have always felt grateful when the authors in question revealed some information concerning the circumstances or events that prompted them to write the book, the purposes or goals they were seeking, and finally some explanation of why they thought their contribution to understanding the ways of God to human beings was really important. In other words, I wanted to know why I should read this book rather than the myriad others that gleam in the theological firmament.

Because of this characteristic or quirk in my own reading habits, I will offer no further apologia for beginning this book with some comments on the circumstances that led to it, as well as a statement of my own purpose and goals in writing it. And I will give special attention to elucidating my reasons for believing that the ideas discussed here from the heart of the Third World have enormous importance for readers in the First World, be they professional theologians or merely companions in the adventure of following Jesus Christ as the dawn of the third millennium of his birth draws near.

The circumstances, then, that eventually led to this work can be traced back to my theological education during the years that immediately preceded the Second Vatican Council, which lasted from 1962 until 1965. The seminary buildings constituted a perfect symbol of the Tridentine church, perched in quiet contemplation on a knoll in the Maryland countryside, and far removed from the problems and distractions of the contemporary world. If anything, the symbolism grew even more striking in the classrooms inside the seminary, where the students faced the daily struggle to understand the mystery of God in Latin, while preparing their mettle to fend off the examination questions of their professors, who had attained a remarkable fluency in that dead language. As with our sylvan location, therefore, our intellectual geography developed miles apart from "the world," in this case a reality located twenty miles to the east in Baltimore and environs.

The one event that breached the walls of this formidable intellectual fortress occurred during my second year of theological studies. It was then that Fr. John Courtney Murray returned to the seminary classroom after seventeen years of writing, lecturing, and editing the periodical *Theological Studies*. His very tall and distinguished appearance, combined with a certain savoir faire, an English accent that belied his New York City origins, and a gift for mellifluent English prose, made his lectures an instant success. Even more memorable, however, from my own point of view, was the experience of working along with Murray as an assistant editor of *Theological Studies*. It was only in the office of that periodical and during the famous "picnics" that Murray sponsored for his staff that I began to become acquainted with and to discuss in depth such worldly issues as the correct relationship between church and state, the problem of religious freedom, the interface of religion and culture, indeed the entire spectrum of issues that were later to surface in the most important document of Vatican II, the *Pastoral Constitution on the Church in the Modern World*. Murray once remarked that we are all apprentices in the uses of freedom; certainly I will always be indebted to him for the beginning of my own apprenticeship in that virtue, which has formed a central axis in my own reflection ever since.

In the ensuing years, during my doctoral studies, I began to explore in considerable depth the scriptural foundations of Christian freedom, which brought me face to face with the profound analysis of St. Paul. In a study of First Corinthians, I was deeply impressed by the revelation of Paul's apostolic psychology, as epitomized in his assertion that "though I am free from all men, I have made myself a slave to all, that I might win the more" (9:19). In this chapter Paul transforms the Stoic notion of freedom in a brilliant restatement of the gospel ethic as freedom for others, a freedom sharply imprinted with a discipline of service. Of course, it is obvious that the particular question of consuming idol-meat in the *macellum* of Corinth is no longer a problem that vexes the modern church; but Paul's much broader synthesis of the issues it raised with regard to questions of freedom, honesty, service, love, and their integration, certainly has great relevance today.

Of equal importance is Paul's energetic defense of Christian freedom in his Letter to the Galatians, which some have not hesitated to refer to as "the gospel of Christian freedom." It is very necessary, however, to emphasize clearly the shadow side of the reality of Christian freedom, an aspect that I had to deal with during my studies. I believe that this dark side was most bluntly and starkly expressed by John L. McKenzie in an introduction to a book on the Letter to the Galatians. "There is surely no less urgency," he writes, "to proclaim and to defend Christian freedom in the contemporary Church than there was in the Church of the apostles." And this situation has come to pass for one reason: "Our church-talk does not deal with human freedom; we are much more facile when we speak of law, which may suggest that we have learned more from the Pharisees than we have from Paul."[1] In other words, it seems that historically Catholicism has much more frequently appeared as a community of law rather than as a community of love, in spite of the fact that the latter obligation was the only one imposed by Jesus Christ on all his followers.

Thus we come face to face with what I consider the basic paradox of the Christian churches: the sublimity of Paul's teaching on the absolute necessity of Christian freedom issuing in self-giving love vis-à-vis the perennial pharisaic temptation to seek the community of security and order that results from the twin bulwarks of fear and the law. Once again, I think McKenzie has expressed it with characteristic if shocking bluntness: "It seems that the proclamation of Christian freedom is more likely to arouse hostility than any other element of the Gospel. The greater the risk of hostility, the more manifest is the urgent need of the proclamation. I think that Paul would be shocked to see the power that the slave Church holds over the free Church."[2]

Finally, the conclusion of my doctoral studies occurred in 1968, coincidentally the same year that the Latin American bishops conference (CELAM) met at Medellin, Colombia, and provided the initial impetus for a theology of liberation for the entire continent. This immediately struck me as a historic development, combining as it did the goal of Christian freedom with the practice of Christian liberation, and my initial enthusiasm for it has gradually developed into what promises to be a lifelong commitment.

In this brief prologue, it is important that I stress from the outset my own position on the issue of a North American liberation theology. It is often asserted as a self-evident truth in theological circles in the United States that we must beware of the error of "importing" Latin American theology, and that the real task is to develop a North American liberation theology which corresponds both to the U.S. context and to the character of the Catholic church in America. My own contention (which cannot be developed at length here) is that the very *beginning* of a North American liberation theology entails a careful and attentive listening to and understanding of Latin American theology, followed by a *second step* of genuine reflection and discernment, and ending in the beginning of a process of national *conversion*. This would include the honest acknowledgment of our frequent resort to chauvinism and militarism in dealing with other nations, of our growing transformation into a people characterized by an ethos of consumerism and selfish individualism, and an increasing attitude and practice of uncaring indifference to the misery and impoverishment of billions of human beings on this planet. And these sins should frankly be called "mortal" in the deepest sense of the term, since they daily inflict untimely death on multitudes of men and women.

At this point, some preliminary remarks appear helpful with regard to the general organization of the book and the interrelationships of the various chapters. The title and subtitle not only express the goal of a church that truly liberates human beings but also stress the epoch-making importance of the new approaches and methods for advancing and defending human freedom in actual practice that are now beginning to flourish in the world church. Thus, a very important point is that I intend to move beyond an emphasis on the theological *meaning* of Christian freedom and to direct the major focus of this book on recent developments relating to the Christian *practice* of freedom or its *praxis*, referring by this term to the dialectical relationship between theory and practice. Included in these forms of activity are the creation and development of liberating theological methods and sources, the discernment and implementation of local and national pastoral strategies, the utilization of liberating educational and evangelizing techniques, the dissemination of supportive official documents and, above all, the revitalization and renewal of structures that will contribute to the development of a Christian community or church that is at the same time liberated and liberating.

Moving to the different parts of the book, chapter 1 analyzes the very influential ideas of John Courtney Murray on Christian freedom and liberation. Especially noteworthy is his assertion that after the Vatican Council's declaration on the minor issue of religious freedom in the secular sense, a second great argument would be set afoot, now on the theological meaning of Christian freedom. Chapter 2 provides an overview of the contribution of liberation theology to both the theoretical and pastoral implications of Christian freedom. Thus the chapter analyzes the indigenous (not European) origin of liberation theology, its major themes, its role as the voice of the Third World, and its essential contribution as a "world theology" for the "world church" which Karl Rahner referred to as the single most important result of the Second Vatican Council.

The third chapter studies a number of authors concerning the basic *methodology* of a liberating theology or a theology of Christian freedom, stressing the fundamental importance of method, no matter what particular themes or concepts are being considered. Chapter 4 follows along the same lines, studying the divergences that result in a theology of freedom as a result of the choice of different *sources* or interlocutors. In both chapters it is shown that the results would be applicable to a liberating theology in any part of the world.

Chapters 5 and 6 also have similar concerns, with the first one stressing the effectiveness of the educational and evangelical tool of *conscientization* (consciousness-raising) as developed by the Brazilian educator Paulo Freire. It also shows the importance of Freire's liberation theology for the reflection/prayer of the Basic Ecclesial Communities (BECs). Chapter 6 studies the origin and importance of the BECs as a new way of being the grassroots church, with lay leadership trained and aided by the clergy and bishops. This model of the church of the future is shown to exemplify and concretize a number of values and traits of a genuine Christian community which may serve as both model and catalyst for the entire church.

Chapter 7 is concerned with the important role of human rights in defending and nurturing freedom throughout the secular world and also within the confines of the church. Thus, in contemporary times it is not only the foremost institution of freedom but also can foster similar institutions and practices of freedom in both church and world.

A final chapter 8 recognizes the importance of official church documents in the acceptance and dissemination of any theology, and thus presents a commentary and evaluation of the 1986 *Instruction on Christian Freedom and Liberation* issued by the Vatican Congregation on the Doctrine of the Faith. It highlights above all the Vatican's approval and encouragement of Christian freedom and liberation for all the different regions and nations of the world. (The text of the Vatican document is included in an appendix for easy consultation by the reader.) In the epilogue, I then conclude with a discussion of the recent encyclical letter of Pope John Paul II, *On Social Concerns*, focusing on its relationship to and its relevance for many of the issues discussed in this book.

Another official document that is deservedly receiving much attention and debate at the present time is the U.S. bishops' pastoral letter on *Economic Justice for All: Catholic Social Teaching and the U.S. Economy*.[3] One of the major accomplishments of this letter is that it boldly and unambiguously speaks out with regard to the greatest challenge to freedom and liberation in the world today: the enslavement of hundreds of millions of people in the gigantic structural prison of misery, suffering and death that constitutes the reality of the Third World.

The bishops begin their analysis by focusing on the role of the United States in the interdependent area of economic relationships. They first mention the importance of just economic relations with all U.S. trading partners as well as with the socialist countries, but move on quickly to the central issue: " . . . without in the least discounting the importance of these linkages, our emphasis on the preferential option for the poor moves us to focus our attention mainly on U.S. relations with the third world."[4]

Lest there be any doubt of who the poor are or what their suffering entails, the bishops paint a chilling and succinct portrait of the world reality:

> Half the world's people, nearly 2.5 billion, live in countries where the annual per capita income is $400 or less. At least 800 million people in those countries live in absolute poverty, "beneath any rational definition of human decency." Nearly half a billion are chronically hungry, despite abundant harvests worldwide. Fifteen out of every 100 children born in those countries die before the age of 5, and millions of the survivors are physically or mentally stunted.[5]

The bishops' response to this situation is developed at considerable length, but they leave no doubt concerning the four basic moral responses demanded of Christians. These include the demands of Christian love and solidarity that must transcend national borders, the need for basic justice so that all may participate fairly in the international economy, and respect for and protection of both political and economic rights as a prime objective for all nations. The fourth element in their moral framework is also the most important: "*The special place of the poor* in this moral perspective means that meeting the basic needs of the millions of deprived and hungry people in the world must be the No. 1 objective of international policy."[6]

In short, I believe the bishops are to be congratulated and thanked for a bold and challenging call to action. But there does not appear to be any significant response either at the grassroots level of the church or among the clergy. Perhaps there has been an atrophy of our capacity for moral imagination and indeed moral indignation before the sheer enormity of the suffering and the oppression of so many human beings in the Third World. Perhaps we need to rekindle the dangerous memory of Jesus of Nazareth, who passionately defended the poor and angrily rebuked their oppressors, hurling at the latter such epithets as you blind fools, hypocrites, whited sepulchres, snakes and vipers (Mt 23). Perhaps there is truth in what Richard Hofstadter has said about the intellectual in America, including the Christian intellectual:

> He becomes comfortable, perhaps even moderately prosperous, as he takes a position in the university or in government or working for the mass media, but he then tailors himself to the requirements of these institutions. He loses that precious tincture of rage so necessary for first-rate creativity as a writer, that capacity for negation and rebellion that is necessary to the candid social critic, that initiative and independence of aim required for distinguished work in science.[7]

Perhaps, finally, what is really lacking in our hearts and consciences today is simply that precious tincture of rage.

Chapter 1
The Legacy of John Courtney Murray

In his introduction to the *Declaration on Religious Freedom*, widely accepted as the major American accomplishment in the Second Vatican Council, John Courtney Murray, that document's principal architect, employed his characteristic lapidary style to highlight its accomplishments. The linchpin of his analysis concerned two arguments. In the first of these, he averred, "the greatest argument on religious freedom in all history happily broke forth in the Church."[1] The debate itself, he goes on, "was full and free and vigorous, if at times confused and emotional. Out of it came the sixth and final text, here presented."

Murray then proceeded to a second debate, which he believed was of greater importance than the declaration's concentration on "the major issue of religious freedom in the technical secular sense." He predicted that "a second great argument will be set afoot—now on the theological meaning of Christian freedom," when "the children of God, who receive this freedom as a gift from their Father through Christ in the Holy Spirit, assert it within the Church as well as within the world, always for the sake of the world and the Church."[2]

It should be emphasized that this further argument was explicitly excluded from consideration in the Council, as is clear in the subtitle to the declaration: *On the Right of the Person and of Communities to Social and Civil Freedom in Matters Religious.* Richard Regan, the author of the most thorough study of the declaration, explains this development that took place in the fifth conciliar text on religious freedom:

> The first change in the new text was the subtitle: the "freedom" to which the schema asserted the right of persons and communities was now expressly qualified as "social and civil." At the request of the Fathers, these words were added to make clear that the freedom in question did not concern the relation of men to truth or to God, or the relations between the faithful and

authorities in the Church, but the relations among persons in human and civil society.[3]

My contention throughout this book will be, to use Murray's phrase, "that a certain indivisibility attaches to the notion of freedom" and that Christian freedom has a most profound and intimate impact on the relation of men to truth and God as well as on the relations between the faithful and authorities in the Church. This is not to deny, but rather to amplify and integrate the notion of social and civil freedom in matters religious, which continues to be a matter of importance and, in some countries, a matter of acute urgency.

To return, then, to this second great argument on the theological meaning of Christian freedom, I will begin with a survey of Murray's own ideas on the subject. It is interesting to note that Murray had to profit from his own experience in this matter, as his intellectual biographer, Bishop Donald Pelotte, has pointed out: "It is only in his very last years that Murray ventured to give a definition of freedom, and then it came after many years of work and reflection, after having himself undergone a long process of liberation."[4] Two articles written by Murray in those last years best express his theological vision of freedom, and also, in my view as a former student, represent his most polished prose style. Since less than two years of life were left to him after the conclusion of the Council and of his own work on the "distracting debate on religious freedom,"[5] his ideas were not developed in any detail, but the foundation and main girders of its intellectual structure are readily apparent.

In those last years Murray was extremely conscious of the fact that the church was moving into a new phase of its history, which he referred to somewhat prosaically as the Age of Renewal. In the foreword to a conference on "Freedom and Man" in 1965, he referred to it as follows:

> The full profile of the new age has not yet emerged into clear definition. One feature, however, already stands out. Freedom is the feature. It is visible on the face that Vatican II has presented to a watching world. It will also be marked on the face of the new historical epoch into which the Council is moving a world that awaits the movement.[6]

In a graduation address delivered at this time, Murray returned to the theme of an Age of Renewal, but he expressed its significance in what appears to be his favorite scriptural source: "Within the Church, and therefore throughout the length and breadth of mankind, Saint Paul's resounding message will be heard with new clarity: 'For freedom Christ has set you free. . . . It was unto freedom, brethren, that you were called' (Galatians 5:1,13)."[7]

In this address, Murray agrees with those who believe that the progress of culture and civilization of the last four centuries has been substantially nothing more than a movement or pilgrimage toward freedom, both civil and religious. He is frank in admitting that the church has not been part of this pilgrimage but has often obstructed mankind's historical movement toward freedom, thus becoming, in a typical Murray *mot juste*, "truants from the school of history."[8] But he is equally candid in rebuking the lack of substance in the cultural and political understanding of freedom, arguing that political discourse on freedom must have more profundity than it achieved in the nineteenth century if it is to be taken seriously today and that the notion of freedom as an absolute is today obsolete. He concludes these introductory notions thus: "Discourse on freedom must have some substance, if it is to be listened to. The practice of freedom must be disciplined by other values, if it is to be worthy of man."[9]

It is illuminating to reflect further on Murray's critique of church opposition to freedom and his consideration of two of the major concrete historical forms in which the problems of freedom occurred. In the sixteenth century it arose as a problem of the church: "The issue was the doctrinal authority of the Church and her right of pastoral guidance. Therefore, the post-tridentine Church laid heavy accent, not on the freedom of the Christian but on the authority of the Church."

In the nineteenth century, the problem of freedom arose again in the guise of the problem of God. Here the concern was human conscience and state power, and whether these were to be considered autonomous from any higher law, including the dominion of God; again, to use Murray's lapidary phrase, it involved "the outlaw conscience and the totalitarian state." Consequently, "the ultra-montane church emphasized, not man's human civil freedoms, but the due subjection of man and society to the ultimate Majesty, the Lord of creation and history, whose will sets limits to the freedom of man and the reach of all human powers."[10]

Murray concedes a certain necessity for both the above reactions in order to preserve human dignity. In the first place, the church rightly opposed the idolatry of mankind as a kind of "divinity in [its] own right." At the other end of the spectrum, she resisted all efforts to reduce humanity to the level of nature (naturalism) or of matter (materialism), as well as to the level of society and history (socialism and Marxism). Despite this, however, the author probes the weaknesses in the church's posture in a paragraph that could serve as a succinct epilogue for Murray's life work:

> Catholic historians, however, are now beginning to recognize that there was also a failure on the part of the Church, her magistery and her people, chiefly the intellectuals. There was a failure to recognize the signs of the times, to look beneath the surface of error and deviation and to discern the

genuine human aspiration that was at work—man's perennial aspiration to possess his birthright of freedom. Condemnations in abundance fell on the errors to the right and to the left. But there was no effort to discern the truth that always lies at the heart of error. Not until Pope Leo XIII, and then only hesitantly, was the effort begun to fashion a doctrine of freedom, human and Christian, out of the Church's own treasury of reason and faith, that would at once speak to the intelligence of man and also solicit his heart.[11]

Murray goes on to insist again that freedom is the first truth about humanity and that its positive personal and social value must be respected, even when it leads to error and evil. Though freedom has been "the forgotten truth" for long centuries, he remained optimistic that the "new age which the Church is entering is to be—such is our hope—the Age of Renewal of this truth."[12]

At this point, I am going to focus on Murray's theological views, first on the personal reality of freedom and then on its fundamental configuration in the social order. Once again, I believe that, despite the lack of extensive development of details in these outlines, they are not lacking in profundity and contemporary relevance. Aside from these more systematic considerations, I will also add some remarks about the question of the development of the doctrine of freedom and comment on Murray's use of Scripture and tradition in grounding his theology.

I have already referred to Bishop Pelotte's observation that Murray articulated a comprehensive concept of freedom only in his very last years. To go one step further, I would suggest that only then *could* he elaborate such an understanding, for it was only during and after the Second Vatican Council that an extraordinarily significant change occurred in Catholic social thought, largely under the influence of the *Pastoral Constitution on the Church in the Modern World (Gaudium et Spes)*. A very astute commentator, Charles E. Curran, has demonstrated that the two famous social encyclicals of John XXIII, *Mater et Magistra* (1961) and *Pacem in Terris* (1963), "show that even at this comparatively late date papal social teaching was based almost exclusively on natural law."[13] He then goes on to point out how *Gaudium et Spes*, issued in 1965, "employs a different methodology without ever explicitly alluding to the significant change which this involves for Catholic social teaching," a methodological change described as "a shift away from a natural-law approach toward a more gospel- and faith-centered approach."[14]

In the commencement address mentioned earlier, John Courtney Murray brings together these two approaches regarding his understanding of personal (not individualist) freedom. The text consists of a single paragraph, which I divide only for the purpose of clarity. In the first part, Murray refers to personal freedom in the light of natural law theory:

Freedom therefore is inwardness, spontaneity, the capacity of a man to find within himself the reasons and the motives of his own right decisions and action, apart from external coercion. Freedom therefore is authenticity, truthfulness, fidelity to the pursuit of truth and to the truth when found. In further consequence, freedom is experienced as duty, as responsibility—as a response to the claims of justice, to the demands of rightful law, to the governance and guidance of legitimate authority.

At this point, Murray moves deftly to an "intimately Christian" understanding where "freedom has a higher meaning than all this. Freedom, in the deepest experience of it, is love. To be free is to be-for-the-others. The Christian call to freedom is inherently a call to community, a summons out of isolation, an invitation to be-with-the-others, an impulse to service of the others."[15] If this is not a complete synthesis, it certainly qualifies as a very succinct and felicitous recapitulation of the Christian understanding of freedom.

In turning now to Murray's understanding of freedom in society, it should be emphasized that the personal and social realities are not separate but are rather closely united with the most intimate of bonds. In his book, *The Problem of Religious Freedom,* Murray was also quite explicit in asserting that the understanding of religious freedom as a personal and corporate human right is not to be found in nineteenth century theologians but is rather the result of the demands of personal and political consciousness in the twentieth century. His argument is stated thus:

The link between religious freedom and limited constitutional government, and the link between the freedom of the Church and the freedom of the people—these were not nineteenth-century theological-political insights. They became available only within twentieth-century perspectives, created by the "signs of the times." The two links were not forged by abstract deductive logic but by history, by the historical advance of totalitarian government, and by the corresponding new appreciation of man's dignity in society.[16]

A number of times in Murray's *oeuvre* there is reference to the "tetrad" of spiritual forces that constitutes and sustains the modern polity. In the historical evolution of this structure, he highlights the importance of Pope John XXIII's development of traditional sources. Leo XIII and Pius XII, in Murray's view, had continually reiterated the triad of truth, justice, and love on which human society is built; John XXIII was the first to add the fourth spiritual element of freedom as equally essential. This doctrine was both traditional and new at the same time: "The tradition has always asserted that the human quality of society depends on the freedom of the Church. In a new and more profound understanding of the tradition John

XXIII affirms that the human quality of society depends on the freedom of the people.... In our age ... the two freedoms are inseparable—in fact, they are identical."[17] Also, the function of truth, justice, and love was seen as assuring the stability of society, while freedom provided the dynamism of progress toward fuller humanity in communal living.

Clearly, then, Murray's understanding of societal freedom is based on natural law, or as he has also expressed it, on the exigencies of reason. One paragraph welds the different elements together very tightly:

> The spiritual order of society is founded on truth—on the true view of man, his dignity, his duties and rights, his freedoms and obligations. This order must be brought into being under fidelity to the precepts of justice, whose vindication is the primary function of the public power as well as the primary civic duty of the citizenry. This order needs to be animated and perfected by love; for civic unity cannot be achieved by justice and law alone; love is the ultimate force that sustains all human living together. Finally, this order is to achieve increasingly more human conditions of social equality, without any impairment of freedom.[18]

The dynamism of freedom ensures, then, that both personal and social freedom is a hard-won achievement, or rather an endless striving which always falls short of its goal. Murray describes this striving in terms of chiseled elegance:

> There is no sudden leap into freedom, whether personal or social. In order to be free a man or a society must undergo a process of liberation. The process is never complete, and it is always precarious, subject to deflection or defeat. Man is never more than an apprentice in the uses of freedom. Their mastery eludes him. The possession of freedom, like the possession of truth, is the term, always only proximate, of an arduous education.[19]

If we inquire into the scriptural sources that Murray uses to ground or at least illuminate his understanding of societal freedom, the results are indeed disappointing. In a number of places, he refers to the "live as free men" text of 1 Peter 2:16 and the Galatians 5:1 text already mentioned, plus the admonition in Galatians 5:13: " ... only do not use your freedom as an opportunity for the flesh, but through love be servants of one another." "The injunction," he says of this text, "following the warning, says the final inexhaustible word about Christian freedom."[20] In *Freedom and Man* and in several other places, he does refer to Romans, chapters 7 and 8. There, Paul cries out for deliverance from "this body of death," which Murray interprets as "the human environment, external and internal."[21] This human environment could refer to the structures of society, although it must be admitted that Murray restricts the good news of freedom to a personal level in the next sentence by quoting Romans 8:2: "For the law of the Spirit of life in Jesus Christ has set me free from the law of sin and death" (Rom 8:2).

One sympathetic critic of Murray's work has stated flatly that "one never finds a serious example of biblical exegesis in the entire Murray corpus on Church-state relations." And he adds his own conviction that, "In a pluralistic society such as contemporary America, an attempt to develop a social ethic which is rooted in Christian faith *without* beginning with biblical symbols and never leaving them entirely behind is, I think, doomed to failure."[22] This is a very disputed position which I do not wish to enter into here. My own view is closer to the more flexible statements of Charles Curran that "in speaking to the broader and pluralistic community, bishops and other Christian spokespersons and leaders might find it more effective to prescind from the specifically Christian," while admitting that "at times even in pluralistic societies it should not always be necessary for Christians and others to prescind from their own unique approaches in addressing questions affecting the whole society."[23]

Curran has also provided what I think is the most thorough critique of Murray's thought, but the positive thrust of his criticism is evident in the final sentence of his study: " . . . Murray's creative genius has made him the most outstanding Catholic theologian in the United States in this century."[24] In my view, also, many of his criticisms are not so much peculiar to Murray as referring to the whole field of theology in Murray's lifetime, as well as to the particular characteristics of the debate in the United States at that time. As regards Catholic theology itself, there has been more change in the two decades since Murray's death than in the previous four hundred years of its history, so that the anticipation of such change would have required truly supernatural prescience of *any* theologians in the mid-sixties. Lacking such a charisma, Murray clearly could not have stepped outside the bounds of history.

Curran's most trenchant criticisms, in my opinion, begin with Murray's view that the American civic unity is grounded on a natural law philosophy. Not only is this untenable as an interpretation of the historical intent of America's founding fathers, but it is also mistaken as the contemporary interpretation of the philosophical foundations of the American consensus. As Curran argues cogently: "Our society exists not only with a religious pluralism but also with a philosophical pluralism. Few if any Catholic theologians would insist on the need for an acceptance of natural law with its epistemological and metaphysical presuppositions as the only foundation for the American proposition."[25]

Closely connected with Murray's emphasis on natural law is his failure to give sufficient attention to the theological reality of sin and its influence on all personal and social reality. In Curran's view, this has led Murray to an overly optimistic and insufficiently critical attitude toward the United States, its institutions and policies. A clear example is his almost total unconcern with economic as opposed to political issues, and little awareness of economic problems in the United States:

> One brief reference to the American economic scene seems to accept the unique American claim to have abolished the problem of poverty. There still exist some depressed areas, but the means for the solution of the problem exist and are known. Even in Murray's day there was evidence that the problem of poverty was not solved in the United States. Murray fails to realize the reality and the extent of the problem.[26]

Along with this, Murray is also seen to have accepted rather uncritically the American ethos regarding the Cold War and the approach to Communism. But perhaps the most telling criticism relates to Murray's attitude toward nuclear war. "At the very minimum," Curran states, "Murray fails to appreciate the horror of nuclear war and all that is involved in it. To cross the atomic threshold could open up the possibilities of a nuclear holocaust."[27]

Granted these limitations, however, it is fitting to close by stressing the positive contributions to a theology of Christian freedom that is the crowning legacy of Murray's life. And, recalling his assertion that, in order to be free, a man or a society must undergo a process of liberation, his work is also concerned with this arduous task, that is, it is also a theology of liberation.

In analyzing what this process of liberation entails, I will first discuss what I believe are the most important contributions in Pelotte's study, and then conclude with my own reflections. After characterizing his own book as a historical and theological analysis of Murray's role in developing a Roman Catholic theology of freedom, Pelotte moves beyond this to a vision of the future:

> The import of Murray's work for future theological and especially ecclesiological discussion, however, remains unexplored. If Murray's achievement is to be taken seriously, theological reflection must now turn to at least three areas of inquiry, that of development of doctrine, that of democratization of the Church, and that of Catholic presence in American secular society.[28]

As regards development of doctrine, the author asserts that future theology must derive from human experience, and must be interdisciplinary as well as collaborative. Clearly, these characteristics are abundantly evident in contemporary approaches to theology,[29] while the really neuralgic issues are to be found especially in the second, but also in the third area of inquiry.

Concerning the democratization of the church, Pelotte believes that the same philosophical and theological principles which led to the reformulation of Catholic doctrine on the freedom of religion and the proper relations between church and state "might also justify a continuing democratization of the Church's internal structures," with the result that the greatest impact of Murray's thought might be on the institutions of the church. He admits that it remains to be seen how this process can be theologically reconciled to the traditional role of the papacy, and concludes, perhaps ironically, by noting that "in thinking through the democratization of Church structures the Catholic community will have the benefit of centuries of Protestant experience." As regards the relation of Catholics to American secular society, the author provides an excellent summary of Murray's style vis-à-vis that relationship:

> For Murray, dialogue between serious men about serious things was the *sine qua non* of civilized society. The end in view was not necessarily agreement but frequently that kind of understanding which is presupposed by honest disagreement. Such Christian realism might well prove an excellent norm for those who have accepted his challenge to commit themselves as Catholics to America's role in history.[30]

To return to the *Declaration on Religious Freedom,* Murray in his introduction to that document also bequeathed us a profound and prophetic vision of the future: "The conciliar affirmation of the principle of freedom was narrowly limited—in the text. But the text itself was flung into a pool whose shores are as wide as the universal church. The ripples will run far."[31] As we attempt to discern those ripples of freedom today, it seems to me that some are striving to utilize Murray's thought to support certain partisan issues or even to bolster different ideological positions. In entering into this discussion, I recognize the dangers and difficulties of the undertaking but believe the dialogue can be fruitful if we emphasize that the major task must be to interpret the signs of our own times as faithfully as he did his.

Beginning with an overview, I certainly hold that Murray's tetrad of attributes referred to above (that is, truth, justice, love, freedom) should be embraced as an excellent modern version of the four cardinal virtues. Their ecumenical breadth also recommends them, for they are just as necessary in the sacristy or chancery as they are in parliaments or presidential palaces.

It seems just as obvious on a general level that he would have plunged with great delight into the elaboration and critique of the cornucopia of issues regarding the relations of church and society that poured forth from the texts of the Second Vatican Council, especially the document on the church in the modern world. There is also no doubt in my mind that he would have roundly welcomed the process of civilized "argument" or dialogue that has developed in the U.S. church as a result of the bishops' pastoral letters on *The Challenge of Peace* (1983) and *Economic Justice for All* (1986). The dissemination of drafts inviting the response of the entire community, the dialogue with leaders of other religions, academics, government officials, representatives of the military, business, labor, and other fields, as well as the publicity generated by the debates in both the religious and secular press, produced a model of profound moral argument which is without precedent in the history of the United States.

A final issue, which has great importance at the present time (and indeed, in every epoch) is the question of the church and Christian freedom. This issue touches upon the essential nature of the church as an evangelical community in which the Spirit of God breathes in every member and in which all share the same call as followers of Jesus Christ. But it also extends to the church's proclamation of the good news *ad extra*, for it cannot honestly and credibly announce and defend human rights and human freedom if it does not put them into practice.

Fortunately, we do not have to speculate here on what Murray's views might have been, for he published them in a brief but profound and comprehensive article in the last year of his life, entitled appropriately "Freedom, Authority, Community."[32] He admitted that the topic was not directly considered in Vatican II, but could readily be deduced from its teachings, since the entire council was a splendid "event of freedom" in the history of the church.

Murray's brilliance in focusing issues is evident in the very first line, where he refuses to begin with a consideration of a "crisis of authority," as many others did, but instead focuses the basic issue as a "crisis of *community.*"[33] "Authority is indeed from God," he asserts, "but it is exercised in community over human persons. The freedom of the human person is also from God, and it is to be used in the community for the benefit of others."[34] He then goes on to define the uniqueness of the Christian community by referring to the Vatican II image of the People of God: "The basic condition of the People [of God] is therefore one of equality in dignity and freedom, established by the common possession of the Spirit." As in any community, authority is of course essential, but it exists *within* the community, as a special ministry to be performed in the service of the community and in dialogue with the community.

The primary function of this ministry of service is unitive, that is, it exists to gather, unite and establish communion. In order to achieve this goal,

Murray points to the need for new structures of communication, such as the Synod of Bishops, and also for reform of the existing structures, such as the congregations of the Roman Curia. He also returns to his own work in Vatican II for a principle that could have many far-reaching implications: "The principle of the Declaration on Religious Freedom—that there should be in society as much freedom as possible and only as much restriction as necessary—applies analogously in the Church. Only 'in necessary things' is unity itself necessary."[35]

Furthermore, with regard to the corrective or punitive function of authority, which while necessary remains merely a modality of the unitive function, Murray advances a very specific proposal drawn from the Anglo-American tradition:

> What comes to the fore today is the need that the corrective or punitive function of authority should be performed under regard for what is called, in the common-law tradition, "due process." The demand for due process of law is an exigence of Christian dignity and freedom. It is to be satisfied as exactly in the Church as in civil society (one might indeed say, more exactly).[36]

Murray certainly does not believe that this more adequate understanding of the ecclesial problem (which includes much more nuance than I have been able to include) will remove the inevitable tension which will continue to characterize the dialogue between authority and the free Christian community. His final conclusion in the article is more modest, more realistic, and more profound: "By situating this perennial polarity within the living context of community, it can serve to make the tension healthy and creative, releasing the energies radiant from both poles for their one common task, which is to build the beloved community."[37]

In closing this chapter, I would like to call attention to a last remark of Murray that can serve as a bridge to the next chapter and indeed to the rest of this book. He was quite aware of the fact that in late 1966 the church was engaged in an era of *assestamento* (adjustment) after the Council and that the forms and modalities by which authority would perform its unitive function and create communion were still problematical. At this precise point, this thinker renowned for his speculative powers called for bold practical experiments, so that the beloved community could learn from its own experience: "The problem is not simply to conceptualize in theological terms the relation between authority and freedom in the Christian community, as it appears in new perspectives; this relation must be lived, in all concreteness and practicality. Thus the experience of life will give vitality to the theology."[38] As we shall see, and as Murray could scarcely have foreseen, this appeal to the experience and the practice of the Christian community would form the dynamic thrust that produced a new theology of freedom and liberation in Latin America and the rest of the Third World. The rest of this book is concerned with charting the course of these ripples of freedom and evaluating their impact, not only on the shores of the universal church, but also and even more importantly on the borders of the wide world itself.

Chapter 2
Latin America's Theology of Freedom

This chapter presents my own reflections on the present and future condition and prospects of another theology of Christian freedom—liberation theology—that has flourished in Latin America over the past two decades. As an introduction to this complex phenomenon, it seems appropriate to recall a conference on the topic that was held in 1986 at Simon Fraser University, near the enchantingly beautiful city of Vancouver in British Columbia. To my knowledge, it was by far the largest interdisciplinary meeting on the issue that has ever been held in North America.

The conference sparked great enthusiasm and euphoria among the participants for a number of reasons. First of all, because of the large number of Canadian speakers and participants, it provided the many guests from Europe, Latin America, and especially the United States with a very penetrating and challenging vision of a specifically Canadian theology of liberation. Also—perhaps because of the neutral setting of a secular university—it was an extraordinarily ecumenical event, with very frank and honest exchanges between Christians of many different denominations as well as with a number of non-Christians and nonbelievers.

But the most important overall result was the conference's ringing rebuttal, in both theory and praxis, of a charge that is now heard in certain academic circles, that liberation theology has passed its peak and is now in the process of fading away into the same ash heap of history as the theological fads of the sixties and seventies. On the contrary, the overwhelming impression created by five major addresses and over seventy seminar talks in every field of academe was that of exuberant, youthful vitality. It was clearly evident that liberation theology, far from bordering on the edge of senility, has now arrived at the threshold of young adulthood, with all the strengths and weaknesses that characterize that turbulent and often painful period.

A single encounter during the conference provides a dramatic example of this youthful and creative *élan*. At the hotel in Vancouver one morning, I found myself sitting at breakfast across from a Chilean priest, Ronaldo Muñoz, who had delivered one of the major addresses of the meeting. After I had informed him that my own theological reflection was carried out in a university setting in New York City, he replied simply that his theological work was situated in the context of one of the poorest *barriadas* or slums of Santiago, the capital of Chile. After working with the people there from dawn to dusk, in the evening he used whatever time remained for theological reflection, but a reflection that was completely suffused with the experience of his suffering and oppressed people. Because of all his activity, I was somewhat surprised to hear that the subject of his book was a spirituality of liberation, but even more astonished to learn that the book would be only one of over fifty volumes on all aspects of liberation theology that had been planned for publication throughout Latin America in the coming decade.

Somewhat stunned by the audacious scope of this project, I reacted by asking what the Latin American theologians would do after all these books were written and published. "When the fifty volumes are finished ten years from now," he answered, breaking into a dazzling smile, "then—we will start all over again!" Muñoz was referring in slightly exaggerated fashion to the insistence of liberation theology on continually reinterpreting theological understanding in the light of changing historical contexts and circumstances.

A related and equally astonishing incident occurred several months after the conference. A notice from Patmos Press in West Germany appeared, announcing "A Theological Event!" in very large letters on its front cover. The event was not the appearance of some new star in the German theological firmament, as would ordinarily have been expected, but rather the *publication in German* of all fifty-three of the books on liberation theology that Muñoz had mentioned. The phenomenon surely must be evaluated as one of the principal contemporary theological "signs of the times," to use the expression that was introduced into common parlance by the Second Vatican Council. For decades and even centuries, the cutting edge of practically all theological discussion has been forged in Europe, especially in Germany, and then exported to provide the dominant ideas and basic texts for the universities and seminaries of the rest of the world. Thus, Jürgen Moltmann and Wolfhart Pannenberg, Karl Rahner and Johann B. Metz, Karl Barth and Rudolf Bultmann, spearheaded, and indeed still profoundly influence, the major theological movements of the twentieth century.

In contrast to these influences, I interpret the Patmos publications as symbolic of a great watershed in theological history, the reversal of a mighty current of ideas that has flowed in one direction for centuries, that is, from the center to the periphery of the world. This stream, again for the first time in the Christian era, is now coursing in the opposite direction, to the center in Europe from the periphery, that is, from the nations of the Third World under the aegis of the nations and churches of Latin America. Thus, one of the major objectives of this chapter (and indeed this entire book) will be to analyze and evaluate the significance of this liberating theology both in its own context and in its repercussions on the rest of the world, especially on my own country, the United States of America.

Theology for a World Church

As a basic approach to a more profound understanding of liberation theology, I would like to concentrate on an article published by the Jesuit theologian Karl Rahner in 1979. He has been acclaimed by many as the most influential Catholic theologian of the twentieth century, and I wholeheartedly share this view. In his article, entitled "Towards a Fundamental Theological Understanding of Vatican II," Rahner concentrated on what he considered to be the two most important transformations that have occurred in the entire history of the Catholic Church.[1] The first of these transformations took place at the very beginning of the Christian era, when the church of the first century underwent an astonishing metamorphosis from its identity as a Jewish sect to that of a church, with its center in the culture and civilization of Europe and the Mediterranean basin. Then the centuries passed and, although many events of great importance occurred, the second great transformation did not take place until the Second Vatican Council (1962-65). In Rahner's own words, "This means that in the history of Christianity the transition from one historical and theological situation to an essentially new one did happen once, and that now in the transition from a Christianity of Europe (with its American annexes) to a fully world religion it is starting to happen for a second time."[2] And thus, for him, the basic theological significance of Vatican II was that it was "the first major official event in which the church actualized itself precisely as a *world church*" (italics are Rahner's). Another way Rahner expresses this thesis is to affirm that "there have only been three great epochs in Church history: First, the short period of Jewish Christianity; second, the period of the Church in the region of Hellenism and European culture and civilization; and third, the period of the Church in which the sphere of the Church's life is in fact the entire world."[3] And, he adds, this third period has only just begun.

Rahner died six years after this article was published, and it is clear that he himself did not develop a theology for this "world church," although he was quite sympathetic to the various theologies that were developing in Asia, Africa, and especially in Latin America. For example, just a few weeks before his death, he wrote a letter to the Cardinal Archbishop of Lima, Juan Landázuri Ricketts, defending the orthodoxy of the Peruvian priest, Gustavo Gutiérrez, one of the leaders in the creation of a liberating theology. Although Rahner did not say he agreed with all of Gutiérrez's ideas, he did hold that they were legitimate within the healthy pluralism that should characterize the correct environment for creative theological work.

At any rate, I here take a step beyond Rahner's analysis and articulate my own thesis as clearly and forcefully as possible: liberation theology in Latin America and other areas of the Third World must be understood as the essential dialogue partner for the creation of a "world theology" that will correspond to the reality of the "world church" that was understood by Rahner as the most important theological result of the Second Vatican Council. A correlative thesis is the following: this dialogue partner has been almost entirely missing from the conversation throughout twenty centuries of Christianity and comprises basically the masses of the poor, the marginalized, the oppressed, the victims, who are now finding and articulating the words to *denounce* their impoverishment, their marginalization, their oppression, and their victimization, and to *announce* their determination and plans of action to cast off these ancient shackles and enslavement forever.

I do not hold that Rahner's concept of a world church is a novel idea. Some time before Rahner's article, I argued in 1975 in the Jesuit weekly *America* that the new task of theology today was for the formation of a "geotheology" or world theology.[4] About the same time, independently, Walbert Buhlmann published *The Coming of the Third Church*, a church he defined as "that of the new nations, now entering as a new element into world history and into the history of the Church, who will be 'surprise pockets' of the near future."[5] One of the greatest martyrs in the history of the Catholic Church, Archbishop Oscar Romero of San Salvador, dedicated his life to becoming "the voice of those who have no voice," that is, the poor and oppressed of his diocese and of his continent.[6] And theologians within the Third World have labored mightily to express the religious aspirations of their own peoples in a number of books with titles such as *The Emergent Gospel: Theology from the Underside of History*[7] and *Irruption of the Third World: Challenge to Theology*.[8] Thus, it is not a question of a failure to articulate the need for a true world theology; it is rather the obvious failure of theologians in the First World not only to recognize the need but to accord it its deserved centrality in their theological work on behalf of the world church.

Furthermore, there are other reasons besides theological ones that warrant the prompt acknowledgment and acceptance of the new interlocutors from the Third World. Although liberation theology is a thoroughgoing ecumenical enterprise, its founders and major authors at present are predominantly Catholic; and the demographic evidence regarding the future of that church (especially as a Eurocentric church) is startling indeed. When the Second Vatican Council ended in 1965, 47 percent of the then 585 million Catholics lived in the Third World. Today, more than two decades later, more than 60 percent of the world's 900 million Catholics live in Asia, Africa, and Latin America and—perhaps the most important point—that proportion continues to increase dramatically as each day passes.

A second demographic factor has to do with vocations to the priesthood, since priests (along with religious women and brothers) must be considered the front line troops in the church's mission to spread the gospel and nourish the growth of religious faith. In this area the Vatican newspaper, *L'Osservatore Romano,* has recently published statistics which show an extraordinary increase in students for the priesthood in the Third World, along with a concomitant drastic reduction in seminarians in the United States, Europe, and other parts of the First World.[9] For example, between the years 1970-1985, the number of seminarians worldwide in the Catholic Church increased by 16.5 percent. However, in Africa and South America the number in that period grew by an amazing 88 percent, while in Asia (particularly India, Korea, and the Philippines) there was an increase of more than 55 percent. Consequently, *L'Osservatore Romano* predicted that by 1995, 15 percent of the world's priests would come from Africa (as compared with 5 percent in 1970) and 7 percent from North America (as compared with 19 percent of all priests in 1970). This led *The New York Times* to speculate that "someday priests from Asia and Africa might have to look after Roman Catholics in countries that once sent off boatloads of missionaries." Although the Vatican survey does not advert to it, the increase in priests in the Third World would also normally result in an increase in the proportion of bishops, thus affecting the church's highest leadership echelons and also its theological views through the bishops' teaching office or magisterium. This would clearly exert profound continuous influence on the world church and its world theology.

Origins of a Liberating Theology

Even if one does not accept the theses on liberation theology I have advanced above, at least the demographic statistics should indicate that it is important for those in the First World to achieve a more comprehensive understanding of this historical phenomenon. At this point, consequently, I will move toward that objective by answering the question, where did liberation theology come from? In other words, what are the origins of liberation theology?

It should be noted, first of all, that the very name "theology of liberation" was the focus of considerable debate among certain Latin American theologians during the late sixties. One of the principal opponents of that name was the Uruguayan Juan Luis Segundo, who contended that such a name would contribute to a distorted perception of the movement as just another fad, like the theologies of secularization, hope, play, and so forth, that flourished in the sixties. Segundo also felt that the name would provide an easy target for the fierce opposition that would inevitably be directed at this theology, an opposition that must be expected for any theology that gives central emphasis to social justice and to social change.[10] At any rate, Gustavo Gutiérrez published the most influential book of the movement, *The Theology of Liberation,* in 1971, and the name is by now generally accepted. However, Segundo's predictions have also come true, and the movement has generated more widespread and violent opposition than any other in recent history.

It is abundantly clear that there are very powerful and well-financed political and commercial interests, in the United States, Europe, and the Third World, that are inexorably hostile to ideas that challenge the status quo or threaten to awaken the masses of the poor to the root causes of their misery. My own preference is to use the term "liberating theologies," a phrase which includes *any* theology which contributes to the authentic freedom of human beings on either the personal, political, economic, cultural or ecclesiastical levels. The political economist William K. Tabb has recently suggested the term "transformative theologies" to include "all those theologies that have in common a commitment to do justice and transform social reality as a fulfillment of the biblical message."[11] I would certainly agree with this, but Tabb himself concludes that insisting on the new term would only create linguistic confusion at this point.

In searching for the origins of liberation theology, it is helpful to begin with the most common misinterpretation. According to Rahner's article, mentioned earlier, the Catholic church had been Eurocentric for roughly nineteen centuries, so that many have followed this traditional path and tried to trace this theology's origins to European sources, usually to the "political theology" developed by the German theologians Johann B. Metz[12] and Jürgen Moltmann. For example, in an otherwise knowledgeable article on the church in Nicaragua published in *The Atlantic Monthly,* Conor Cruise O'Brien writes confidently that "by 1979 liberation theology had been around for a little over a decade, since its beginnings, in Germany, in 1967."[13] No further information is provided by Mr. O'Brien as to why that particular year was chosen, who the purported German founder was, or indeed whether the writer had any first-hand knowledge whatever about liberation theology. Although it does not appear to be true in the case of Mr. O'Brien, in many instances this tactic for establishing the origins of liberation theology in Europe is an ideological device for pigeonholing it in comfortable, familiar categories and finally dismissing the movement as "nothing new" and therefore not worthy of further analysis or dialogue. This, then, is the ideological tactic that I am opposing most emphatically in this chapter.

The mention of Johann B. Metz, whom I consider to be the best of contemporary European theologians, leads me to mention that he is on the board of directors of the Patmos firm that is translating the fifty-three volumes on liberation theology into German. The board included its own description of the roots (*die Würzeln*) of liberation theology in the Patmos advertisement, as follows:

> The source and point of departure (*Ursprung und Aufgangspunkt*) of liberation theology's reflections is not to be found in a political doctrine, nor in a philosophical theory, nor in an analysis by the social sciences. It arises rather from a compassionate encounter with a marginalized and an oppressed people. The profound spiritual experience of a poor and at the same time believing people has opened the eyes of faith for the Church in Latin America and for its theologians. They have discovered the Crucified One in the midst of the many who are crucified by the misery that surrounds them. In the poor of the entire continent they have recognized the ruler of the world, who has identified himself with the least of his brothers and sisters (Mt 25:31-46).[14]

Another astute analyst of the Latin American scene, Gregory Baum, has also recently published his observations on the origin of liberation theology. He asserts emphatically that it originated from new religious experiences, which "took place among Latin American Christians struggling for justice—either on a small scale attempting to improve their living conditions or on a larger scale as part of a movement to reconstruct the social order."[15] That these experiences were *religious* is shown by their realization that God was on their side and in solidarity with all of the poor and the outcasts. Thus, in their reading of the Bible they showed great interest in "the story of the exodus, the divine covenant in the desert, the prophets' call to social justice, Christ's proclamation of God's coming reign, Christ's solidarity with the lowly and simple people, which eventually led to his execution, and Christ's resurrection in which God vindicated him and with him all the victims of history."

Of course, Baum continues, there were priests working among these struggling Christians, and some of these were theologians. Although they had been trained in European universities, most of them did not occupy positions as university professors but rather described themselves as "organic intellectuals," a concept popularized by the Italian Marxist, Antonio Gramsci. Baum regards this designation as referring to "intellectuals who do not serve the promotion of mainstream culture but instead identify themselves with the people at the base and try to think through and articulate the insights of theological literature." After insisting on the essentially ecumenical nature of the resulting theology, Baum concludes with what I think is a very felicitous and succinct description of liberation theology: " . . . an interpretation of the Christian message, generated by popular groups and articulated in systematic form by theologians, that brings out, in the Latin American context, the this-worldly, critical, transformist or revolutionary meaning of the divine promises revealed in Scripture."

It should be obvious that I completely agree with Baum's description and am in total disagreement with a superficial and historically inaccurate attribution of liberation theology to European sources, especially as a technique for minimizing its importance. Thus, I am going to stress and try to demonstrate in depth its originality and its development as an indigenous creation within Latin American religion, culture and history.

Stages of Liberating Theology

An excellent procedure for illuminating this originality and creativity is to study the continuous eruption of various forms of liberating theology that traverse the continent's history, reaching back to the earliest years of the Iberian conquest. Here I rely on the work of the Argentine historian Enrique Dussell, whose research has uncovered the lineaments of six major stages in Latin American theology.[16]

Dussell calls the first stage (from 1511 to 1553) a "prophetic theology" because it consisted essentially of a series of passionate Christian protests against the enslavement and brutal oppression of the Indians by the *conquistadores*. In November of 1511, the Dominican friar Antonio de Montesinos preached a powerful attack against the Spanish oppressors and an equally impassioned defense of the rights of the Indians. This eloquent demand for justice resulted in the eventual conversion to the cause of the Indians of one listener to the sermon, named Bartolomé de las Casas, in 1514. Dussell states flatly that "this prophetic conversion of a thinker who would afterwards be so prolific in his writings as well as so profound and practical in his conclusions could be considered the birth of the Latin American theology of liberation."[17] This prophetic period began to come to an end, however, in 1553, which marks the foundation of the first universities in Mexico City and Lima. This led gradually to a "theology of colonial Christendom," which abandoned the prophetic denunciations of de las Casas and instead evolved an ideological justification of the conquest and of the crimes against the Indians.

In the third epoch, the pendulum swung back to another era of authentic liberation theology, called a "Political Theology of Emancipation," that arose during the period when most of the nations of Latin America achieved their political independence from Spain and Portugal (from 1808 to 1831). The goals of this movement were not primarily scholarly, but rather reflected the efforts of a broad spectrum of professors, priests, religious, and secular leaders of various kinds to formulate and disseminate theological justification for the wars of independence, as well as to provide religious motivation for taking part in the struggle for political freedom. Because of the chaotic conditions caused by war, the liberation theology produced did not take the form of books or articles, but rather of speeches, sermons, pamphlets, tracts, and other forms of ad hoc literature.

The fourth and fifth theological periods noted by Dussell consisted of another conservative neocolonial period (from 1831-1930), which was largely on the defensive against the many new developments in Western thought and against the incursions of an aggressively missionary Protestantism, followed by an epoch characterized by a more progressive mentality and referred to as the "New Christendom" (from 1930-1962). The latter name refers to the movement's attempt to revive the era of colonial Christendom by means of a new, more vital and modern approach. The major characteristics of the new approach included the rapid spread of Catholic Action, the founding of theological faculties and social centers, the creation of youth and labor organizations, the formation of the Latin American Bishops' Conference (called CELAM) in 1958, and finally a widespread interest in and development of biblical studies.

During this stage, the basic theological approach was still heavily dependent on European models, both on the theoretical and on the pastoral level, and thus had not yet arrived at a clear social and historical understanding of the uniqueness of the Latin American *realidad*, which would not take place until the following period. However, in support of my thesis concerning the originality of Latin American theology, I would emphasize that this New Christendom era led to the creation of a vast and varied *infrastructure* (containing all the elements just mentioned), which provided the essential framework necessary for the birth of the contemporary liberation theology.

From the People or the Intellectuals?

Two further comments on the origin of liberation theology may be helpful, one regarding the popular level and one on the intellectual level. On the popular level, it is clear that the basic pastoral strategy of the Latin American church, beginning with Brazil in the 1950s, has been the formation and cultivation of basic ecclesial communities (BECs, known as CEBs in Portuguese and Spanish).[18] These are small groups of Catholics with lay leaders who meet regularly for services which include prayer, worship, and the application of Bible teachings to their lives in a process known as conscientization. This process was developed by the Brazilian educator, Paulo Freire, and is defined in his book, *The Pedagogy of the Oppressed.* Both the technique of conscientization and the pastoral strategy of basic Christian communities will be discussed at length in subsequent chapters of this book.

The various observers and students of these groups express their relation to liberation theology in one of two ways. Either it is asserted that the "base communities are liberation theology put into practice" or "liberation theology has emerged from reflection on the experience of the base communities." The first one clearly stresses the priority of liberation theology, while the second stresses the priority of the experience of the base communities. But if we look more closely, it is evident that the two assertions are by no means in opposition to each other, but rather that there is an ongoing and profound dialectical relationship between the base communities and liberation theology, resulting in a symbiosis that stimulates constant growth and maturation in both partners in the dialectic. Furthermore, an enormous literature has arisen concerning the BECs, which have flourished not only in Latin America but also in Asia, Africa and even (with substantial adaptations) in the developed nations of the West. It is abundantly clear, then, that the Latin American pastoral strategy of Christian base communities, intimately linked with liberation theology, has made and will continue to make a very significant and original contribution to Catholic ecclesiology and thus to the church itself on a worldwide level.

With regard to the intellectual origins of liberation theology, my remarks are based on the ideas of Juan Luis Segundo, who has recently cemented his reputation as the most creative and prolific liberation theologian with a massive, three-volume work on Christology.[19] Segundo is also the earliest proponent of a contemporary liberating theology in Latin America, as is evident in a series of lectures he delivered in Montevideo as far back as 1959.[20]

In a brief but significant article, originally given as a speech in Toronto, Segundo, as the most important participant in the liberation movement, has presented his own description of its origins. I begin with a text that succinctly summarizes his view:

> Contrary to the most common assumption, Latin American theology, without any precise title, began to have clearly distinctive features at least ten years before Gustavo Gutiérrez's well known book, *A Theology of Liberation*. This was a kind of baptism, but the baby had already grown old.
>
> The real beginning came simultaneously from many theologians working in different countries and places in Latin America, before the first session of Vatican II. In any case, these developments began some years before the Constitution *Gaudium et Spes* in 1965, which, to a great extent, was used afterwards as an official support for the main views of this liberation theology.[21]

Segundo then proceeds further and specifies the exact place of origin of this theology as the politically autonomous Latin American universities, while the dramatis personae included students, faculty members, and various groups of intellectuals and professionals. In the universities, these individuals enjoyed political freedom to support variant political ideas, or as Segundo puts it, "above all to unmask, through all kinds of intellectual tools, the mystifying ideologies used by our governments to hide and to justify the inhuman situation of the majority of our population."

Since the majority of those involved were Catholics, this "de-ideologizing" resulted in a kind of religious conversion for many with regard to the social consequences of their religious beliefs, because traditional Catholicism in Latin America had evolved along very individualistic lines, as is true in many other parts of the world also. For the students and others

> . . . could do nothing except include theology—the understanding of Christian faith—into the ideological mechanisms structuring the whole of our culture. And when I say "the whole of our culture," I mean by that, that even though ideologies are consciously or unconsciously developed in the ruling classes which benefit from them, they also pervade the whole of society since they are introjected even into the minds of those who are their victims. Unlearned and so incapable of utilizing developed tools of ideological suspicion in a culture considered impartial and the same for all social classes, poor and marginalized people were led by the culture to accept distorted and hidden

oppressive elements which justified their situation and, among all these elements, a distorted and oppressive theology.[22]

Thus, Segundo continues, "before knowing anything about political theology, if it existed at all at the time, the university student, using above all the
notion of the social function of ideologies, had already discovered that our
whole culture, whatever the intention of constructing it may have been, was
working for the benefit of the ruling classes." A further discussion of
ideological suspicion and the method of liberation theology is given in the
next section of this chapter.

Either Content or Method?

Turning from the question of the origin of liberation theology, we take
up a question that follows logically: What is this theology about? Or what is
its content and substance? And here we have to chart a careful course
through a dangerous Scylla and Charybdis with regard to theological content and theological method.

On the one hand, there are some theologians who evaluate and
pigeonhole liberation theology as merely one more example of a theological
approach that is concerned with certain distinctive themes, after the manner of a theology of work, a theology of hope or a theology of play. On the
other hand, liberation theologians oppose this interpretation by insisting
that the most important aspect of this theology is not its content or themes,
but rather its theological method. As Segundo expresses it in his book, *The
Liberation of Theology,* "the one and only thing that can maintain the liberating character of any theology is not its content but its *methodology.* It is the
latter that guarantees the continuing bite of theology, whatever terminology may be used and however much the existing system tries to reabsorb it
into itself."[23]

My own conclusion is in agreement with Segundo that the method of a
liberating theology is of primary importance. At the same time, however, I
would also insist on the enduring importance of the themes, events, and
doctrine that it selects and elaborates in distinctive fashion from the sources
of Scripture, the history of Christian tradition, and contextual analyses.
Consequently, I am going to consider both issues, turning here to theological content and then to theological method in chapter 3.

A useful survey of the content of liberation theology may be found in
the book of Roger Haight entitled *An Alternative Vision.*[24] Haight recognizes
that liberation theology is not a complete systematic theology and also that

there are many different kinds of liberation theology. As a consequence, he rightly expands the traditional understanding of "content" to include not only themes or categories but also general characteristics, experiences, suppositions, and principles. Although this approach does not result in a neat conceptual package, it does arrive at a more accurate overall picture of the reality of liberation theology. What follows, then, will be a selection of the most important elements in Haight's analysis, together with my own reflections on these elements.

The first and most important experience is the same one that I have just mentioned from the advertisement for the German translation called "The Liberation Theology Library." That is the compassionate experience of poverty, or to put it more exactly, of the impoverishment of vast masses of people because of domestic and foreign economic systems. For the fact is that the majority of the people of Latin America live in a situation of permanent destitution, of mortal danger, because of lack of essential food, potable water, sanitation, decent shelter and even the rudiments of health care, literacy, and education. Because of this situation, the German theologian, Jürgen Moltmann, has referred to the vast urban slums that surround each of the cities of the Latin American continent as "circles of death," since such conditions involve not only misery but death itself, especially to the weakest and most vulnerable, that is, the children. Unlike their colleagues in the north, the Latin American theologians cannot escape this omnipresent horror, and this explains a certain passion and urgency which permeates all their work.

Second, and in keeping with its very title, liberation theology places great emphasis on the important biblical themes of freedom and liberation, especially freedom from the appalling social and structural sinfulness I have just described, as well as liberation from what are clearly seen to be the profound roots of personal sinfulness. A concrete example is evident in *The Pedagogy of the Oppressed* (Freire's most famous book), which aims at overcoming the sense of fatalism that has been imposed on the poor by the ruling classes and which enables them instead to become free and creative agents in the fulfillment of their own destiny. Connected with this is the profound realization that it is in this world and not in some other supposedly "religious" world that men and women are called to act and to fulfill God's will.

Another way of expressing all this is to note that in liberation theology there is a strong emphasis on historical consciousness, with its openness to social and personal change and opposition to a fixed and static world view. In close harmony with this is its constant stress on the social nature and social responsibilities of human existence, which puts it in sharp contrast with a religious sensibility such as that which prevails in the United States and which is characterized by a pervasive individualism tending toward self-ishness.[25] Such a social consciousness emphasizes the effects of one's environment and social status on the most basic assumptions of one's world view, including the religious or theological dimension, and devotes considerable attention to a critique of unexamined ideologies. It emphasizes, too, that human society is a "social construction,"[26] not a fixed creation of God or nature, and that accordingly it can be reconstructed in ways that promise greater justice and greater participation for all its members.

Thus, it was inevitable that liberation theology should turn more and more to the social sciences, both for a macro- and microanalysis of the theologian's social context, as well as for possible models and strategies for social change and even radical transformation of societies that frustrate the liberty and well-being of their members. It was also inevitable in this context that Latin Americans should enter into a dialogue with Marxism, which represents the most comprehensive and influential alternative to capitalism on the analytical level in the contemporary world. Clearly, there are many lights and shadows in the chiaroscuro of this dialogue, but this is clearly preferable to the U.S. relationship to Marxism, which has been brilliantly characterized by Richard Hofstadter as part of "the paranoid style in American politics."[27] A notable exception to this style is the carefully researched and balanced study of Marxism by Arthur McGovern.[28]

Some of the characteristic theological themes or emphases of liberation theology can only be touched on briefly at this point. Major importance is given to the biblical notion of the kingdom of God, a vision of societal existence marked by justice, peace and loving collaboration. This does not mean an idolatrous baptism of any one polis as the kingdom, as facile criticisms suggest, but rather the recognition, in the example of Jon Sobrino, that states which murder their own citizens with impunity are certainly further from the eschatological kingdom than states which abjure and punish such flagrant genocide.[29] Other significant concepts include the universality of God's grace in the world (that is, it is not limited to the various channels of the Christian churches), the close relationship between liberation or salvation from personal sin and from oppressive social structures, and a very strong insistence that the essence of Christianity consists in love, the love of God and neighbor. Many liberation theologians hold that in the contemporary world the most important and difficult area of Christian love of neighbor is to be found in a commitment to the struggle for justice, especially justice for the masses of poor and suffering human beings in the contemporary world.

A final word may be said regarding spirituality, understood as the interior life of prayer, worship, and union with God, united to the practice of holiness in one's entire life and vocation. Liberation theology is sometimes charged with neglecting this dimension of Christian life because of its interest in social or political issues. The reply to this charge is that spirituality applies to the whole of one's life, and this includes action of some kind in the struggle for justice, which cannot avoid social and political issues. Also, because of the opposition, danger, and frustration encountered in this struggle, a very profoundly rooted spirituality is necessary, with greater depth and courageous perseverance than is usually required in more tranquil and less dangerous forms of Christian witness. In my opinion, this approach to spirituality does not constitute some kind of novelty but rather a retrieval of the authentic biblical spirituality that is obvious in the lives of the Hebrew prophets and of Jesus of Nazareth.[30]

Glimpses of the Future

In concluding with an assessment of the impact of liberation theology, my emphasis will be on the future, since I believe that its contemporary impact is beyond doubt. Not only does a veritable library of books and articles exist on this topic, but one can hardly pick up a serious theological journal without encountering an article or review related to the subject of liberation.

My concentration on the future first focuses on the Third World in general, and then on the more specific area of Latin America. We can refer to this endeavor as a quest for "the signs of the future," which may be considered a complement to Vatican II's call to discern "the signs of the times."

The impact of liberation theology in a more general or global way has been aptly and succinctly expressed by Ignacio Ellacuria: "The full and integral salvation of the Third World, of the world of the poor, is a great historical challenge. Responding to this challenge should be regarded as the fundamental charism of the Latin American Church."[31] Ellacuría, a theologian who has labored for many years in El Salvador, develops this thesis at some length, but the following text summarizes his argument:

> Is it not true that this decisive turning towards the poor is the mission of the Church in Latin America, and of the Latin American Church within the universal Church? In Latin America "the poor" are not a fringe group; they are a majority. In a real sense they define what Latin America is: poor in health, poor in education, poor in living standards, poor in having a say in their own destiny. By virtue of the universal vocation of the Gospel and by virtue of the historical summons specific to the region in which the Latin American Church lives, it must be the Church of the poor. If it were to be that

in truth, then it would give impetus to a new historical form of Christianity that should be transmitted to the universal Church. And this new form will be transmitted, if it acquires the necessary drive and tension.[32]

Rather than remaining on this level of general statements, I will focus on two specific contemporary events that clearly reveal the important impact of liberation theology on the universal church. I am referring to the publication of the Vatican Congregation for the Doctrine of the Faith's *Instruction on Christian Freedom and Liberation* (dated March 22, 1986) and Pope John Paul's personal *Letter to the Brazilian Episcopal Conference* (dated April 9, 1986). Both of these documents provide abundant evidence of the impact of liberation theology both on the universal and the Latin American church, an impact which shows every promise of continuing and developing in the immediate and long-range future.

In the document on Christian freedom and liberation,[33] which is divided into one hundred paragraphs, a number of important statements on liberation themes occur at the very beginning. In the first paragraph, the gospel, which is the charter and normative expression of the essential faith of Christianity, is said to be "by its very nature a message of freedom and liberation." In the second paragraph, the theme of freedom and liberation is said to be "at the heart of the Christian message." Thus I would emphasize as forcefully as possible that it is extremely difficult to conceive how an official church document could present a *stronger* endorsement of any position than to refer to it as the "heart" or "very nature" of the message that the church exists to transmit.

Several other important observations are made in the second chapter regarding the theme of Christian freedom and liberation. First of all, the document explicitly limits itself to what it calls the *"principal* theoretical and practical aspects" of its theme and then enunciates what is probably the most important single statement in the instruction: "As regards applications to different local situations, it is for the local churches, in communion with one another and with the See of Peter, to make direct provision for them." There are at least two important consequences of this statement. On the one hand, the Latin American church could have and indeed already has seen this as an approval of the liberation theology that has flourished in their own "local church," including both the work of theologians as well as that of bishops in their conferences at Medellin and Puebla and in many local documents. Thus, it has been widely embraced and disseminated as an official endorsement of the latter's work, which, considering the hierarchical teaching structure of the Roman Catholic Church, will entail far-reaching repercussions, that is, impact for the future.

On the other hand, recalling the position noted above, that freedom and liberation are at the heart of the gospel message, this can also be read as a challenge to all the other regions of the world, including the United States, to develop their own liberation theologies. A U.S. liberation theology, then, could not avoid facing the accusation made by many Latin Americans that this country is guilty of various forms of military, economic, and cultural invasion of Central and South America. This, too, if it is taken up by U.S. theologians and citizens, could have considerable impact on Latin America's future.[34]

Such knowledgeable observers as Gustavo Gutiérrez and Leonardo Boff have noted that an even more important endorsement of liberation theology occurred in a letter sent by Pope John Paul to the bishops of Brazil shortly after the above document was published. The letter was composed after a very intense meeting of several days with the Brazilian hierarchy in Rome. During that time, the topics included what the pope himself referred to in his welcoming speech as "the red-hot question of liberation theology," noting also that "when purified of elements which can adulterate it, with grave consequences for the faith, this theology of liberation is not only orthodox but also necessary."[35]

During the Roman visit, the pope appears to have gained a renewed confidence in the orthodoxy and pastoral sagacity of the Brazilian episcopacy, which is generally acknowledged to have been the most progressive in Latin America over the past two decades. His remarks on liberation theology are to be found in parts 5 and 6 of the seven-part letter he wrote them after the Roman visit.[36]

The pope first asserts that, given the necessary relation with Scripture and tradition, "the theology of liberation is not only timely but useful and necessary," and that it should constitute a "new stage" in the church's long history of theological reflection. He then moves on to the statements that so elated Latin American theologians and especially the bishops of Brazil:

I think that in this ["new stage"] the Church in Brazil can play an important and at the same time delicate role: that of creating the space and conditions for the development of a theological reflection that fully adheres to the Church's constant teaching on social matters and, at the same time, is suitable for inspiring an effective pastoral praxis in favor of social justice, equity, the observance of human rights, and the construction of a human society based on brotherhood, harmony, truth and charity.

After noting that this reflection should include a critique of unbridled capitalism as well as of state capitalism, he goes on to stress that "such a function, if realized, will certainly be a service the Brazilian Church can render to the nation, and to Latin America, as well as to many other world regions where similar challenges present themselves." And to all this Pope John Paul then adds his own prayer that God "may help you to be unceasingly watchful so that the correct and necessary theology of liberation can develop in Brazil and in Latin America. . . . "

I think these texts are sufficient to manifest the reasons for the joy and hope felt in Latin America at the pope's recognition of their special charism. In realizing this task, Brazil, the south's emerging superpower and the world's largest Catholic nation, had been dubbed the spearhead or cutting edge of human liberation. Above all, episcopal prestige and endorsement have been given to liberation theology *within the Latin American church,* which has enormous importance, given the hierarchical institutions of the Catholic Church. Considering also the approval given *for the entire church* by the Vatican instruction on Christian freedom and liberation, the auspices are excellent for the profound development and massive expansion of liberation theology throughout Latin America and the world. If John Courtney Murray were writing today, he might well suggest that the ripples of Christian freedom he had glimpsed in 1965 had now assumed the proportions of a tidal wave.

Chapter 3
The Method for Liberating Theology

At first glance, the somewhat arcane issue of theological method may appear to have little if any connection with the practice of Christian freedom and to be of little relevance or interest for those actually struggling for the liberation of the poor in Latin America or in any other part of the world. Rather, it would appear to be of concern only in academic circles, for those who have the leisure to pursue the truth for its own sake in the quiet corridors of universities and seminaries.

Despite these initial reactions, it should become evident in the course of this chapter that liberation theology's greatest achievement and its major contribution to the world church has been precisely to overcome this truncated and profoundly alienating understanding of theology. And it has achieved this by creating a method of doing theology which is intimately linked not only with orthodoxy but also with orthopraxis, that is, the liberating action which will provide the ultimate test of orthodoxy. Although it has often been neglected in the course of the history of the church, this retrieval of the importance of orthopraxis follows in the same theological tradition as Christianity's charter document, the Sermon on the Mount: "Not everyone who says to me, 'Lord, Lord,' shall enter the kingdom of heaven, but he who does the will of my Father who is in heaven" (Mt 7:21).

One of the pioneers in the articulation of this method, Juan Luis Segundo, has constantly emphasized the utmost importance of the fact that "the one and only thing that can maintain the liberative character of any theology is not its content but its methodology. It is the latter that guarantees the continuing bite of theology, whatever terminology may be used and however much the system tries to reabsorb it into itself."[1] At this point, then, I begin with a consideration of method in the writings of Gustavo Gutiérrez, J.L. Segundo, and Jon Sobrino, since they have clearly been the leaders in the profound articulation of method. In the latter part of this chapter, I go on to consider theologians from other areas in order to achieve a synthesis that will contribute to a "world theology" for the world church that was discussed in chapter 2.

Method in Gutiérrez and Segundo

Gutiérrez's *A Theology of Liberation*[2] was the first encounter with this new movement for many in the English-speaking world. Its first part is devoted to the clarification of his methodology, which he believes is both traditional and new. An important point Gutiérrez makes at the beginning of this attempt is that theology is an activity common to all believers, even though it may consist in "a rough outline of a theology" or a "pre-understanding of that faith which is manifested in life, action, and concrete attitude."[3] Clearly, then, his method is not intended merely for academics or professional theologians, but also for all who try to lead a Christian life.

In clarifying his approach, Gutiérrez first considers two classical expressions of theological method: theology as wisdom and theology as rational knowledge. The former was intended to serve for growth in the spiritual life and was basically a reflection on Scripture. Because of monastic and Greek philosophical influences, however, it tended to be removed from any worldly concerns. Gutiérrez perceives a dichotomy opening up between this approach and that of a more rationalistic theology around the fourteenth century, with *The Imitation of Christ* serving as a paradigm of the split.

Theology as rational knowledge, he continues, began in the twelfth century and reached its zenith in Albert the Great and Thomas Aquinas. In this transition theology became "an intellectual discipline, born of the meeting of faith and reason."[4] It should be strongly stressed that Gutiérrez regards both of these classical expressions as valid and as permanent tasks for theology. At the same time, he asserts emphatically that "both functions must be salvaged, at least partially, from the division and deformations they have suffered throughout history."[5]

Gutiérrez next defines his own method as "critical reflection on praxis," and stresses that this does not involve a new content but a new way of doing theology.[6] The following points appear to me to be central to his approach. First, he begins with the fact that the Christian and the Christian community are called to a definite praxis, that is, to "real charity, action, and commitment to the service of men."[7] In the Latin American context, the most striking sign of the times is clearly that of massive human suffering, and so the praxis is further qualified as the attempt to eliminate such suffering. For Gutiérrez, theology is a reflection on this definite praxis. It is a second step or—in the oft-quoted phrase of Hegel—"it rises only at sundown."

Moreover, theology must be critical both of society and of the church in the light of the Bible. Thus it serves the purpose of freeing both these institutions from various forms of ideology, idolatry, and alienation, while at the same time preventing pastoral practice from degenerating into mindless activism. Clearly, such an approach qualifies as prophetic, since it seeks to discover the profound meaning of historical events "with the purpose of making the Christian's commitment within them more radical and clear."[8] Consequently, critical theology is open to the world and to all of human history, with the result that it will always be changing and constantly be in a process of renewal.

Lastly, Gutiérrez places great stress on the element of hope in his method. Instead of being "the caboose of the present," theology will continue to be reflection "in the light of the future which is believed in and hoped for" and thus "part of the process by which the world is transformed."[9]

Juan Luis Segundo's views on method are expressed with greatest clarity in his work, *The Liberation of Theology*, although it appears to me that he has been utilizing the method ever since his first published theological works.[10] In this book Segundo is forthright in adopting a conflictive stance and stating the differences which characterize a "liberating" theology as opposed to what he calls "academic" or "classical" theology, that is, theology as he sees it practiced in the centers of learning of the West.

To express his liberating methodology, Segundo utilizes the concept of the "hermeneutic circle." The same term was previously applied to the exegetical approach of Rudolf Bultmann, but Segundo believes that his method corresponds better to the strict sense of the circle. On its most fundamental level, the method involves "the continuous change in our interpretation of the Bible which is dictated by the continuing changes in our present-day reality, both individual and societal."[11] If present reality is to change, one must be to some extent dissatisfied with it and thus raise questions concerning it that are "rich enough, general enough, and basic enough to force us to change our customary perceptions of life, death, knowledge, society, politics, and the world in general."[12] Once these new and more profound questions are posed to the scriptural texts, it is essential that our interpretation of the texts change also; otherwise, the new questions would either receive no answer or else answers that are conservative and useless.

This preliminary description of the method is further clarified by the delineation of four steps that are essential to its proper exercise:

Firstly there is our way of experiencing reality, which leads us to ideological suspicion. *Secondly* there is the application of our ideological suspicion to the whole ideological superstructure in general and to theology in particular. *Thirdly* there comes a new way of experiencing theological reality that leads us to exegetical suspicion, that is, to the suspicion that the prevailing interpretation of the Bible has not taken important pieces of data into account. *Fourthly* we have our new hermeneutic, that is, our new way of interpreting the fountainhead of our faith (i.e., Scripture) with the new elements at our disposal.[13]

The concept of "suspicion" here is derived from Paul Ricoeur and is based on Segundo's hypothesis that ideologies connected with current social conditions and vested interests may be unconsciously ruling our present theological ideas and pastoral practice.

It is important to note that the first stage of the circle always involves the experience of a definite problem, and an act of will or commitment on the part of the subject to find a solution to the problem. Segundo concludes from this that "a hermeneutic circle in theology always presupposes a profound human commitment, a *partiality* that is consciously accepted—not on the basis of theological criteria of course, but on the basis of human criteria."[14]

At this point it is obvious that the hermeneutical circle is in need of considerable clarification, so that its procedures may be understood more precisely. To accomplish this, Segundo considers in some detail the works of four writers: Harvey Cox, Karl Marx, Max Weber, and James Cone. His objective is to determine whether they have succeeded in completing the four steps in the circle and, if not, to point out precisely at what point they have failed.

The true meaning of the circle can perhaps be best illustrated by considering the treatment of Cone, since he is adjudged to be the only writer who has completed all four stages. As regards the first stage, there can be no doubt that Cone is partial, that is, totally committed to the black community and its struggle for freedom. Clearly, Cone has experienced the problem of racism and is determined to find a solution and to attempt to change the reality of racism.

When he reaches the second point of the circle, Cone manages to achieve a high level of suspicion with regard to the whole American superstructure, including the dominant theology. This appears clearly in his charge that American white theology "has been basically a theology of the white oppressor, giving religious sanction to the genocide of Indians and the enslavement of black people."[15] The central ideological weapon that Cone uncovers is white theology's pretense of "color blindness,"[16] an approach which effectively disguises the racial roots of oppression.

Cone then moves to the third point in the circle, by committing himself to uprooting the mechanisms of ideology in white theology and thus to fashioning a theology that corresponds to the perspective and aspirations of the black community. This leads directly into the fourth point, as he presents a new interpretation of Scripture based on the richer and more profound questions that have been raised.

Segundo's entire book is actually a nuanced attempt to perform the same task as Cone. Instead of Cone's "white theology," he deideologizes the "classical" or "academic" theology of the West; and instead of speaking for the black community, he speaks for the suffering masses of the Third World in Latin America. In my view, the key to his method is what may be called an ideological dialectic, that is, an exposure of unconscious or conscious ideologies that sacralize the status quo, while at the same time clearing the ground for the creation of new and more efficacious ideologies that will be open to change. A great deal of attention has been given in Segundo's published work to the implications of these principles for ecclesiology, but that is beyond the scope of this chapter.[17]

The Approach of Jon Sobrino

The basic principles of Sobrino's approach are to be found in his presentation at a meeting in Mexico City,[18] while their actual utilization in theologizing is evident throughout his books on Christology.[19] Two questions are considered of crucial importance by Sobrino in the Mexico City address. First, what is the interest of the theologian? Why does one do theology in the first place? Also, for whom is one theologizing and from whose perspective? Obviously, this presupposes that theological activity is never neutral; it always has a practical and ethical dimension, whether this is explicit or implicit. Sobrino concludes that in Europe the predominant interest has been to recover the meaning of a faith that was threatened, and that this was liberating for certain elites. In Latin America, the basic problem was to recover the meaning of a real situation that was not only threatened but in actual misery. The interest, therefore, was to "aid in transforming the reality of sin. The adversary in theology has been not so much the 'atheist' as the 'non-person'."[20]

A second basic question concerns the influence of the Christian reality on theological understanding. This presupposes that the Christian reality is always in the process of realizing itself in history. The question then becomes: What different effects does this Christian reality have on the actual concrete functioning of theological understanding in Latin America and Europe?

In responding to both questions, Sobrino utilizes a tripartite framework, which is based on the actual history of Jesus. I note in passing that the actual "following of the historical Jesus" (i.e., Christian praxis) is the crucial *locus theologicus* throughout his books on Christology. Each of the three aspects of the history of Jesus is also related to the method of theological understanding.

The first area of discussion concerns the liberating character of the history of Jesus, which leads to the question of the *liberating* character of theological understanding (as opposed to a possible *alienating* character). The next element concentrates on the dialectic between the present and the future of the kingdom of God proclaimed by Jesus, which brings us to the problem of the relation between theory and praxis. The third element concerns the dialectic of cross and resurrection in the life of Jesus, which leads to the problem of the epistemological break within theological understanding.

With regard to the liberating character of theology, Sobrino utilizes for his comparison the two "moments" of the Enlightenment. He believes that the major emphasis in European theology has been a response to the challenge of the first moment symbolized by Kant, where liberation is seen as the freeing of reason from all authoritarianism and where its basic interest is rationality. The Latin Americans, by contrast, orient themselves to the second moment of the Enlightenment, symbolized by Marx, where liberation is seen as the freeing of reality from suffering and where the basic interest is not rationality but transformation. Clearly, the latter involves not only a new way of thinking but also a new way of acting.

Such a bifurcation of interests, Sobrino continues, has important repercussions; for European theology tends to harmonize the reality of massive suffering, for example, with the demands of reason, in order to demonstrate that it is meaningful to believe in God in a world of suffering. But such an approach can, in fact, have an alienating rather than liberating function; for often it leaves the reality untouched and in that sense justified or justifiable. On the other hand, the Latin Americans focus rather on the need to transform the sinful situation and thus to confront it in a manner that is as real and free of ideology as possible. In summary form, "the first viewpoint can lead to seeking the reconciliation of meaninglessness only within the subject himself or herself; the second viewpoint sees reconciliation as possible only in the solution of the crisis of reality itself, or at least in the attempt at a solution."[21] This diversity of perspectives explains also why the Latin Americans seek aid in finding solutions not primarily from philosophy but from the social sciences, since these analyze the reality and mechanisms of human suffering and provide possible concrete models of liberation from that suffering. It also explains their greater awareness of the status of theology precisely as knowledge. Because of possible ideologization, they stress the real effects that a certain kind of theology has on society, and not merely the intention that the theologian has in doing theology.

Sobrino devotes the second major part of his essay to a problematic mentioned above, the relationship between theory and praxis in the advancement of the kingdom. European theology is seen as primarily interested in transmitting a body of truths or meanings, that is, it is fundamentally theory or a history of theory, even when it is reflecting on theory and praxis. The Latins, however, stress the need first for a contact with reality before reflecting on the theology implied in that contact. Furthermore, for them "it is not only a question of thinking beginning with experience, but of thinking beginning with a definite experience, beginning with a praxis that not only is influenced by the suffering in the world . . . but which starts with the transformation of that suffering."[22]

Sobrino admits that European theology has also stressed the need of orthopraxis flowing from orthodoxy, but believes that it still concentrates on thinking rather than action and that it has replaced an orthodoxy of affirmations by an orthodoxy of method. Also, in Europe the "following of Jesus" is usually relegated to spiritual theology; its role as a means of "knowing" Jesus has been largely ignored in contemporary systematic Christologies. For Latin Americans, however, it is the real following of Jesus (i.e., praxis) which permits knowledge of the reality of Jesus: "method in its most profound sense is understood as the unity of knowledge as activity and knowledge as content."[23] In summary, the method is not to think about but actually to follow the way of Jesus, that is, Christ is "truth" insofar as he is "way."

At this point the question arises: What "way" is to be followed that permits an understanding that is distinctively Christian? In other words, what "way" moves from the present to the future of the kingdom of God? This introduces the third major division of Sobrino's exposition, the integration of the "epistemological break" into theological understanding; for the way from the present world to the kingdom of God can be understood either as a progressive development of the present order or as a contradiction and transformation of the present. For Sobrino, it is clear that theological understanding has to be contrary to natural understanding. This epistemological break is found in Scripture in its affirmation of the transcendence of a crucified God.[24] Another way of stating this fact is that theological understanding must undergo "conversion" in its own functioning. Without this, it will seek to develop universal standards of interpretation within which it tries to verify the truth of faith, "but it does not suspect that the first thing faith does is put these universal standards in question."[25]

Sobrino then delineates a number of consequences of the epistemological break which have influenced Latin American theology. In a continent where love, reconciliation, and justice are not apparent, but where the situation of vast masses of people is catastrophic, theology is much more dialectical than analogical: like is not known by like, but by the dissimilar. "Liberation" can only be understood dialectically, in opposition to lived oppression, and it is in the situation of sin and oppression that one seeks to find God.

Furthermore, Greek thought had assumed that wonder and the positive structure of reality were what moved man to know. For Latin Americans, the primary motivation is rather that of sorrow, since present history is understood as the continued history of the passion of God; thus the groans of the oppressed occupy a privileged position as the motive for theological thinking. And instead of a system which coherently integrates the data of revelation and the data of history, this theology seeks to respond to a situation of widespread sorrow by striving to eliminate the causes of sorrow.

Another consequence has to do with the question of theodicy, or the reconciliation of God and human suffering. The Latins have historicized and politicized the question, so that it is not merely concerned with natural catastrophes but with human decisions and systems of oppression. Moreover, they view the problem not as a justification of God but as the justification of man in a world of injustice. Consequently, the solution is not to be found in "thinking" about God in a way which reconciles God and suffering, but rather in the task of constructing a world according to God's will and experiencing the reality of God in this attempt. And the question of theodicy is viewed as essentially practical: to the extent that faith in the God of Jesus leads to the real overcoming of suffering, to that extent is God justified, even when there is no theoretical reconciliation of God and suffering. From this perspective, knowledge of God is connatural: whoever tries seriously to do justice to men and women is on the way to God.

The phenomenon of the "death of God" leads to a fourth consequence. In Europe, this phenomenon functions as the most radical expression of the crisis of meaning within a theistic culture. It also serves to highlight what is most distinctive in Christian thought; for "the crucified God marks the dividing line between an authentically Christian theology and any religion, philosophy, or ideology whatever, since it is the most radical expression of God's assumption of history, not in the ideal but in the real order."[26]

However, the "death of God" is seen in Latin America in a different concrete mediation than that of Europe, namely, in the "death of man." If the death of God is the expression of a crisis of meaning, then the death of man is the expression of a crisis in reality itself, so that the epistemological break is not so much in the death of God as in the death of the oppressed. Thus the mediation of the absolutely Other is that which functions as really other: the oppressed. Through the latter is discovered what is typical of the God of Jesus: "his availability to become other, to submerge himself in history and thus to make real and credible his last word to mankind, his word of love."[27]

A last consequence concerns the basic aporia or paradox of all serious understanding, such as, in Christian history, the paradox or aporia of creator and creature, liberty and grace, faith and works. In Latin America, the basic aporia is between the gratuity of the kingdom of God and its human realization (a modern equivalent of the problem of grace and liberty). Since the realization takes place in a world of suffering, the task is necessarily conflictive, and the most positive element in reality—love which searches efficaciously for justice—appears impotent before the most negative factor—sin and injustice.

Aporia means literally "without a way"; from this perspective there appears to be no way for love to triumph over injustice. The problem is not resolved by thinking but once again by praxis: to know theologically in the presence of an aporia is to open a way. Thus, Latin American theology tends to opt for concrete social and political solutions (e.g., socialism). This differs from the European emphasis on "eschatological reserve," which tends to relativize all concrete programs, since they do not constitute the definitive kingdom of God. Latin theology admits this but insists that partial and functional solutions are essential in order to solve the aporia. Christian faith, in this view, is not an ideology, but it provides the *source* of partial and functional ideologies.[28]

In conclusion, while admitting the positive achievements of European theology (e.g., those which led to Vatican II), Sobrino faults it for its lack of self-criticism. This appears in its historical anachronism, namely, in its assumption that a theological understanding that was liberating in certain historical situations must continue to be such in different historical situations. It is also seen to be guilty of geographical anachronism, that is, it was not aware that it was theologizing from the geopolitical center of the world, ignoring the fact that the world is a totality in tension between center and periphery and that, from a Christian perspective, it is the periphery (the poor) or the repercussions on the periphery that is the privileged place for theological understanding.

Sobrino also alludes to a difference between the two theologies with regard to their relation to the sources of faith. Obviously, for both there is a first moment of acceptance of the Christian faith. But the Europeans tend to clarify reality from the sources; for the Latins, the sources are not seen as sources previous to the analysis of reality and liberating praxis, but rather as sources which illumine reality insofar as they themselves are illuminated by it. In brief, there is a constant dialectical interplay between the sources of revelation and real Christian existence.

From Sobrino's perspective, the most fundamental divergence between the different theologies lies in the overcoming of dualisms. In Europe, this has often occurred on the level of thinking (e.g., spirit-body, person-society, transcendence-history). But what Latin American theology has attempted is the overcoming of the most radical dualism of all: that between the believing subject and history, between theory and praxis, not on the level of mere thinking, but on the level of real existence. A final sentence sums up the entire article:

> Fundamentally, Latin American theology has tried to recover the meaning of the profound biblical experiences concerning what it means to know theologically: to know the truth is to do the truth, to know Jesus is to follow Jesus, to know sin is to take away sin, to know suffering is to free the world from suffering, to know God is to go to God in justice.[29]

Sobrino's analysis is considerably more nuanced than the foregoing outline indicates. For present purposes, however, it can be seen to pull together in a synthesis the elements of method presented by the other theologians noted above. It also has the advantage of uncovering, on a profound level, the basic differences between the Latin American approach and other traditional methods in theology. Before evaluating its possible contribution to world theology, I would now like to consider briefly the work of several North American theologians who have written recently on the problematic of theology and praxis.

Developments in North America

Charles Davis has published an important article on the subject of praxis.[30] In large part, Davis is expounding the views of others, but the basic thrust of his analysis of praxis is very similar to that of Sobrino. Also, he sees the question as a serious challenge to all of theology, and points to a number of the crucial questions it raises.

In my opinion, however, the article is ultimately disappointing, in that Davis does not really expatiate on the kind of theology that would reply to the questions he has posed. He does insist that a renewed praxis is necessary and that it "must be conscious as united to theory." Moreover, he notes that Christian praxis "demands a critical analysis of present society, intended to uncover the contradictions latent within it," and includes "the actualization of the conflict thus uncovered."[31] However, to cite one example, he does not respond to the problem posed earlier that an acceptance of the mediation of faith by praxis means that "theology loses its boundaries as an independent discipline, because the only appropriate context for the conscious articulation of praxis is a theory of the development of society in its total reality."[32]

Matthew Lamb has also published an article on the problem, which performs a valuable service in clearly outlining five different methodological approaches to theology.[33] Like Davis, he believes that "theory-praxis goes right to the core of the entire theological enterprise."[34] After an analysis of the four other models in contemporary theology, he discusses a theology based on "critical praxis correlations," which he himself appears to favor. This approach affirms that "praxis is not only the goal but also the foundation of theory" and that "only an authentic religious, moral, intellectual and social praxis can ground an authentic theology."[35] Moreover, the approach calls for "orthopraxy as the foundation of orthodoxy" as well as the relating of theology to other human knowledge and action not by the mediation of philosophy but by "the praxis of a wide-ranging interdisciplinary collaboration."[36] Lamb uses the term "emancipatory" praxis frequently, and this appears to correspond to the Latin American use of "liberating" praxis, at least on a formal level.

Lamb's major contribution to the development of a theology of "critical praxis correlationships" appears to be the distinguishing of different tasks within it as either foundational-methodological, epistemological-organizational, or empirical-communicative. However, aside from the question of the clarity and utility of these distinctions, he does not contribute much detail for the understanding of a praxis-grounded theology. In this respect, it should be stressed that the author himself refers to his survey as "only a beginning."[37]

In the much larger framework of his book on method, David Tracy is another author who has turned his attention to the question of a "practical theology."[38] In Tracy's view, fundamental and systematic theology are concerned with the construction of present meaning, while historical theology reconstructs past meaning for the present. From this perspective he envisions practical theology's task as "to project the future possibilities of meaning and truth on the basis of present constructive and past historical theological resources."[39] It is doubtful to me that any of the Latin Americans mentioned above would accept this as a total description of their task of theologizing.

Tracy also proceeds to a critique of contemporary theologies of praxis from his revisionist perspective. His major objection is that they do not challenge the neo-orthodox model of their predecessors. Thus he asks: "Why cannot that critical commitment so admirably articulated in the critical interpretations of the social and political realities of our common experience, also be employed to interpret critically the possible conceptual incoherencies of traditional Christian symbols?"[40] If we confine ourselves to the Latin American theologians under discussion, the answer to that question is that they have employed and are continuing to employ a critique of the Christian tradition and symbols that is at least as penetrating as any that I know in Western theology.[41]

But the charge of neo-orthodoxy does give a clue to the real divergence between Tracy and the Latin Americans. In his description of the neo-orthodox approach, Tracy observes that it insists "upon the theologian's own faith as an existential condition of the possibility of theology."[42] The Latin Americans certainly would insist on this, as is obvious in the authors treated in this article. Since Tracy himself does not, my guess is that the Latin Americans would consider him not as a theologian at all but as an apologete or philosopher of religion. In his critical review of Tracy's book, Avery Dulles acutely points to this key issue in his final question: "Is Christian praxis a constitutive element in the systematic understanding of faith?"[43] Tracy's revisionist stance clearly compels him to say no; for the Latin Americans, the answer is just as clearly a resounding yes.

In general, Tracy's treatment of a theology of praxis is the least developed in his book, reading as it does as a kind of brief appendix to other very erudite and comprehensive chapters. Again, it should be acknowledged that he characterizes his views in this chapter as "merely anticipatory."[44] In my view, a continuation of discussion on this issue will reveal that Tracy's views on theological method and those of the Latin Americans are mutually exclusive; but this does not rule out the possibility of fruitful dialogue.[45]

Another North American, Gregory Baum, appears to have entered into a much more profound conversation with Latin American theologians than any of those mentioned, and also to be closest to them in method. Baum calls his approach "critical theology," noting first that it entails "a sustained dialogue with the critical thought of the late Enlightenment,"[46] which corresponds to Sobrino's "second moment" of the Enlightenment. Further, he states that it is a "reflection on praxis," which is "applicable to every area of theology—moral, dogmatic, ascetical, and so forth." Like the Latin Americans, Baum is very aware of the possible alienating effects of religion, as the title of his book indicates. He, too, is critical of the privatization of Christianity, and sets forth his own intention of regaining the "double dimension of personal-and-social in the gospel."[47]

Baum is careful to point out differences in his method and that of the Latin Americans. For example, he notes the differences in social and class analysis required in North America, as well as the different forms of historically based symbols and of political commitments (e.g., the "reformist" approach is seen as acceptable, as well as the "radical" stance). Neverthe-less, the basic methods appear to be the same, and Baum admits as much when he says they are "structurally" identical.[48] This structural identity is defined very clearly when he asserts that both methods "are reflections on faith-conversion, they are grounded in social commitment in favor of the oppressed, they raise consciousness, lead to social involvement, and regard themselves as the reflective or contemplative component of the liberating human action, in which God is redemptively present to the sinful world."[49] Although the term "praxis" is not used in this sentence, it is clearly implied throughout.

Baum's two-year effort at producing a "theological reading of soci-ology," the subtitle of his book, shows that he shares the Latin American predilection for dialogue with the social sciences. Even the divergences he mentions concerning different social analyses, and so forth, are faithful to the Latin American principle of theologizing out of one's own historical and geographical milieu. Thus the further development of Baum's theology will be an important test case for the applicability of the Latin American method in other parts of the world, especially in the developed world.

Concluding Observations

One fact that clearly emerges from this survey is that the question of praxis is surfacing from many different perspectives as a key issue in theological methodology today or even, as Lamb maintains, *the* central issue. It should also be clear that the concept of praxis has provided the linchpin in the structure of an original and indigenous Latin American theology during the past fifteen years, that is, during the time when it ceased to be a mirror-reality, merely reflecting the theological views of the developed nations, and began its course as a source-reality, faithful to its own history and culture.[50] Because of their unswerving concentration on praxis, then, it seems entirely probable that the Latins have an important contribution to make to the problematic that is now coming to the fore in Western theology.[51] This contribution may be discerned not only in the im-portant area of method in theology, but also in the actual *doing* of praxis-based theology. The present study may at least be of some service in open-ing up the parameters and uncovering further nuances in the contemporary debate on praxis.

Furthermore, this study may help to dissolve some false impressions concerning Latin American theology that occasionally arise in the West. The difficulty may be illustrated by a humorous anecdote related of the late

Cardinal Jean Daniélou.[52] On a visit to Buenos Aires, Daniélou was asked
for his opinion of the theology of liberation. The cardinal is reported to have
answered that he saw it as a "sub-sub-sub-division" of moral theology.
Thus it was a part of theology that studied the moral act, a part of moral
which studied the social act, a part of that area which studied the political
act, and a part of the latter which studied the problems of underdeveloped
nations. I hope it is clear from the whole tenor of this survey that Daniélou
was profoundly mistaken; what is at issue is not merely the ethics of
development (or of liberation) but the entire structure, method, and content
of contemporary theology.

Again, my primary purpose has been to present ideas from the
periphery that show promise of advancing the dialogue in world theology
with regard to theological method. However, I would like to conclude with
some general observations of my own.

The Latin Americans, in my judgment, have provided a perspective
from outside the orbit of the North Atlantic community which gives a
unique, perhaps unparalleled, opportunity for a penetrating critique of the
Western theological enterprise. Such an optic has not been available for
many centuries; indeed, even the quarrels of the Reformation may now be
seen as essentially an intramural Western debate.

Quite clearly, this does not mean the overthrow of Western theology or
the abandonment of its long and fruitful tradition. But it certainly does offer
abundant opportunities for a purification, for a deepened sensitivity, especially on social issues, for the posing of radical questions about the real
role and concrete impact of theology and the theologian on church and
society, and thus for progress in the never-ending development of theological understanding. The need for a "view from the outside" may be illustrated from a study by the sociologist Joseph P. Fitzpatrick. In a perceptive
discussion of the interrelatedness of religion and culture, he especially emphasizes the fact that "we have the tendency, once we are brought up in a
culture, to project our moral judgments into the culture of others, to judge
them according to the standards which prevail in our own way of life."[53]
Theologians, we may suppose, are not exempt from this human tendency to
accept our particular social constructions as ultimate reality, as the way
things are.

A good concrete example of utilizing the view from outside may be
seen in an essay by Avery Dulles entitled "The Meaning of Faith Considered in Relationship to Justice."[54] Dulles analyzes central elements of
the understanding of faith in both Catholic and Protestant tradition, then
indicates how the tradition is enriched by recent developments in liberation
theology. He honestly states his reservations about aspects of the movement, but Dulles' basically sympathetic attitude suggests that he is open to
further dialogue with regard to his criticisms.[55]

A second observation concerns the neuralgic issue of ideology. Gregory Baum has recently stated flatly that "theologians can no longer stand back from the ideological critique of the Christian religion, to which the sociologists have led them."[56] If this is true, the question of "interest" posed above and the possibility of unconscious ideologies would seem to be urgent issues in the contemporary practice of theology. Thus it appears extremely salutary for theologians to pose for themselves questions such as the following: For whom is one writing in this work, and from whose perspective is one writing? What is the basic reason for selecting a certain topic and developing it in a certain way? What are the actual results that may result from one's work, for the church or society or both? Cui bono, or who benefits from certain directions and emphases?[57]

Clearly, a pedestrian but honest reply might be that one wants to publish rather than perish. Or one could say that one's purpose is to pursue the truth at all costs, wherever it leads and whatever its effects. But this is precisely the attitude that the sociology of knowledge has revealed to be intellectually naive, with its ever-present potentiality for canonizing relative positions as absolute truth. I would judge that a salutary capacity for "ideological suspicion" now appears to be an essential weapon in the intellectual armory of the theologian.

There is, however, another side to the ideological coin. Schillebeeckx has observed that "in contemporary society it is impossible to believe in a Christianity that is not at one with the movement to emancipate mankind."[58] But to effect such emancipation, one has to develop and implement practical strategies for social transformation, that is, ideologies in a neutral sense. Without these, the commitment to emancipation remains on an abstract, and ultimately alienating, level.

Such ideologies are not to be found in Scripture, although an urgent motivation to find and implement them may be discovered there. Rather, they are obtainable through the discernment and utilization of the best models of analysis available at a given point in history, most probably in a framework of interdisciplinary collaboration. It should be frankly recognized that there is no absolute certainty that the models are correct, and they are open to modification and even rejection as a result of actual praxis.

Further, a crucial point is that a certain élan and perseverance are essential for an effective commitment to social transformation. Here the emphasis in European political theology on "eschatological reserve" becomes problematic; for while it attempts, laudably, to protect the absoluteness and gratuity of the kingdom of God, it tends to cast a relativizing pall on all human efforts to realize that kingdom, thus undercutting the enthusiasm and determination needed for an effective historical project. Ironically, the movement to overcome the alienating "privatization" of Christianity may thus be fostering a more subtle but no less effective form of alienation.

Another general conclusion is that an incorporation of the Latin American emphasis on praxis and social justice into theology, including pastoral theology, could have an enormous impact on the church and the world it serves, no matter how the praxis-theory debate develops. For a key weakness in the church at present appears to be the tendency to issue "statements" on social issues without a real plan for the implementation of social teaching at the grass-roots level. But only such orthopraxis (perhaps better, Christo-praxis) and continuing reflection on it appear capable of moving toward a primary objective of the contemporary church: a true synthesis of faith and justice.[59]

As for the praxis-theory debate itself, it seems plausible to assume that both the method of "critical theory correlationship" (as represented by Tracy) and that of "critical praxis correlationship" (as represented by Baum and the Latin Americans) will continue to develop and flourish. Although the approaches are fundamentally divergent in emphasis, there seems to be no compelling reason why they cannot engage in collaboration and fruitful dialogue in the future; for the dialectical relationship of theory (or meaning) and praxis is a fundamental human and theological necessity. In this regard, I would agree with the classic statement of Teilhard de Chardin: "The contemporary point of view is that if the 'true' religion exists it should be recognizable . . . by this sign: that under its influence and by its light the world as a totality takes on a maximum of coherence and a maximum of interest for our taste for action."[60]

At any rate, it is my conviction that a true world-theology is being born in our time and that an era of theological imperialism is rapidly expiring. By speaking of world-theology, I do not intend to advocate a false or premature universalism, nor am I attempting to coopt or domesticate the challenging voices from the periphery that are now reaching the centers of the West. But it appears evident to me that the process toward an interdependent planetary culture is irreversible, and that at the same time this will be characterized by a diversity never before experienced and a consequent enrichment from areas previously ignored. Indeed, this may be the beginning of the era envisioned by Dietrich Bonhoeffer during his own struggle with oppression,

> when men will once more be called on to utter the word of God that the world will be changed and renewed by it. It will be a new language, perhaps quite non-religious, but liberating and redeeming—as was Jesus' language; it will shock people and yet overcome them with its power; it will be the language of a new righteousness and truth, proclaiming God's peace with men and the coming of his kingdom.[61]

Chapter 4
Sources for a Theology of Freedom

In chapter 2, I advanced the view that at present liberation theologies in Latin America have arrived at the stage of young adulthood. Aside from the reasons proposed then in support of this statement, I would like to explore in this chapter other reasons for discerning a growing maturity within the movement. Ironically, these reasons do not refer to a growing consensus and uniformity among the different authors throughout the continent, but rather the opposite: many are branching out and following different routes, and at the same time these differences have resulted in significant areas of constructive criticism. One of the leaders in this development has been Juan Luis Segundo, and his criticism of Latin American colleagues has drawn sharp rebukes from other theologians.[1] In my view, however, this capacity for mutual criticism is a sign of maturity in the movement as well as a very necessary practice for the long-range development and deepening of any liberating theology, that is, any theology that contributes to genuine liberation and creative freedom.

Of even greater importance than these disagreements, however, is the relationship between this chapter and the previous one, which was concerned with the crucial issues of theological method. In this chapter we are concerned with the equally significant question of the *locus theologicus*, that is, the source or sources that provide theology with the materials for the creation of a systematic understanding of the faith that will illumine and contribute to the search for Christian freedom and liberation. A secondary question focuses on the criteria for identifying genuine sources, especially in the context of theological education.

It goes without saying that the major sources for any Christian theology consist of the revealed word of God in Scripture, as well as the rich history of the interpretation and application of Scripture, including the writings of the magisterium, that is referred to as tradition. An increasingly important source, moreover, in recent times has been discovered in Christian experience, both of individuals and indeed of the whole church, viewed under its designation as the People of God. Aspects of this experience include its context (e.g., rich nations or poor nations), its praxis (e.g., different approaches to seeking justice or establishing solidarity with the poor), and its tools of interpretation (e.g., the social sciences are now included with philosophy as interlocutors).

Praxis and the Sources

As a heuristic device for understanding the different approaches that are currently developing in liberation theology, I will now analyze some important recent articles. A helpful beginning is a study by the Argentine Jesuit, Juan Carlos Scannone, who considers himself to be "a philosopher at the service of the theology of liberation."[2] I am especially concentrating on the third part of his article, where he discusses various currents (*corrientes*) and moments within this theology.[3]

Following the generally accepted presupposition that all liberating theology should be intimately related to praxis, Scannone distinguishes four major currents, which are differentiated precisely by the different modes of praxis from which they derive their origins and subsistence. Thus, we have the following major movements: (1) theology that is drawn from the pastoral praxis of the church; (2) theology that concentrates on the praxis of revolutionary groups; (3) theology that begins with historical praxis; and (4) theology that derives from the praxis of the peoples (*pueblos*) of Latin America.

The first approach coincides with the viewpoint of an important group of the Latin American bishops, stressing the evangelical character of liberation and emphasizing a biblical and ecclesial focus. Its preferred mediation in theological discourse is not the socioanalytical one but rather the ethical-anthropological one. Also, because its major interests are in safeguarding the tradition and maintaining ecclesial unity, it tends to give less attention to articulating a theology for lay persons, whose mission demands a commitment to politics.[4] Scannone considers this approach to be a genuine liberation theology, at least in the broad sense of that term.

The second group, whose starting point is revolutionary praxis, is quite critical of the first approach, accusing it of spiritualizing the language of liberation and emptying it of socioanalytical content and historical "bite." The most conspicuous examples of this approach include Hugo Assman and participants in the Christians for Socialism movement. They utilize a Marxist analysis, according to Scannone, but they do not accept dialectical materialism on the philosophical level, which would clearly be atheistic. This kind of reflection occurs among Christians who have been radicalized by revolutionary action which, it should be stressed, is not necessarily violent.

Scannone criticizes this type of reflection because theological thought "arrives too late" to be able to criticize the ideological presuppositions of the revolutionary political option which has been previously adopted. The option is used as a standpoint to criticize the formulations and institutions of the church and also revolutionary deviations, but the option itself is not questioned and thus for all practical purposes is absolutized.

Consequently, Scannone continues, this current loses touch with both the hierarchy and the masses of the people, tending to become a language only sociologically Christian put at the service of the class struggle. It is thus a continuation of the radical current of the theology of secularization, which ends up by disfiguring and at times eliminating the difference between church and world. We will return to the relationship with Marxism later on. For the moment it is enough to point out that some liberation theologians have succeeded in a far more positive dialogue with Marxism than the above criticism suggests.[5]

The third approach is one that directly continues the perspectives opened up by the book of Gustavo Gutiérrez, *A Theology of Liberation;* it is radical in its goal of the structural transformation of Latin American society, but also consciously faithful to the church and the theological tradition. However, it is not only a question of a reflection made in communion with the church, "but also, and especially, of the communitarian and collective subject of the theological reflection: that subject of reflection is the ecclesial base communities."[6] Scannone includes a brief discussion of the use of Marxist social analysis in this movement, but his critique appears to be rather simplistic.

The last approach, from the praxis of the Latin American peoples, has as its most conspicuous representative Lucio Gera. Perhaps the central point of difference from the third approach is to be found in the understanding of the word "people." The second and third approaches understand the people above all as a class or oppressed classes in the capitalist economic structure. The fourth approach, without denying the validity of class analysis, conceives the people as above all a historico-cultural phenomenon, that is, the communitarian subject of a history and a culture. Scannone treats this in more detail than the other approaches, especially its intimate relationship with popular religion, and it is clearly the one he prefers, obviously influenced by the deep roots of Argentine populism and the ambiguous legacy of Peronism.

It is interesting to compare the foregoing analysis with a study of tendencies in liberation theology written a few years later in Chile by Cristián Johansson.[7] Johannson's criteria for distinguishing the tendencies are based on the following questions: "What aspect of reality has the greatest influence on the task of theology; who is the recipient of the theological reflection; what or whom is being served by theology?"[8] Thus, his central point of distinction is the concept of "hermeneutical place," and he presents three possibilities: (1) praxis and the poor as hermeneutical place; (2) praxis and the faithful people as the same; and (3) the culture as hermeneutical place.

For the first position, Johansson cites only one author, Ignacio Ellacuría.[9] To summarize, this position holds that the materially poor, who by the action of evangelization are becoming the spiritually poor, are the place where the Christian God becomes present in an irreplaceable manner, since the poor are an essential part of the kingdom of God and indeed enjoy priority and absoluteness in that kingdom.

The second group contends that the "hermeneutical place is praxis itself insofar as in it takes place the transcendent presence and the salvation of the Lord, who is the ultimate criterion of discernment." However, it is not just a question of the praxis of individuals or groups, but that of the whole faithful people of God, of which the groups form part. Furthermore, the praxis and culture of the people are the primary hermeneutical place for theoretical thinking about liberation, which includes theological thought. The only source given for this tendency is the Juan Carlos Scannone quoted above.[10]

On an even broader level, the third position attempts to determine both the richnesses and the deficiencies of contemporary culture, with the goal of finding paths toward a culture which is liberating and human. The task of theology is to penetrate into the value nucleus of a culture, bringing into being a dialogue between the gospel and culture and aiming at the evangelization of the culture.

Also, the new culture is already in a certain sense present in the contemporary culture, that is, in the life of the people. Furthermore, one of the most visible features of Latin American culture is its religiosity, which constitutes its fundamental value nucleus. Popular religion, then, is an essential hermeneutical place for theological reflection. The major authorities cited for the different elements of this position are Bonaventure Kloppenburg, Jon Sobrino, and Gustavo Gutiérrez.[11] Further comment on Johansson's analysis and that of Scannone will take place after consideration of the important views of Juan Luis Segundo on this issue.

Two Different Theologies?

Segundo's article is very important because it concerns the basic method of any liberating theology anywhere in the world, and also because it has serious implications for the parallel questions of the option for the poor and the hermeneutic privilege of the poor, which are also preoccupations of the Christian churches on a global level. The article was published in France under the title "The Two Theologies of Liberation," and the seriousness with which he views the gap between the two may be clearly seen in the following quote:

> No doubt, both (theologies) share the same global intention of liberating and humanizing those who suffer the most from unjust structures on our continent; but this cannot conceal the fact that we are faced here with two different theologies under the same name: different in scope, different in method, different in presuppositions and different in pastoral consequences.[12]

The basic difference involves the choice of a theology that is intellectual, that is, uses the social sciences and ideological criticism as essential interlocutors for dialogue, and one that is popular in the Spanish sense of arising from the common people. It should also be noted that Segundo believes that a very important shift occurred during the early or middle seventies, which involved a transition from the first or intellectual approach to the second or popular one. And he points out that some very important liberation theologians, such as Gustavo Gutiérrez, Leonardo Boff, and Jon Sobrino, have participated in this shift, a shift with which Segundo is in profound disagreement.

He locates the origins of the first or intellectual approach in the Latin American universities of the early sixties, some years before the Second Vatican Council's *Constitution on the Church in the Modern World* and without any influence at all from European political theology, a misinterpretation of many European theologians. It was in the universities that faculty and students "became free to support any kind of political ideas, and above all to unmask, through all sorts of intellectual tools, the mystifying ideologies used by our governments to hide and to justify the inhuman situation of the majority of our population."[13] And, of course, for Christian students and the theologians working with them, the reigning theological system appeared to be part of this mystification and thus a major contributor to legitimating oppression and injustice. The result was that "this ideological suspicion . . . became a source of a new vision about what theology should become and about how a theologian was supposed to work to unmask the anti-Christian elements hidden in a so-called Christian society."[14]

It is also important to stress that this approach was meant to affect the *whole of theology*, with its studies of God, the church, sacraments, grace, Christology, and so forth. The students and theologians were not preoccupied with forming a new theology that talked about liberation or made this theme its center, in preference to any other theological theme. Also, it was intended to reach the *whole of society*, although at a different pace for the different social classes. It is important to stress this long-term and far-reaching goal: "As theologians, we believed at that time, and some of us still believe, that this movement among the most active and creative members of the church could eventually reach, sooner or later, all oppressed people on our continent, through the pastoral activities of a church following a new line and carrying out a new message."[15]

The second or "popular" line of liberation theology was influenced by the growing impact of popular and populist movements in the seventies, and shifted the focus or context of theology from the middle class of the universities to the common people, the poor. The method of this approach has been well articulated by Leonardo Boff: "In a Church that has opted for the people, for the poor and for their liberation, the *principal learning of theology* comes from the contact with (grassroots) people. Who evangelizes the theologian? The faith witnessed by faithful people, their capacity to introduce God in all their struggling, their resistance against the oppression they customarily have to suffer."[16] In accordance with this view, Boff published a book about a new ecclesiogenesis, that is, a church born from the poor, and Gustavo Gutiérrez entitled his latest book *The Historical Power of the Poor.*[17] These are but two of the many theologians who had begun to comprehend their true task as that of bringing unity and structure to the faith of the people, as well as furnishing a foundation and defense of the people's practice of the faith.

But it is important to note that not all theologians were in agreement with this particular approach to becoming an "organic intellectual" of the poor. These were the ones (like Segundo himself) who "refuse to give up the first critical function which comes out of a suspicion that theology, like other all-pervasive cultural features, can and perhaps should be considered an instrument of oppression and, hence, as a non-Christian theology. Facts point so obviously in that direction that theologians belonging explicitly to the second line cannot but raise the same central suspicion."[18]

This is precisely the reason why Segundo criticizes a number of theologians who have made the shift from the first to the second approach. And it is important to stress that these theologians are certainly acknowledged to be among the best authors in the field of liberation theology: Leonardo Boff, Jon Sobrino, and Gustavo Gutiérrez. Since I noted at the beginning of this chapter that constructive criticism constituted a sign of theological maturity, it is worth examining these critiques in greater detail.

In an article already cited, Leonardo Boff, a Brazilian Franciscan, discusses his experience of dialogue with poor and uneducated members of Basic Ecclesial Communities in the very underdeveloped state of Acre on the frontier between Brazil and Bolivia. At one point, Boff asked these people: "How did Jesus redeem us?" And many people answered "through his cross" or "through his suffering."

Now does Boff *learn from* these poor people or does he manifest *ideological suspicion* regarding their answers? Here is the text from Boff:

> I asked myself: why do (grass-roots) people immediately associate redemption with the cross: Undoubtedly because they have not learned the historical character of redemption, that is, of the process of liberation. Perhaps it is so because their own life is nothing but suffering and crosses, the cross society has managed to make them carry on their shoulders. . . . A Jesus who only suffers is not liberating; he generates the cult of suffering and fatalism. It is important to relocate within the mind of common people the cross in its true place. . . .[19]

Clearly, Boff, who in the quote mentioned earlier stated that the principal learning of theology comes from grass-roots people, is in practice criticizing the people's theology and emphatically asserting the theology that should replace it. Consequently, it seems clear to me that a basic incoherence is evident in Boff's theological approach and that this should be corrected. Thus, I agree completely with Segundo in an important conclusion for the universal church regarding learning from contact with the poor: "I do not know if you perceive that there is an undoubtedly involuntary contradiction between the claim of having been evangelized by the poor and taught by them, and, on the other hand, the pretension of relocating in people's minds the true meaning of the cross and suffering. How can a passive and fatalistic conception of God evangelize the theologian?"[20] Another way of expressing this problem is Segundo's view that serious theologians in Latin America (clearly including himself) avoid "reducing theology to more or less superficial and spontaneous answers to the problems which Christian people *perceive* in their everyday life and which they bring forward when they meet in Basic Christian Communities."[21] The crucial issue here is the question: does liberation theology fall into the trap of "romanticizing" the poor or, from another perspective, of "sacralizing" the poor?

Before proceeding further with this question, however, we must inquire whether other theologians besides Boff have made the shift to the common people or whether it is an idiosyncrasy peculiar to him. And indeed, a similar process may be observed in the writings of Jon Sobrino. In an address on theological method delivered at Mexico City in 1975, Sobrino refers to the context of the university as the place of origin of liberation theology. From this university context an important methodological characteristic arises, which Sobrino describes as follows: "We think that Latin

American theology is more conscious than European theology of its very status as knowledge. Obviously, this is the problem of the ideologization of theology, in regard to which Latin American theology is more sensitive than European theology."[22] This sensitivity, Sobrino goes on to say, is the reason why liberation theology uses the social sciences in a way similar to the use theology made of philosophy in times past. For the social sciences constitute the valuable cognitive tools which are necessary for the process of de-ideologizing, but "tools which because of their complexity and subtlety are beyond the grasp of the majority of people."

But in a later article included in the same volume, Sobrino shows that he has shifted to the second line of liberation theology. Note that the subtitle of the article is "The Poor: The Theological Locus of Ecclesiology." Here Sobrino asserts that "thus the Church of the poor encounters the historical place of conversion, the place of the other and the power to become the other."[23] Segundo's conclusion is worth quoting at length:

> The process of becoming the other in the Church thus occupies the theological position that the social sciences and their instrumentality for de-ideologization held in the first variety of liberation theology. Up to a point, it is interesting that the second line returns to philosophy in a certain way, because it finds in philosophy the means to establish the theological rationale for becoming other among common people. One can observe, for example, the profound influence of the philosopher Emmanuel Levinas as much in Enrique Dussel as in Juan Carlos Scannone, two of the outstanding theologians of the second line.[24]

Another result of the shift to the second line that is very important is the fact that it has resulted in a serious decline in the quality of theological production, again in some of the acknowledged leaders among liberation theologians. As an example, Segundo points out that the most recent book of Gustavo Gutiérrez, *The Power of the Poor in History*, "could not be considered, even by a long shot, to be of the same intellectual quality that characterized *A Theology of Liberation*," and he goes on to state, rather sharply, that "anyone who ignores the context and shift we are studying would think that the theological quality of Gustavo has markedly diminished and that the work does not rise above a certain level of debatable propaganda, although it is of a quality beyond that which characterizes ordinary people and what they do." The exact same comparison is then applied to the theological production of Leonardo Boff; books of his such as *Christ the Liberator*, and especially *The Passion of Christ—The Passion of the World*, are far superior in quality to his more recent works, which are concerned "with new ecclesial forms and a church which is born of the people."[25]

A few conclusions may be suitably appended here. First of all, Segundo's critique, in my opinion, clearly refutes the schemata presented in the articles of Juan Carlos Scannone and Cristián Johannson, discussed above. In one sense, the latter two analyses are remarkably similar; they are both identifying "hermeneutical places" for the divergencies in liberation theology and differ merely in the choice and evaluation of the "places." But neither author seriously considers the importance of ideology criticism of theology itself, and thus their studies are of little lasting value.

Also, I began this section by stating my heuristic purpose for understanding the various approaches that are developing in Latin American theology. I hope that we have been enabled to discover how important this dialogue is for theology and the church in that continent. In my opinion, the choices made with regard to the options I have mentioned will lead either to a new period of creative energy and the profound development of liberation theology, or to an exhaustive repetition of the answers of the past, the subsequent end of liberation theology, and incalculable damage to the enduring cause of human freedom.

Liberation and the Crisis of Theology

This mention of human freedom leads directly into a discussion concerning the most fundamental division within Latin American theology and the root cause of a crisis in that theology. The division and crisis are based on a question that probes still more deeply than the ones in the preceding section: does the study, publication and dissemination of theology contribute to the advance of liberation and consequent freedom for human beings, or does it lead to an increase in their oppression and eventual enslavement? It should be obvious that this question is also fundamental for theology in every area of the world, as the recent Vatican *Instruction on Christian Freedom and Liberation* has pointed out.[26] The catalyst for this analysis is another important article by Segundo, which was published in a little-known Brazilian periodical and to my knowledge never translated into English.

The structure of this article is based on the four steps of the hermeneutic circle, a subject which has been analyzed in many other studies.[27] Moreover, throughout the work, Segundo adopts a long-range analysis of the future of theology on the southern continent, thus employing another of his methodological principles: searching for solutions that are complex and far-seeing rather than those that are simplistic and immediate in scope. An important focal point also is the formation and education of theologians, who will be the future religious leaders in Latin America.

He begins by acknowledging quite frankly that Latin American theology is in a state of crisis because of a vacuum, "which coincides, paradoxically, with an international prominence that is without precedent."[28] One of the major causes of the vacuum is that so far theology has been programmatic, that is, intent on discussing goals and methods as well as defending itself, but neglecting its basic task: the rethinking of all of theology with a view to liberation.

Consequently, when it is a question of the formation of future theologians, a foreign theology is usually imported, since there is no local systematization that could be compared in seriousness and scientific rigor with those elaborated in Europe. How, then, is a liberation orientation included in the curriculum? "In the most illogical manner imaginable," replies Segundo, that is, by extra reading or by adding a course on liberation theology to a curriculum based completely on other norms and values. What is needed, on the contrary, is a "different way of realizing the total task of theology, a way of questioning, in a critical manner, the whole field of theology."[29]

Segundo's response, to create a new and original way of thinking theologically, is based on the hermeneutic circle in a somewhat dense manner, and here I can only mention the more significant ideas. The first point of the circle includes a prior commitment, and here Segundo is adamant: "The concrete manner in which a student or a professional begins to study theology, to pose questions to revelation, constitutes a political-social option *in every case*. . . . One takes sides even when one claims not to do so. One chooses a group, a class, an area which theology, like all human thought, is going to serve, however neutral it may claim to be."[30]

Some conclusions follow from this first point of the circle. The important question for each theologian to ask is then: for whom are you thinking? for which group, party, or human interests are you posing problems? Thus, Segundo believes that theology must be judged by a pretheological criterion; to follow Christ's example in the gospels we must first ask what is good or what is bad for human beings. Clearly, then, we will have to think and learn with nontheologians and non-Christians, who are asking the same questions. A corollary of this regards the life-style of the theologian: what classes or groups does he or she live with or associate with, and what kind of ideas and interests are the ones that dominate his or her daily life?

The second step of the circle involves the suspicion that the culture is hiding and disguising its true problems through a kind of cultural "false consciousness" or ideology in the pejorative sense. Segundo then presents what he calls a new definition of this step in the hermeneutical circle: "it consists in the systematic application of ideological suspicion to the commonplaces of a culture which oppresses human beings."[31] Without this ability, theology will be deficient and even false because it will not be in contact with reality or with the real problems of a culture.

Moving to the third and fourth steps of the circle, it is clear that they are nothing else but the application to theology of the first two steps. This is necessary because religious ideas are part of the commonplaces of a culture and manifest the same phenomena of false consciousness as the culture, along with their corollary of human oppression. The third and fourth steps of the circle exist precisely to rectify and transform such religious ideas so that they may serve to destroy oppression in a culture.

But there is great difficulty in accepting the third step as a hermeneutic condition, Segundo holds, and that lies in our unending quest for security and certainty. "In spite of all declarations," he says bluntly, "theology is not practiced in order to help to solve the problems of history, but to assure the orthodoxy of future ministers and, through them, to maintain the orthodoxy of the faithful."[32] The third step, then, is a direct threat to this kind of security, because its primary criterion is not orthodoxy; rather, that criterion is to accept from theology only that which appears to be liberating. Segundo is quite emphatic in stating that "I can believe only in a liberating God and a liberating revelation. Moreover, I know that, to the extent that this functionality is lost sight of, even momentarily, theology becomes conservative and oppressive, as happened with the theology of the Pharisees."[33] Segundo admits that the individual may not always be able to discern immediately this liberating impact, and may have to put some things "in parentheses" until it is seen more clearly. But he is adamant that the relation to liberation is crucial: "I only ask that they give me guarantees that this relation is the central criterion of what they are teaching me. I only require that I be permitted to ask about this relation without the question being seen as a mark of heterodoxy or rebellion."[34] Another way of expressing the same idea is to say that liberation precedes and judges theology, and that this statement is an act of faith.

This brings us to the fourth point of the circle, which is the same ideological critique of society as was made regarding culture in general in the second step. Segundo presents an interesting example of this approach:

> We expect every systematic attempt in theology to arrive at truths that are considered universal and valid for all times. The critical instruments we possess, the systematic employment of suspicion, have taught us that such attempts always tend, consciously or unconsciously, to sacralize the existing order as universal and to adapt human attitudes to that order in the name of God and of the revelation of God.[35]

Somewhat unexpectedly, Segundo concludes his article by trying to put an end to the "myth" that there is no room in a liberating theology for systematic theology. Actually, the task that is necessary is to rethink, in a liberating, coherent, and systematic way, all the themes presented by revelation. Finally, he insists, "I judge that the greatest challenge today for Latin American theology is to systematize in a liberating way Christology, eschatology, ecclesiology, soteriology, all the great classical themes of theology."[36]

Concluding Remarks

In general, I think this discussion of the different approaches of liberation theology will help to clarify attempts to create a liberating theology in other parts of the world. For example, more attention may have to be given to the kinds of pretheological values that people bring to the study of theology, which will greatly influence what "real knowledge," in Newman's sense, they are going to obtain in their study.

At this point, however, I concentrate on two aspects of the chapter which I think deserve emphasis and clarification. The first aspect has to do with Segundo's article on the hermeneutic circle. On one level, this article is important because it reveals the most basic division or divergencies in present-day theology in Latin America and also, in my opinion, in North America. These are not primarily found in the various "theological places" mentioned by some of our sources; rather they are to be found in the radical opposition that exists between a theology that is liberating and encouraging freedom and creativity, or one that is oppressive and supporting oppression and slavery.

Consequently, I think the most important question a teacher of theology (or preacher or catechist or parent) can ask is: does *this* study, *this* publication, *this* material for teaching, *this* method of teaching, promise to contribute to the real liberation and consequent freedom of human beings, or does it promise the opposite, any of the myriad forms of slavery that abound in the contemporary world? If that question were posed seriously by the reader, I would consider this chapter (or this book) to have been successful and worth the effort.

Another aspect of this chapter is concerned with the question of the "hermeneutical privilege of the poor." Although I cannot develop this in detail, I would like to suggest a via media between the positions of Segundo and those who hold that the poor can evangelize and teach the rest of the churches. As was said above, I agree with him that the theologian must remain critical regarding the theological views of the poor. I agree, not for any theoretical reason, but because in my years working in the Third World, I had ample—almost daily—experience of the frequency with which very poor people internalize the dominating beliefs of their oppressors, and also of the depth and the tenacity with which those views are defended.

At the same time, the poor also appear to have a deeper understanding of some aspects of the gospel message than others (including theologians) precisely because of their situation of poverty. Here I refer to the excellent study and survey of the literature on the hermeneutical privilege of the poor by Monika Hellwig.[37]

At the end of this work, Professor Hellwig concludes that "there must usually be a catalyst or mediator who engages the poor and oppressed in the process of 'conscientization'." With such mediation, she continues, certain attitudes are expressed which ring true to those who have meditated on the gospels. These are listed as particularly significant:

(a) The poor know that they are in urgent need of redemption.

(b) The poor know not only their dependence on God and on powerful people but also their interdependence with one another.

(c) The poor rest their security not on things but on people.

(d) The poor have no exaggerated sense of their own importance.

(e) The poor expect little from competition and much from co-operation.

(f) The poor have no exaggerated need of privacy.

(g) The poor can distinguish between necessities and luxuries.

(h) The poor can wait because they have acquired a kind of dogged patience born of acknowledged dependence.

(i) When the poor are exposed to the gospel, they interpret it very concretely and readily see it as having historical, practical import. An example of this is the ease with which Martin Luther King could invite his followers to identify with the exodus theme and with the nonviolent protest of Jesus as seen by John Wesley.

(j) When the poor have the gospel preached to them, it sounds like good news and not like a threat or a scolding.

(k) The promise of future salvation is truly present joy and therefore incipient salvation to the poor.

(l) The really (desperately) poor can respond to the call of the gospel with a certain abandonment and uncomplicated totality because they have so little to lose and are ready for anything.

(m) The fears of the poor are more realistic and less exaggerated, because they already know that one can survive very great suffering and want.[38]

Consequently, I believe that there is room for dialogue and a certain amount of mutual learning between theologians of the intellectual, de-ideologizing tendency and those who find enlightenment through direct contact with the poor. However, I would reiterate as strongly as possible that there really does exist a place where "between us and you a great chasm has been fixed" (Lk 16:26), and that consists in how one evaluates the importance of the question mentioned in the first part of my conclusions: does *this* study, *this* publication, *this* material for teaching, *this* method of teaching, promise to contribute to the real liberation and consequent freedom of human beings, or does it promise the opposite?

Chapter 5
Paulo Freire as Liberation Theologian

The year 1991 marks the commemoration of one hundred years of the modern era of Catholic social thought, or in more contemporary terms, of Catholic political theology. It was in 1891 that Pope Leo XIII inaugurated this epoch with the publication of his encyclical *Rerum Novarum*, which constituted for that time a courageous protest against the exploitation of working men and women and a prophetic defense of the rights of labor. At the same time, Leo spearheaded a new direction in Catholic theology which has to rank as one of the most fruitful and significant in the entire history of the church.

But if we analyze this remarkable history in greater detail and with the advantage of hindsight, it is readily apparent that it suffers from at least one serious drawback. The interlocutor in the documents, that is, the one who is instructed and exhorted to act for justice and to aid the poor, is almost always white, usually wealthy, and often very powerful both politically and socially. Since the social teaching is also characterized by a tendency to emphasize public order and stability, especially with regard to the lower classes, it conveys a rather somber message to the poor and powerless masses that form the majority of the world's population. Their only recourse, it would seem, is to hope and pray for conversion on the part of the powerful ones who exploit them, while at the same time meekly accepting their own suffering as a following in the footsteps of a crucified Lord.

From this perspective, it becomes readily apparent that the Latin American church has given birth to one of the most original and far-reaching developments in the entire century of social teaching. This lies not only in the elaboration of liberation theology, which aspires to be the "voice of the voiceless" throughout the continent. But even more important than this has been the creation and actual implementation of a praxis that has enabled the wretched of the earth to discover *their own voice* and thus their own dignity and their own capacity for participation and action. For elaborating this technique, which is called conscientization, and dedicating his life to implementing it on a world scale, I believe that the Brazilian educator, Paulo Freire, must qualify as one of the most creative geniuses of the twentieth century.

Freire's Background

In this chapter, I first examine some aspects of Freire's life which appear helpful for a more profound understanding of his thought and propose a general overview of his theory and method. This serves as an introduction to a more detailed analysis of his approach on three levels: first, as regards education and popular culture; second, with respect to its theological and pastoral implications; and lastly, its contribution to sociopolitical analysis and transformation. In the course of this I hope to provide convincing evidence that Freire must be considered one of the most creative pioneers of a contemporary liberation theology.

Several experiences in Freire's early life provide an illuminating background for his later work.[1] He was born in Recife, a port city in Brazil's infamous Northeast—an entire region that comprises what can only be called the Calcutta of Latin America. The depression dominated his grade school years. His subpar academic performance and resultant two-year delay in advancement were diagnosed by his teachers as mild mental retardation, although the true cause was simple hunger, induced by his middle-class family's straitened economic plight. When these circumstances improved, he earned degrees in philosophy and law, eventually gaining a post as counsel for local labor unions. His experience in adult education seminars with workers in the notorious *favelas* or slums of Recife led him to the discovery of his eventual vocation as an educator.

His initial efforts in adult literacy campaigns produced excellent results, but by 1963 the Brazilian oligarchy came to the realization that his work was actually "subversive of the democratic order"; Freire was promptly jailed for seventy days and then exiled. After laboring with UNESCO and the Institute for Agrarian Reform in Chile, he departed in 1969 to teach at Harvard and later to act as consultant in Asian and African education for the World Council of Churches at Geneva. During the 1980s he has been associated with the Institute of Cultural Action, an organization which he was instrumental in founding.

A number of sympathetic readers of Freire's book, *The Pedagogy of the*

Oppressed, have complained about the difficulty and obscurity of his prose style. Thus, it will be helpful at the outset to listen to an eyewitness describing his method of teaching literacy in actual practice:

> Freire would go into a village and enter into conversation with people. He would ask them to help him to observe the village life. He would have them help him take pictures of scenes of village activities which were familiar and common to most of the villagers. The villagers would then come together to see the pictures. Freire would ask them to describe what they saw in detail, writing words under the pictures as they reflected on what they were seeing and feeling.
>
> Then Freire would question the villagers about the contradictions in the explanations they were giving about why things were the way they were. For example, in one village, the people described the harvest as being very poor. Freire asked them "Why?" Some of the villagers said: "Because the land is tired." Freire asked them why some of the land seemed to be very productive and other parts of the land seemed tired. They explained that the rich farmers had fertilizer and they didn't. Freire then asked them how that was the case. The questions and answers continued, leading to issues related to their life situation. The topics discussed ranged from those which were primarily theological, political, or economic in nature to those which were basically philosophical in nature.
>
> Frequently, villagers gave fatalistic answers. Freire would always come back to the contradictions that the people themselves had exposed. The people then began, as a result of this process, to think for themselves and to become aware of alternative ways of viewing and coping with what had seemed to be insurmountable problems for themselves and their communities.
>
> In the process, people learned to read, to care, and to have a sense of worth. Freire called what happened to them *conscientização* (conscientization).[2]

This apparently simple procedure has given birth to an enormous body of theoretical elaboration and commentary, as well as to creative applications to many cultural situations other than that of literacy training. I now turn first to a discussion of Freire's method as an educational tool.

Out of the Culture of Silence

The conception of education (whether for literacy or at any other level) that Freire has fiercely opposed all his life is what he terms the "narrative" approach, where the student is perceived as a receptacle or container to be filled by the teacher: "The more completely he fills the receptacles, the better a teacher he is. The more meekly the students permit themselves to be filled, the better students they are." Another term for this approach is the "banking" concept, where the student receives, files, and repeats the "deposits" that have been doled out to him by the teacher; similarly, in this approach, knowledge is viewed as "a gift bestowed by those who consider themselves knowledgeable upon those whom they consider to know nothing."[3]

The onslaught against such educational practice recurs constantly throughout Freire's work, sometimes to the point of satiety. It is firmly rooted in his anthropology, which is diametrically opposed to behaviorist or positivist conceptions, or indeed to any model of man which emphasizes his role as passive object. For Freire, human beings always are—or can be—the subjects, the agents, the transformers, of themselves and their world: "Only men, as 'open' beings, are able to achieve the complex operation of simultaneously transforming the world by their action and grasping and expressing the world's reality in their creative language." Thus, in place of the banking concept, Freire advocates an authentically dialogical or "problem-posing" education, wherein "men develop their power to perceive critically *the way they exist* in the world *with which* and *in which* they find themselves. . . . the teacher-student and the students-teachers reflect simultaneously on themselves and the world without dichotomizing this reflection from action, and thus establish an authentic form of thought and action."[4]

Thus far, this could be viewed as a common enough conception of liberal education. But Freire is not speaking merely about the training of a cultured elite; the principles apply to *all* men and women, especially to the *marginados* in the periphery of society who have been submerged by society in what he refers to as a "culture of silence." In this respect, Freire quotes with approval the Brazilian priest Antonio Vieira: "Let's begin with this last word, *infans; infans* is the one who does not speak. . . . This was the situation in Brazil for many years, and this, in my opinion, was the main cause of all its ills. The fact that the sick man cannot speak forces the doctor to guess, which makes it even more difficult to prescribe."[5] Consequently, conscientization can and should allow the humblest peasant to speak his own word, thus emerging from the culture of silence. Since "there is no true word that is not at the same time a praxis" and "to speak a true word is to transform the world," he can thus become the agent and creator of his own destiny.

It should be noted, too, that a culture of silence exists also in the developed countries, where "ways of thinking become as standardized as ways of dressing and tastes in food. People begin thinking and acting according to the prescriptions they receive daily from the communications media rather than in response to their dialectical relationships with the world."[6] Although Freire does not emphasize it, this Western mode of false consciousness is already far advanced in the Third World, superimposing yet another cultural layer of silence upon the existing one.

The critics who have accused Freire of obtruding his views on illiterates and others may find some justification because of the use to which his method has been put by certain disciples. However, it must be stressed that such practice is directly contrary to the principle of genuine dialogue that he inculcates in all his writings.

To sum up his educational accomplishments, he has created and continues to refine his "practical method" and it is being utilized by thousands upon thousands of those engaged in teaching throughout the world. And what is really revolutionary about his method is that he has pioneered ways of bringing literacy to the great majority of the human race, those millions who had been plunged, without their volition and seemingly without hope, into the obscure depths of the culture of silence.

The Educator as Theologian

Apart from education, the implications of conscientization for the churches and their pastoral and theological tasks in Latin America also merit careful consideration. This is not the place to attempt an overview of the religious situation there; however, I will utilize the analysis of a knowledgeable interpreter, Philip Berryman. In an article noting that all indicators point to a continuing, massive urbanization of the churches, Berryman singles out three characteristic approaches of various elites which he believes will be of continuing importance for the future of religion on our neighboring continent.

The first of these involves *identification with the people* on the part of pastoral agents, students and professional persons, which immediately recalls Freire's insistence on communion with the people noted previously: "This means breaking with a bourgeois life style and an attempt to share the life of the popular class in a barrio. There is an attempt to discover the life of the community, to appreciate its values, to share its problems. Such a posture tries to be non-paternalistic, learning and receiving before giving and teaching."[7]

If the participants are interrogated as to their ultimate purpose in this project, a second characteristic is revealed, for they almost invariably reply: *concientización*. Berryman considers this effort of immense potential value, because of the phenomenon of urbanization, in which large masses of people are uprooted from their ancestral heritage and traditions, and thus become easy prey of anomie and of both official and commercial propaganda in the city.

As the people dialogue on their situation and seek avenues of change in the process of conscientization, an inevitable process of politicization occurs, which leads to the author's third characteristic: *the formation of base-communities or base-organizations.* In this connection, Berryman observes: "If one of the magic words in the Latin American Church today is *concientización,* the other is *comunidad de base.* . . . In many places the *comunidad de base* is formed around a series of dialogues of evangelization. People come together, perhaps for bible study, perhaps for a discussion that begins with some basic situation or theme. People have a sense of belonging and they get the opportunity to express themselves, to say their 'word'." The similarity of these three approaches to Freire's educational technique is strikingly obvious. The major difference is the constant use of the Bible as a catalyst for the groups, resulting in a specifically Christian form of conscientization.

This view of pastoral practice is also reflected in the documents of the Latin American bishops. César Jérez and Juan Hernández-Pico have pointed out that "Freire's philosophy strongly influenced the documents in which the Latin American Bishops Conference at Medellín in 1968 sought to apply the teachings of Vatican II to their own continent. He can be considered one of the most important influences on the Latin American scene—as much, we may venture to say, as Che Guevara."[8]

Even a cursory reading of the Medellín documents strongly supports this view. For instance, the bishops note at the outset that "the lack of political consciousness in our countries makes the educational activity of the Church absolutely essential, for the purpose of bringing Christians to consider their participation in the political life of the nation as a matter of conscience and as the practice of charity in its most noble and meaningful sense for the life of the community. . . . This task of *'concientización'* and social education ought to be integrated into Joint Pastoral Action at various levels."[9] Further on, they insist that "justice, and therefore peace, conquer by means of a dynamic action of awakening (*concientización*) and organization of the popular sectors, which are capable of pressing public officials who are often impotent in their social projects without popular support."[10] And in their response to the critical problem of illiteracy, the bishops present what can only be termed a paraphrase of Freire:

The task of educating these our brothers does not consist in incorporating them into the cultural structures existing around them, which can also be oppressive, but in something much deeper. It consists in equipping them so that they themselves, as authors of their own progress, develop in a creative and original way a cultural world attuned to their own abundance and which is the fruit of their own efforts; especially in the case of the Indians it is necessary to respect the peculiar values of their culture.[11]

In the English translation of the document, moreover, conscientization is referred to more often as "awareness"; in general, then, it can be said that the urgent need for such awareness and action flowing from it permeate all sixteen Medellin documents from beginning to end.

Aside from this enormous impact on pastoral strategy, Freire's influence has also been acknowledged by leading proponents of the "theology of liberation," which is now flourishing throughout the southern hemisphere. Gustavo Gutiérrez refers to his work as "one of the most creative and fruitful efforts which has been implemented in Latin America," and offers his own summation of the process of conscientization: "[The oppressed person] makes the transfer from a 'naive awareness'—which does not deal with problems, gives too much value to the past, tends to accept mythical attitudes, and tends towards debate—to a 'critical awareness'—which delves into problems, is open to new ideas, replaces magical explanations with real causes, and tends to dialogue."[12] Gutiérrez also utilizes key concepts of Freire at pivotal points in his theology, for instance, in his description of the "new man," that is, "the kind of man who critically analyzes the present, controls his destiny, and is oriented toward the future";[13] later on, moreover, the Freireian dialectic of denunciation-annunciation forms the keystone of the author's conceptualization of utopia and its relationship to political action.[14] Finally, Gutiérrez presents a succinct critique of conscientization which I believe has considerable merit: "Freire's ideas and methods continue to be developed. All the potentialities of conscientization are slowly unfolding, as well as its limitations. It is a process which can be deepened, modified, reorientated, and extended. This is the task in which in the first place the founder of this movement, as well as many of those who in one way or another have participated in it, are involved."[15]

Juan Luis Segundo, whose many books have propelled him to the first rank of liberation theologians, is also a collaborator with Freire. In *Our Idea of God,* Segundo discusses with approval Freire's theory of literacy training, and offers some interesting observations on his own conception of its relationship to evangelization:

> . . . it is not possible to give the gospel as it really is, that is, as a liberative interpretation of history, without making man a *subject* of that history rather than an object of it. Without this process of consciousness-raising, the task of evangelizing and catechizing runs the risk of being a cultural invasion: i.e., the learning of new words that do not correspond to life's realities, and mere conceptual games that leave intact old alienations stemming from fear, en-

slavement, and ideology.... This intimate and necessary connection between evangelization and political conscientization ... destroys any false
hope of having an "aseptic" evangelization.[16]

But perhaps Segundo's principal utilization of Freire occurs in connection with the sacraments, which he understands basically as a "communitarian pedagogy of liberation," similar in every respect to Freire's
pedagogy of liberation. Like Freire, he believes their objective should
always be problem-posing and never "deposit-making," which he rejects as
"alienating magic" that denies the Christian people the opportunity to
speak their own word. The analogies with conscientization in his elaboration of what he considers to be authentic sacramental practice should be obvious: "On the occasion of each sacrament it should present the Christian
people with their present, concrete, existential situation. It should pose this
situation as a problem that challenges them and calls for their response.
And it should also show divine revelation to be an element capable of helping them face up to this challenge."

The community's response, in turn, must take place on two levels: that
of intellectual awareness and understanding, and that of action. "When the
Christian community organizes itself in sacramental terms, it orients itself
toward action designed to meet an historical challenge in a reflective and
critical way."[17]

Many other examples could be cited of Freire's relationship to these
and other liberation theologians. However, the above should suffice to illustrate my own view that conscientization is a crucial element—perhaps *the*
central element—in all the theologies of liberation.

Freire's impact, then, on both the pastoral and theological enterprise
in Latin America—the world's most populous Catholic continent—is undoubtedly of capital importance. And although he is not, and does not aspire to be, a professional theologian, a survey of his views concerning theology would seem to be appropriate in concluding this section. As will become
evident, he rates as an excellent amateur theologian.

As might be expected, Freire emphasizes the need to distinguish between authentic and alienating religion: "Religion ... which embodies this
transcendent meaning of man's relationship with others, should never
become an instrument for his alienation. Precisely because he is a finite (in
the sense of incomplete) and indigent being, man finds in transcendence—
through love—his Source, who liberates him."[18]

Alienating religion can be indigenous, as in his childhood recollections
of priests who went about exhorting the peasants to be patient in their misery, for it was God's will that thus they merit heaven. Freire's reaction to
this is explosive: "How could we make God responsible for this calamity?

As if Absolute Love could abandon man to constant victimization and total destitution. That would be a God such as Marx described."[19]

But there are also imported brands of alienation. Freire alludes to the North American palliative of "The Family That Prays Together Stays Together," and notes that often in Latin America such a praying family "has no house, no job, no bread, no clothes, no health care, nor education for the children" and that "the moment they start to talk about those things, their sincerity is called into question by those who not only hold political, economic, and ecclesiastical power over others, but want to control their minds too."[20]

In the search for a more authentic Christianity, Freire believes that theology plays an indispensable role, but that a renaissance is urgently needed: "Never, perhaps, have we needed a theological rebirth as much as today. But we need one that, taking advantage of the jolt that the Death of God theology gave to our medievalized theology, will go well beyond it."[21] And it is one of Freire's strongest—and most controversial—convictions that a renewed theology can only emerge from within the Third World, inasmuch as First World theologians are too intimately linked to the status quo to produce anything but pessimistic theologies, which deny man's capacity for growth and liberating change.

It is important, however, to note carefully his definition of the Third World, since it is broader than the usual understanding of the term:

> . . . the very concept of a Third World is ideological and political, not merely geographical: the First World has, living in its bosom and in jarring contradiction with itself, its own Third World—just as this latter has, within itself, its First World, represented by the ideology of domination and the power of the dominating classes. In a word, the Third World exists wherever there is a world of silence, of oppression, of dependence, of exploitation, of violence done by the dominating classes to the oppressed.[22]

Within this more global context, Freire explicitates the fundamental characteristics of the theology he envisions: "Only from the Third World, too, in the sense I am giving it here, can a utopian theology emerge, a theology of denouncing and announcing, implying prophecy and hope. A theology that serves the bourgeoisie cannot be utopian and prophetic and hopeful. On the contrary, that sort of theology would create a passive, adjusted man waiting for a better life in the hereafter."[23] The basic reason that the metropolises of the First World cannot produce a theology that evidences these utopian, prophetic, and hopeful tendencies is because for these societies the future is merely more of the present: continuation as metropolises.

Thus, if I may summarize, his projected theology will be thoroughly permeated with hope for a new future for mankind. But it is important to stress the *kind* of hope that is being suggested:

> A kind of theology in which hope would be a waiting but not a searching would be profoundly alienating, because it would presume that the average man abdicates his praxis in the world. . . . it would see man as a mere spec-tator, limply waiting for salvation, not working it out. . . . A fatalistic hope, in which we accept the status quo, contains a fatal contradiction: the absurd dichotomy between worldliness and other-worldliness (transcendentalism). I do nothing in this world but wait for what will come: the pure, the just, the good. In that way I make myself an accomplice of injustice, of unlove, of the exploitation of men in the world, and I deny the very act of love by which God, the Absolute, limits Himself by seeing some value in men—limited, un-finished, and incompleted as they are—as beings that choose, as sharers in his creative work.[24]

An inevitable corollary of this theological approach is that it will issue in conflict and division for, as Freire puts it, we will be damned as enemies of Western Christian civilization. However, this important problem may best be postponed for more detailed treatment in the succeeding section on the sociopolitical implications of Freire's theories.

Another critical corollary is that an emphasis on *individual* conversion in the church is not sufficient. In Freire's view, that approach is based on a fundamental illusion, namely,

> that it is somehow enough to change men's and women's hearts, that they need not attack and change the unjust social structures. Only the innocent, though, are deluded enough to believe that exhortations or humanitarian works, or a brilliant syllogizing all in mid-air, can actually change the world by changing men's hearts. The astute ones know perfectly well that the proc-ess works the other way around, and that such mental games only distract us from the radical transformation of social structures—which then may (but may not, too!) lead to a change of hearts.[25]

A last area to be considered is the ecclesiology, or model of the church, that would harmonize with his projected theology. Here Freire sees only three possibilities from which a choice must be made: the traditionalist, reformist, or prophetic models. As might be expected, the traditionalist image is vigorously rejected:

> It is missionary in the worst sense of the term, a "conqueror" of souls, and ob-sessed with death. Hence it finds a masochistic pleasure in constantly harping on sin, on eternal fire, on damnation without hope of redemption. It views death as a charnel house where human beings have to atone for their sins: the

more they suffer, the more they are purified for heaven and an eternal repose. It sees work, not as what men and women do to shape the world as they construct it and construct themselves, but as punishment they must pay for the fact of being men and women.[26]

The "modernizing" church, although it is more efficient and streamlined than the first model, is also finally rejected:

> The bad side of the modern and modernizing Church . . . is not so much its eagerness to update its techniques as its political preferences, which though usually disguised, are unmistakable. Like the traditionalist Church, of which it is a new version, it is loyal, not to the dominated social classes, but to the power elites. . . . Whereas the traditionalist Churches alienate the dominated classes by portraying the world as hostile to them, the modernizing Church alienates them in a different way, by supporting reformisms that only preserve the status quo.[27]

Freire's choice is wholeheartedly for the prophetic model, which he discusses at some length. In general, it reflects the utopian, hopeful, and prophetic perspectives that were sought for in theology itself:

> Today's Latin American Christians who belong to this line will disagree at times, especially over the tactics to be used, but they are in general those who, rejecting the innocence we described above, commit themselves to the oppressed classes and stay firm in that position. . . . The prophetic Church . . . will never let itself be made a "refuge" for the oppressed masses, alienating them still more with hollow-sounding denunciatory speeches that are nothing but bla-bla-bla. On the contrary, it will invite them to a new Exodus.[28]

It appears to me that Freire's theological vision has already been— and will continue to be—implemented by men like Gutiérrez, Segundo, Boff, Miguez Bonino and others. Since it is considered by them an ongoing process—what Bernard Lonergan refers to as the discipline of "communications" and Karl Rahner as "practical theology"—it will undoubtedly undergo a lengthy period of expansion and purification through its reaction to criticism. I return to the theological question at the end of this chapter.

The Impact on Society and Politics

From all that has been discussed thus far, it should be clear that the most volatile and controversial area in Freire's work does not concern merely its educational or religious dimensions, but above all, its sociopolitical implications. Here lies the basic reason for his expulsion from his homeland and other countries; however, it should be noted that such exile is not without some value, since it enabled his thought to reach a wider, global audience.

In this area, I believe the basic motif that dominates all of Freire's thought in the sociopolitical area is that of *marginality*, that is, the desperate plight of the vast majority of mankind, although his principal focus is Latin America. The following passage illuminates his understanding of the situation of marginality and its causes:

> Admitting the existence of men "outside of" or "marginal to" structural reality, it seems legitimate to ask: Who is the author of this movement from the center of the structure to its margin? Do so-called marginal men, among them the illiterates, make the decision to move out to the periphery of society? If so, marginality is an option with all that it involves: hunger, sickness, rickets, pain, mental deficiencies, living death, crime, promiscuity, despair, the impossibility of being. In fact, however, it is difficult to accept that 40% of Brazil's population, almost 90% of Haiti's, 60% of Bolivia's, about 40% of Peru's, more than 30% of Mexico's and Venezuela's, and about 70% of Guatemala's would have made the tragic *choice* of their own marginality as illiterates. If, then, marginality is not by choice, marginal man has been expelled from and kept outside of the social system and is therefore the object of violence.[29]

Since the situation is intolerable and is obviously not going to be changed by those who benefit from it, the agents of structural transformation must be the marginals themselves, hence Freire's *Pedagogy of the Oppressed*. The qualities that should characterize this struggle are presented at length in "Cultural Action and Conscientization":

> [It] tends to be dynamic rather than static; tends to life rather than death; to the future as a challenge to man's creativity rather than as a repetition of the present; to love as a liberation of subjects rather than as pathological possessiveness; to the emotion of life rather than to cold abstractions; to living together in harmony rather than gregariousness; to dialogue rather than mutism; to praxis rather than "law and order"; to men who organize themselves reflectively for action rather than men who are organized for passivity; to creative and communicative language rather than prescriptive signals; to reflective challenges rather than domesticating slogans; and to values which are lived rather than myths which are imposed.[30]

The other aspects of conscientization have been treated earlier in this chapter.

Freire's Liberating Theology

I will not try to summarize here the many facets of Freire's thought that I have presented. Rather, it seems most fruitful to perceive in sharper focus his relationship to liberation theology. Clearly, this has not been a relation of dependence on the part of either interlocutor; rather, it appears to be a question of symbiosis or of parallel journeys to the same goal, which has resulted in many fruitful exchanges along the way.

An excellent example of this relationship may be found in comparing the ideas of Freire presented here with the work of Gustavo Gutiérrez in his book, *A Theology of Liberation.*[31] Although the original Spanish edition of this book was published more than fifteen years ago, it still endures as a kind of founding document of the movement known as liberation theology. And perhaps the most important aspect in the book (and the one most ignored by his many opponents) concerned his definition of the term "liberation," which consists of three interpenetrating levels of meaning.

On the first level, liberation expresses "the aspirations of oppressed peoples and social classes," at the same time that it emphasizes "the conflictual aspect of the economic, social, and political process which puts them at odds with wealthy nations and oppressive classes." I believe it would be difficult to find a more succinct recapitulation of the sociopolitical thought of Freire than that we have just been considering. It may be noted that Gutiérrez does not jettison the concept of development so popular in the sixties, but does insist that development finds its rightful place and potential fruitfulness within "the more universal, profound, and radical perspective of liberation."[32]

On the next level, liberation can be understood within the context of a vision of history and a distinctive anthropology: "Man is seen as assuming conscious responsibility for his own destiny. This understanding provides a dynamic context and broadens the horizons of the desired social changes. In this perspective the unfolding of all man's dimensions is demanded—a man who makes himself throughout his life and throughout history. The gradual conquest of true freedom leads to the creation of a new man and a qualitatively different society." Again, this conception of history as a process of human liberation is characterized by ongoing conflict, since it understands "that the step from an abstract to a real freedom is not taken without a struggle against all the forces that oppress man, a struggle full of pitfalls, detours and temptations to run away. The goal is not only better living conditions, a radical change of structures, a social revolution; it is much more: the continuous creation, never ending, of a new way to be man, a *permanent cultural revolution.*"[33] I believe that Freire would consider this as a very apt statement of the philosophy of history and the anthropology that we have considered in this chapter as the foundation for his pedagogical techniques and for the ultimate aims of all truly liberating education.

Finally, on a third level Gutiérrez sees the term *liberation* as a better way of expressing the reality of profound theological insights than the word *development*. In the biblical sources, he envisions Christ as the one who liberates from sin, which is the "ultimate root of the disruption of friendship and of all injustice and oppression." Thus, "Christ makes man truly free, that is to say, he enables man to live in communion with him; and this is the basis for all human brotherhood."[34] Once again, these remarks could be understood as an echo or at least a rearrangement of Freire's own statements with regard to theology.

The keystone of Freire's thought and the leitmotif of his educational career have centered around the quest for human liberation as the great ideal that energizes all of humanity today. We have listened to his reflections on that search on the level of education, especially for the masses of the poor, in his understanding of a Christian theology that responds to the cry of the poor, and in his lifelong criticism of and struggle against oppression and domination in contemporary society. We must, therefore, confer on Freire belated recognition as one of the outstanding *compañeros* in the worldwide fraternity of theologians of liberation.

Chapter 6
Practice of Liberation in the Grassroots Church

A number of theologians in Latin America have in recent years adopted an academic schedule that may appear strange and even threatening to their colleagues in North America. One-half of each year is devoted to the customary scholarly activities of teaching, research and publication; the other half, however, is dedicated to pastoral work with the very poorest people of the society and of the church. The eventual goal of this bifurcation of interests is to allow the experience of the poor to fecundate and enrich their theological reflection and vice versa, in the dialectical process known as *praxis*.

One of these theologians, Fr. Clodovis Boff of Brazil, has pursued his pastoral activity among the Indians of the Amazon basin deep in Acre, the westernmost state in Brazil. These Indians were members of what are now known as Basic Ecclesial Communities (BECs), the new form of ecclesiology that has been pioneered in Brazil and has by now spread to every corner of Latin America. As a result of this experience, Boff published a fascinating article entitled "The BECs and the Practices (*Práticas*) of Liberation,"[1] from which I have taken the title of this chapter.

The process of organizing and nurturing many thousands of these Basic Ecclesial Communities provides another example of an original creation of the Latin American church, on a par with and intimately related to the process of conscientization discussed in chapter 5. Right from the beginning of their formation, these communities have adopted Freire's approach as an essential hermeneutical tool for the reflection on the Bible that is central to their weekly liturgies. As a consequence, the dispossessed poor of the continent now possess a grassroots church which enables them to become agents of their own destiny and architects of their own liberation both in the church and in their local community or nation. In this chapter I will discuss the origins and procedures of the BECs, and also present my own conclusions with regard to their significance for Christian communities in the United States and elsewhere.

Background of the Communities

The Latin American communities consist of a dozen or few dozen members each and emphasize the active participation of each person in prayer, worship, reflection and action, while creating strong community bonds through this relationship of dialogue and sharing. The number of existing BECs has been estimated at between 100,000 and 150,000; however, it is difficult to obtain exact numbers since many struggle to survive in the context of oppressive regimes which would be glad to identify, and, in some cases, destroy them or their leaders.[2]

It is also difficult to pinpoint the religious and cultural factors that provided the background for the BECs, especially since the nations of Latin America have very diverse social and religious histories. It seems clear, however, that many of the movements which preceded and contributed to the Second Vatican Council (1962-65), such as Catholic Action, the Young Catholic Students and Workers, the biblical and liturgical renewals, and various organizations for social justice, also provided fertile soil for the BECs.

There is, also, general agreement that early forms of the communities began first of all in Brazil. The historian Scott Mainwaring points out that the communities did not come into being from specific plans, but developed from pastoral practice and experience. Thus, he writes, the bishops in their General Pastoral Plan

> certainly did not envision the base communities as they ultimately evolved. It did not define the base communities beyond stating that they would become the lowest-level organization within the Church. The writers revealed no vision that the base communities would become as politically relevant as they did or that they would be primarily for the popular classes. . . . The base communities were originally intended as a means of strengthening the Church's presence, not as a new form of the Church. They were intended to encourage faith in a secular society, not to change the society.[3]

The Brazilian theologian and anthropologist, Marcello Azevedo, has also published a very thorough survey of the origins and process of formation of the BECs in Brazil, which goes beyond the scope of this chapter. However, the author has himself given a succinct overview of his work: "I hope that my historical approach has made clear the *slow gestation* of BECs, their gradual emergence over the course of thirty years. We have glimpsed their early roots, their formative stages in real-life experiments and experiences, and their unfolding development on the practical and theoretical levels. I hope it is clear that the BEC is a *new* and *significant* fact in the Brazilian Church."[4] After his historical analysis, the author moves on to a detailed semantic, missiological, and finally ecclesiological study.

Furthermore, there can be no doubt that the Second Council of Latin American Bishops, held in Medellin, in 1968, was of enormous importance. In this application of Vatican II to their own context, the bishops stated unambiguously that "the Christian ought to find the living of the communion to which he has been called in his 'base community,' that is to say, in a community, local or environmental, which corresponds to the reality of a homogeneous group and whose size allows for personal fraternal contact among its members."[5] It is noteworthy, however, that the bishops used the expression "base community" and never "ecclesial base community" in their reference to the communities. Thus, it appears that at Medellin the emphasis still centered on the *sociological* aspect of small communities of the poor, and had not yet arrived at an *ecclesial* understanding of their significance as a full expression of all the characteristics of the local church. This new dimension of BECs gradually became established in the decade after Medellin, but did not find its full acceptance until the next conference of Latin American bishops at Puebla, Mexico, in 1979.[6]

Description of the BECs

In moving to a more detailed description of the BECs, two important considerations should be kept in mind. First of all, there is no preexisting theoretical model which determines the origin or growth of the communities. This point has been stressed by all observers and expressed very succinctly by José Marins: "There will be of necessity a great deal of pluralism in the formation and structure of the BECs. The more they become part of their social sector and are faithful to the people in their environment, the more they will be distinct with an originality and personality all their own."[7] An important difference in the way different groups relate to secular society has also been outlined by a North American observer, Daniel H. Levine:

All CEBs stress spiritual values and Bible study, but the lessons they draw from the Bible and the way they link spiritual understandings and group life to social and political issues range across the entire gamut of alternatives. At one extreme, CEBs have been closely associated with revolutionary movements in Nicaragua and El Salvador, providing motivation, organized support, and a recruitment ground for more general political movements. In the middle are experiences like Chile or Brazil, where CEBs, strongly promoted and protected by the churches, have spurred religious renewal while sustaining alternative spaces for democracy in heavily authoritarian societies. The other extreme is taken by cases like Colombia, where CEBs are often organized in authoritarian and clerically controlled patterns.[8]

A second consideration relates not merely to pluralism but also to the different levels of development and maturity that actually exist in the concrete histories of the communities. To illustrate this, I refer briefly to three levels or stages in the development of Brazilian BECs.

The first level may be characterized as a community of prayer and reflection on the Bible. The primary interest here lies in the religious formation of the group and strengthening of religious and sacramental life. The second stage begins when, in addition to the above, the community becomes involved in charitable actions within the group, helping those most in need, building collective facilities like dispensaries and schools, and so forth. This can be termed a community of mutual aid. The final level occurs when the political awareness of the group leads it to demand reforms in society; at this stage it can be designated as a community for social change.[9]

Speaking from his experience in Brazil, Carlos Mesters distinguishes three different ways in which the communities he has worked with reflect on the Bible.[10] He summarizes these as follows:

> In the first situation the group involved comes together solely for the sake of discussing the Bible; the Bible is the only thing that unites them and they stick to it. In the second situation the people focus on the Bible, too, but they come together as a community. In the third situation we have a community of people meeting around the Bible who inject concrete reality and their own situation into the discussion. Their struggle as a people enters the picture.[11]

Mesters' conclusion is that all three of these factors—the Bible, the community, and the real-life situation of the people—are essential elements for Christian theological reflection. If any one of them is lacking, as in the first two communities mentioned above, he believes that they have no future as a Christian community. He is also convinced that it is unimportant whether the groups start with the Bible, or the community, or the real-life situation, as long as all three factors are included. Mesters also discusses in detail a number of characteristics of the people's interpretation of the Bible which could serve as catalyst for discussion in communities in other parts of the world.[12]

My own experience with coordinators and members of BECs in Mexico, Panama, and Nicaragua generally supports Mesters' conclusion that the three elements of Bible, community, and reality constitute the essential elements in the theological reflection of the communities. But I found sharp disagreements among them with regard to his statement that it makes no difference which of the three elements comes first. Some coordinators believed that reflection on the Bible must come first in order to provide Christian meaning for any subsequent community actions. For others, it was essential to begin with a reflection on the situation along with some community action for change. They believed that only in this way could the people be enabled to return to reflection on the Bible and to understand it from the viewpoint of the poor and their struggle for justice. This position reflects the views of several prominent Latin American theologians such as Gustavo Gutiérrez, who asserts that theology (reflection) is the "second step" after action,[13] and Juan Luis Segundo, who sees a specific commitment as a necessary first step in the method of theological reflection that he refers to as the "hermeneutic circle."[14]

My own conclusion from observing the BECs is similar to that of Mesters. First of all, it would be a very rare event for a group of Christians to engage in common action with no background of Christian symbols and reflection on them at all. Thus it may be a false question to ask whether action or reflection should come first. But more importantly, I think that the position of Mesters offers greater freedom to assess the strengths and weaknesses of different communities and to adapt the method in a creative way in accordance with this assessment. The method then would respect the diversity and different levels of development of BECs mentioned earlier.

In order to provide more concreteness regarding the BECs, I now add some details from my own contacts with clerical, religious, and lay coordinators as well as with actual members of the communities. It should be noted that the three countries I visited—Mexico, Panama, and Nicaragua—have a relatively long history of organizing and developing communities, and thus may not be typical of other Latin American countries. Also, my experience in the three countries was limited, and thus is not intended as a total picture of the communities.

First of all, it should be stressed that prayer and religious hymns are very important to the life of the BECs. As Cardinal Paulo Arns has expressed it, "People do not come to the BECs where there is no praying or singing. They may come four or five times to organize practical things, but nothing further will come of it." Especially impressive are the new popular hymns that express the aspirations and hopes of the common people and are sung with great enthusiasm. Their prayers of petition, too, are startling in the very concrete nature of their appeals: for clean water, a just wage, a primary school, an independent union, police protection, and so forth.

Another important feature is the development of well-organized programs for the training and continuing education of lay "coordinators" or "animators" (the word "leader" is never used). The programs include national and province conferences, workshops, courses, and the publication of popular literature on Scripture reading, religious education, and social analysis. Of particular importance are the weekly meetings among twenty or thirty coordinators from the same area, at which they discuss both past and upcoming meetings of their groups. A key element of the meeting is the distribution and discussion of a typed or xeroxed *morral* (literally, a saddlebag that contains food for the people on their journey). This is a two-page summary, sometimes in popular dramatic form, of topics for the next meeting. For example, *morrales* that I encountered in Mexico discussed the causes of unemployment in the barrio, developing more friendly relations with neighboring BECs, and learning from the situation of other BECs in Nicaragua. This well-developed system of organization seems to provide an antidote against the temptations to sectarianism or politicization of the BECs, which were seen as the main dangers to the communities in the Puebla meeting. It also represents an impressive building of lay leadership at the grassroots level, clearly a most pressing need in the Latin American church.

Finally, the most vivid impression I received in talking to BEC members in very poor barrios was the great sense of dignity they had gained from their experience in the communities. Those who a few years ago had accepted their designation as "brutes" or "animals" in society now spoke and acted with confidence, honesty, and an awareness of their unique value as persons. Also, in all the meetings I attended, the majority of both coordinators and BEC members were women, a fact which in the long run should have profound consequences in both society and the church.

Concluding Data on the Communities

Before turning to the question of the BECs in the United States, I want to add some remarks on the data and conclusions in the study of the communities by Marcello Azevedo. With his background as both a social scientist and a theologian he has produced the best single work on the grassroots communities thus far, one which other scholars will have to start with. Obviously, I can select only a few items from a very rich study.

I have already noted Azevedo's oft-repeated observation that the BECs are a new and very significant fact in the Brazilian church and in the world church, and that he values them very highly. In this positive context, his criticisms of the movement have greater force and credibility. Thus, he notes that much of the literature on the BECs is very enthusiastic, with such exclusive emphasis on the pastoral strategy of the BECs that other strategies and forms of church life are seen to be downgraded and perhaps eliminated entirely. A common theology appears to have been developed that justifies the phenomenon and presents it to the church as the best way of being church.[15] Azevedo opposes this trend vigorously, as may be seen in the following: "There is no realistic future for BECs in an exclusive or overly optimistic emphasis on the restricted base as the best or only form of Church, however sound or unsound may be the theological argument offered for this position. In this pastoral perspective, many people are irretrievably *left outside,* or *programmatically excluded.*"[16]

Along the same lines, he notes that many bishops, priests and religious have little confidence in the apostolic future of the parish. But Azevedo appears to agree with the views of Felix Pastor that the coexistence and integration of parish and BECs is the correct approach to solving the tensions between them:

> Far from trying to destroy or replace the parish, Basic Groups should aim for its renewal and vivification. . . . With the Basic Communities, the parish acquires a new life. It loses its merely administrative connotations and accentuates its ecclesial meaning when it is turned into a center of communitarian animation and a symbol of the real-life communion existing between the diverse communities.[17]

Another criticism that surfaces in various ways is the need to take full account of the cultural identity of the people. Given the author's training in cultural anthropology, his warning is somber: *"The nonperception of this cultural dimension* may well pose the greatest threat to BEC development and make the whole effort precarious. Herein may lie the strong appeal of sects, evangelical groups, and spiritism even when they are ambiguous, fail to attend to the material needs of the people, and sometimes push an ideologically packaged, fundamentalist approach to the Bible."[18] This leads Azevedo to some rather sharp criticism for those who concentrate on analyzing social injustice and abstract from the cultural realm entirely. This results in community members who "would be *sociopolitically aware,* but gradually *uprooted from their popular Catholicism,* the latter failing to become fully historical. They would involve themselves in partisan politics on the basis of one or another ideology, inwardly and perhaps even outwardly dissociated from their BECs and potentially liable to alienation from their faith."[19]

Closely connected with this is the use of cultural analysis, but practiced in a naive, idealized and synchronic (rather than diachronic) fashion, that envisions the poor as an idyllic, immutable reality impervious to other influences. Azevedo's critique of this should be matter for profound reflection not only by Latin American pastoral agents but by anyone who seeks to understand the situation of the poor throughout the Third World. This text is part of a critique of the work of Paulo Süss:

> The implication is that the popular world is not affected or influenced by the forces of the modern world, except in terms of economic oppression and structural injustice. These forces are viewed as "the system," and only from that standpoint are they to be given consideration by theology. But real-life experience shows us the ever accelerating impact of contemporary reality on every aspect of the lives of the simplest and lowliest people everywhere. The communications media reach everywhere, as do the tentacles of the economic process that is being implanted arbitrarily but inexorably. Ritual and festal Catholicism is on the decline in the rural interior, succumbing to the timetables of movies, TV, and radio. The hit series are watched avidly there, just as they are watched in Rio de Janeiro and São Paulo. Their impact is even more intense in the poor urban peripheries, where the type of job available and the reality of joblessness are thoroughly undermining the structure that Süss describes as "popular."[20]

Azevedo also clearly asserts that it is the *whole Catholic population* of Brazil that is the subject of popular Catholicism, and not merely the members of the BECs, who constitute a relatively small percentage of that population. He notes that the Brazilian bishops speak glowingly of the dynamic features of the BECs, and declare that future evangelizing activity will have to develop in conjunction with the communities. The author then proceeds to express his reservations frankly: "The formulations of the Brazilian bishops are very optimistic. Even more optimistic are the views of theologians and pastoral agents working directly with BECs. Yet one cannot help but feel a bit uneasy when one hears such euphoric projections about a phenomenon that is so recent, so quantitatively small (taking in perhaps four million people), and restricted to a specific stratum of the population."[21] The author's solution to this difficulty, which he refers to as the *great challenge,* is to find ways to carry the fundamental spirit of the BECs to all the other social milieus in the church, to the parishes, the movements and to whole dioceses.

Finally, a very important subject that is developed at great length by the author is "the broader challenge of evangelization in Brazil." Here he provides important analyses of the relation of BECs to the entire socio-political context, in which he critiques the historical projects of both Marxism and liberal capitalism. Here I can provide only one example of what he sees as a new and Christian dialectical synthesis:

> The newness will lie in not looking to those two spurious products for support, capitalism and Marxist socialism, on which there is a remote Christian influence. The newness lies in recapturing at its source the original current of the gospel message, which has in time been perverted by Christianity itself, and frequently by the Church. We must see the Christian inspiration at its sources and recapture it for present-day reality, without paying tribute to the two polarizing forces that are dominating and destroying the world. This is a project on the macroscale of time. It is up to lay Christians especially to believe in it and start laying the foundations for it. And here BECs can have an important role.[22]

BECs and the U.S. Experience

In turning to the "reality" of the church in the United States, I want to emphasize that I am not advocating a wholesale importation of the Latin American experience. Clearly, any development of small Christian communities must be faithful to our own political, social and cultural history. Yet the examples of the BECs in our neighboring church certainly challenge the U.S. church at a very fundamental level. What is the *operative* model of the U.S. church today, especially in the urban and suburban parishes that serve the vast majority of Catholics? Is it an almost totally institutional or sacramental model, or some amalgam of the two? Does it even seriously consider creative strategies at the level of the local church to incarnate effectively elements of the church as herald, as servant, and as communion/community both for the benefit of its own members as well as for the good of all the human beings in their neighborhood or region? Frankly, I do not see how a serious Catholic today, lay or clerical, can escape without lapsing into bad faith a confrontation with this "sign of the times" from the majority of the world church, that is, the church of Latin American and the Third World.

At the same time, it is important to acknowledge that there already exist many examples of vibrant small communities in the United States. Perhaps the most dramatic example of these are the charismatic communities, but we can include Marriage Encounter, Cursillo, Christian Life Communities, Catholic Worker and allied groups, and others. There are also any number of peace and justice communities, engaged in public education, lobbying, solidarity with oppressed people, research, and caring for the immediate needs of the poor. Whether all these communities have anything to learn from the Latin American experience can only be decided by the members themselves.

Whatever the principle of formation of small communities may be, I presuppose here that their goals include development of the faith and spiritual lives of their members as well as some form of commitment to social justice. In this context, I find the distinction made by the Canadian survey of "Communities for Justice" to be quite helpful. The author distinguishes between "popular Christian communities" and "progressive Christian communities." The former include persons who are actually experiencing various forms of poverty and/or oppression—that is to say, they are communities *of* the poor and oppressed. The second category includes those (usually middle class and professional people) who are engaged in actions of support for poor and oppressed peoples; thus, they are communities *for* the poor and oppressed.[23]

At this point, therefore, I discuss popular communities in the U.S. church and afterward consider the progressive communities. The most obvious example of popular communities may be found in the Hispanic church in this country. Although it is often ignored, this church has great importance, as may be seen in the statement of Enrique Dussell: "Demographic projections based on birth rate and immigration indicate that by the year 2000 fifty percent of U.S. Catholics will be of Latin American origin."[24]

It is important to emphasize at the outset that the fundamental concepts of the Latin American BECs are already an essential part of the pastoral strategy of the U.S. Hispanic church. Convincing proof for this assertion can be found in the manual for the formation of BECs published by the Secretariat for Hispanic Affairs of the United States Catholic Conference, where the authors assert that as of 1979 there were already more than twelve thousand BECs actually functioning in the United States.

Since Hispanics constitute such a large part of the U.S. church, it seems reasonable to assume that their pastoral strategy will continue to influence the pastoral strategy of the non-Hispanic church. I suggest that this will happen on a number of levels. First, it will challenge the non-Hispanic church to develop its own creative strategies for developing authentic Christian community within the many large, impersonal parishes that exist today. This problem will be referred to again when we consider the applicability of BECs for the non-Hispanic church.

On another level, the approach could be the providential means for making the voice of the poor heard in the non-Hispanic church and thus making possible its conversion to the cause of the poor. This is especially important since the majority of the U.S. church belong to the middle and upper classes, thus far with little contact or interest in the "base" or marginalized classes. The BECs in their ever increasing numbers will serve as living reminders that no Christian community today, especially those that form among the middle and upper classes, can consider itself authentic unless it is distinguished by a passion for and commitment to social justice for the poor.

On a third level, the experience of the BECs could provide models for other groups that have been marginalized within the U.S. church, such as women, blacks, native Americans, and the urban and rural poor. Again, there is no question of simple translation: rather it involves an openness to learn from fellow Christians in the same national church and creative adaptation to historical and cultural circumstances. Again, such adaptation can only be done by the actual members of marginalized groups.

Are the insights of the BECs applicable to the middle class and upper class sectors of the U.S. church? That this is a very important question may be seen clearly in the recent social analysis of United States society presented by Joe Holland and Peter Henriot. After analyzing the evolution of capitalism into its present phase of "national security state capitalism," they propose a strategy of response by the church to this development which includes the basic Christian communities as an essential element. And, the authors conclude, "the church of the United States can learn much . . . from the Latin American church and its strategy of basic Christian communities."[25]

To achieve clarity in this discussion, certain important facts should be kept in mind. As J.B. Libânio has pointed out, "The research on the BECs shows that they are mainly located in socially deprived rural and urban areas. Few *comunidades* exist among the urban middle and upper classes."[26] Clearly, the situation in the United States is quite the opposite, and I now turn my attention to the "progressive" communities mentioned earlier among the middle and upper classes.

Just as in the discussion of the Hispanic church, the first thing to note is that there is already a strong movement underway in the United States for the development of such communities. In their annual meeting of 1979, the National Federation of Priests' Councils selected the formation of small Christian communities as their key pastoral strategy. In a handbook entitled "Developing Basic Christian Communities," the president of the NFPC, James Ratigan, states flatly that "Catholic priests in the 1980's will not be able to accomplish the task of evangelization unless there is a dramatic (radical) restructuring of the parish. The need for smaller faith communities is essential."[27] He also notes that "Basic Christian Communities are by no means an exclusively Hispanic phenomenon. There have been basic communities for over fifteen years in virtually all parts of the U.S."[28] The council has also formed a task force to document models of different types of successful small communities, as well as to create workshops and a speakers' bureau to aid in the formation and growth of new communities. At this point I offer some reflections on the contents of the handbook published in 1980 by the NFPC.

The contributions of Virgilio Elizondo and Frank Ponce are concerned with Hispanic BECs in the United States and are not germane to the present discussion. However, Ponce does raise a question in his essay that is never satisfactorily answered: Are the BECs only for Hispanics in the United States or are they suitable for the whole church? While emphasizing that the BECs do indeed work for Hispanics and presenting a wealth of information regarding their formation, he concludes that "whether they will work for the larger U.S. Catholic Church is less clear at this point."[29]

More helpful are the observations of Thomas Peyton, which reflect thirteen years of experience in forming voluntary communities within parish structures in the United States. However, Peyton seems to *presume* that his methods would work in any parish. This argument would be much more effective if he had included some data or concrete examples of the success or failure of small communities in non-Hispanic parishes.

A much more concrete picture is presented by David Killian in "Basic Christian Communities in Boston," where he worked within the structure of the nonterritorial parish of the Paulist Center Community. At various times the number of participants in this parish ranged from a thousand to fifteen hundred.

It is interesting to note that the small groups here (called *Koinonia* communities) gradually came into being not because of some previously worked out pastoral plan proceeding from the top but because of the expressed needs and frustrations of some of the more articulate members of the parish. The next key step was to initiate meetings of small groups of parishioners so that they could discuss their experiences of alienation due to the size of the parish (as well as other complaints). Killian observes that "at the end of the session participants concluded that this forum was exactly the type of opportunity for sharing that they wanted."[30] In the beginning, four *koinonia* communities were formed, all drawing their membership from a cross-section of the city of Boston.

Once again, however, a desire was expressed by some parishioners to relate to others in small groups in the same neighborhood, where they shared common problems and social needs and could cooperate in seeking solutions. Killian concludes: "As a priest I have taken special joy in seeing lay people assume responsibility for their church. I have rejoiced that they have been eager to become partners in ministry. . . . In the coming years,

Koinonia can be a part of the wide development of Basic Christian Communities in our country."[31]

In another article, Arthur Chavez described the formation of "little parishes" within the territorial parish of Our Lady of Guadalupe Church in Albuquerque, New Mexico. It is not clear from the article whether this is a Hispanic parish, but Chavez's concluding remarks appear to have relevance for any part of the U.S. church:

> The challenge of the 1980's is that every parish uniquely has to begin a process of not simply understanding their structure, but of building new structures to meet the needs of the people. . . . The Basic Christian Community, the Koinonia experience, or the model of the Little Parish may work for some, and be a special answer for the problems the local church is having in being an effective instrument. For others it may be something else. That which is most necessary is corporate discernment led by the Spirit and action for the Kingdom of God.[32]

I have already referred to the great number of small Christian communities that already exist in the non-Hispanic church in the United States. These communities also clearly differ from those in Latin American in that their membership is largely composed of the middle and upper classes. Given all this, it is quite difficult to discern what any particular group here might learn from the experience of the Latin American BECs. Recognizing, then, that any fruitful borrowing is up to the judgment of the U.S. communities, I here present my own reflections.

One of the key features of the Latin American BECs has been its emphasis on the importance of discovering and encouraging the growth of genuine lay leadership and genuine lay ministries. This appears to me to have great applicability to the U.S. scene. The U.S. church has a large number of well-educated, talented, and committed laity who are quite capable of assuming leadership roles and developing new forms of ministry. In fact, many of them are doing just that at the present time, both with and without the consent of the hierarchy. Also, the women's movement is very strong in the United States and it is obvious that feminists are not going to seek out clerical leaders for their communities. Finally, present vocation statistics make it clear that there will be in the near future a serious shortage of priests in the U.S. church, making the question of lay leadership a very urgent issue on the U.S. agenda.

But what will be the role of bishops and priests vis-à-vis this lay leadership? Again, the Latin American experience has been instructive. The clergy (or many of them) have aimed at a new collegial type of relationship, based on genuine dialogue with the people and fraternal response to their real needs. They have put their talents, training, and resources at the service of the communities, in order to discover, train, and encourage genuine lay leadership and lay ministries. This is similar to the strategy of the intelligent missionary who aims at putting himself or herself out of a job in favor of indigenous leadership. There is as yet no way of determining whether the U.S. clergy will decide on a similar style of leadership in the future; that decision, however, may be crucial for linking future communities to the official church.

I also believe that the method of faith reflection has important lessons for the United States. It is the reflection on "the reality" that I think is most needed in middle class and upper class BECs, which are often insulated from poverty and situations of injustice. Fortunately, the article on social analysis by Holland and Henriot, mentioned earlier, provides an excellent vehicle for achieving this type of reflection in the United States. Both elements, then, would ensure that the BECs developing in the United States would not only be faith communities but also justice communities, aware of and committed to the cause of the poor or oppressed. The formation of such communities will be the great challenge to all members of the U.S. church in the decade ahead.[33]

Chapter 7
Human Rights as Bulwark of Freedom

A quarter of a century ago, Pope John XXIII began his epoch-making encyclical letter, *Peace on Earth,* with a declaration addressed both to the church and to all humanity that provides an indestructible foundation for both the establishment and the institutional defense of human freedom:

> Any human society, if it is to be well-ordered and productive, must lay down as a foundation this principle, namely, that every human being is a person, that is, his nature is endowed with intelligence and free will. By virtue of this, he has rights and duties of his own, flowing directly and simultaneously from his very nature. These rights are therefore universal, inviolable, and inalienable.[1]

And in the very next paragraph the pontiff proceeds to buttress this declaration securely grounded in human reason with at least an equally important principle that is derived from Christian revelation: "If we look upon the dignity of the human person in the light of divinely revealed truth, we cannot help but esteem it *far more highly.*"[2]

In this chapter I discuss the relevance of these statements of Pope John in two important areas. The first is concerned with the creation of organizations throughout Latin America dedicated to the defense and enhancement of both civil and socioeconomic rights. These serve as a model or inspiration for other parts of the world, since they continue to be effective despite the cruel repression of dictatorships and other authoritarian regimes.

In the second part I concentrate on the statement that Christian revelation leads the church to value human dignity together with its concomitant inviolable and inalienable rights "far more highly" than any human society does. From this I draw the obvious theological conclusion that the church will be held to a far higher standard for the promotion and defense of human rights within its own ecclesial society than it proclaims for observance in secular or explicitly atheistic societies.

Human Rights in Latin America

In the efflorescence of theology that has occurred in Latin America in the last two decades, the topic of human rights does not constitute a central explicit theme. Often this lack of attention derives from the exercise of what is called "ideological suspicion." That is to say, it is the suspicion that North American emphasis on human rights (understood as individual freedoms) serves as an ideological mask to conceal the massive human suffering on the socioeconomic level that envelops millions of human beings in the southern continent as well as to disguise North American complicity in contributing to this situation of misery.

This has led the Uruguayan theologian Juan Luis Segundo to complain that "if any country could apply to the rich nations the economic and political mechanisms which they now apply to us, then we would be the ones who would go to investigate—hypocritically, to be sure—the violations of human rights in those countries." And he concludes that "the tragedy of the situation is that the ones who determine and control the defense of human rights . . . are the very ones who make human rights impossible in three quarters of the planet."[3]

When it has reflected theologically on human rights, Latin American theology has from the beginning adopted a creative and original stance by placing great emphasis on two key approaches or contexts for the understanding of rights: (1) the reality or situation in which human rights are fostered must be conceived as one of *structural sin* or, in the words of the Medellín conference, of institutionalized violence; (2) the primary emphasis in human rights policy must be given to socioeconomic rights, which in the concrete order means the *rights of the poor*. That this bipolar approach has gradually begun to influence the social teaching of the U.S. Catholic bishops is quite evident in their pastoral letters of 1983 and 1986, while the impact on the thinking of Pope John Paul is clear in his recent encyclical letter, *Sollicitudo Rei Socialis*.

Granted that the concept of structural sin is gaining increasing acceptance, what is peculiar to the Latin American situation is the acute urgency of a Christian response to transform the unjust structures. This urgency results from a primal and unavoidable characteristic of Latin American reality: the vast majority of human beings in the continent live in situations of deprivation and suffering which simply cannot be evaded. Ignacio Ellacuria has expressed this succinctly: "Who the poor are in the real situation of the Third World is not a problem whose solution requires scriptural exegesis or sociological analysis or historical theories. . . . As a primary fact, as the real situation of the majority of humanity, there is no room for partisan equivocations."[4]

In the context of human rights, it is also glaringly obvious that the reality of structural sin consists in an overwhelming deprivation of socioeconomic rights: food, clothing, housing, medical care, literacy, work, security, and the barest minimum of recreation and culture. Although there may be sincere disagreement on how to change the structures that cause this misery, a consensus exists that, negatively speaking, the situation demands immediate opposition. That is to say, it constitutes the very antithesis of the kingdom of God and requires of the Christian conscience a loud and unconditional "no."

The commitment to the rights of the poor had been boldly proclaimed at the Latin American bishops' conference at Medellín in 1968. In their next conference at Puebla, Mexico, in 1979, the bishops dedicated an entire chapter of their final document to "A Preferential Option for the Poor," and declared unequivocally: "We affirm the need for conversion on the part of the whole Church to a preferential option for the poor."[5] Here and in other places in the document, the bishops caution that the commitment to the poor is "preferential but not exclusive." Lest this seem to absolve the rich of their responsibility, however, the text clearly states the implications of the option for them: " . . . the witness of a poor Church can evangelize the rich whose hearts are attached to wealth, thus converting them from this bondage and their own egotism."[6]

Human Rights and Pastoral Practice

I have already noted that for ideological reasons theology in Latin America has manifested a certain reticence regarding traditional human rights language. On the level of the church's day-to-day pastoral activities, however, there has been a very widespread explicit emphasis on rights language, as well as on strategies for the promotion and defense of human rights.

The Chilean theologian Segundo Galilea, for example, has noted that "the fight for human rights in Latin America has in recent years become such an everyday aspect of the church's pastoral activity on the subcontinent that it has come to be *identified* with her understanding of her mission to mankind."[7] He then reviews the countries where church-sponsored human rights centers and networks have been established on a permanent basis; among those analyzed are the Vicariate of Solidarity in Chile, the Assembly for Human Rights in Bolivia, the Church of Solidarity in Peru and Mexico, and a number of organizations in Brazil, of which the best known is entitled the Campaign for Brotherhood. Galilea also emphasizes that such work for human rights has led directly to one of the most outstanding features of Latin American Christianity in recent years: it has become a persecuted church and a church of the martyrs. Thus, he adds, "although the churches in Latin America have suffered sporadic persecutions since the independence of their respective countries, persecution takes a different form nowadays, because it originates from the church's active support of human rights, and not from her defense of her own rights, as happened in the nineteenth century."[8]

A parallel development, moreover, along the lines of the human rights centers, is the ever-increasing volume of episcopal statements, especially of bishops' conferences, in defense of human rights. Galilea goes so far as to say that now "virtually every time the bishops speak on temporal matters they refer to the human rights problem."[9] And on the level of lay persons, the most important figure is clearly the Argentine Adolfo Pérez Esquivel, who has earned worldwide acclaim as well as the Nobel Peace Prize for his nonviolent approach to human rights theory and practice.[10] Pérez also has considerable organizing skill, as may be seen in his founding of an organization called SERPAJ (the Spanish acronym for "Service for Peace and Justice"), whose purpose he himself describes as "the defense of the human person and the right of the people to their own identity, to self-determination and, above all, to a dignified life." His organization now has flourishing branch offices in Brazil, Mexico, Peru, Colombia, Chile, Bolivia, Uruguay, Nicaragua and Panama, countries which together with Argentina contain more than ninety-five percent of the inhabitants of Latin America. A few articles have also been written on other networks for nonviolent change, and I believe that this nonviolent approach is one of the least understood and least appreciated human rights phenomena in contemporary Latin America.

During recent years also more and more attention has been given to what I consider a unique Latin American contribution to the human rights tradition, and that is its constant stress on the human rights of the poor. This has been succinctly described by Galilea as follows:

> The Church's struggle for human rights is not primarily concerned with public, political and intellectual liberty, but with the basic rights of workers, peasants and natives. In contrast to these basically "human" rights, the right to dissent and the right to a free press are luxuries. In Latin America we are

dealing with the right to work, to earn a minimum wage, to be fed, to acquire a basic education, not to live in permanent insecurity, not to be systematically deprived and discriminated against and to have workers' organizations. In Latin America, the rights of man are the rights of the poor.[11]

Although discussion of this continues to flourish in theological and pastoral publications, I think the best synthesis of its meaning on the ethical level has been provided by the American theologian David Hollenbach. Hollenbach strongly supports the position that the "societal effort to implement and to institutionalize rights should adopt the following three strategic moral priorities 1) The needs of the poor take priority over the wants of the rich. 2) The freedom of the dominated takes priority over the liberty of the powerful. 3) The participation of marginalized groups takes priority over the preservation of an order which excludes them."[12] Hollenbach goes on to argue that these normative ethical standards are more helpful for policy decisions than the lists found in the Universal Declaration and in *Pacem in Terris,* precisely because they consciously acknowledge the fact of conflict between the claims which different persons make on the community. This conflict between the needs of some and the wants of others must be seen as one of the dominant characteristics of modern society, and an adequate human rights policy cannot ignore it if it is to be responsive to the actual situation. This stress on the rights of the poor, both in South and North America, should be considered one of the most challenging areas for the development of human rights theory and especially for implementation in policy and institutions in the years ahead.

Human Rights in the Church

My final reflections concern the question of human rights within the institution of the Catholic church, which requires a brief historical survey as a context for the discussion.[13] It should be made clear at the outset that the church's reaction to the U.S. Declaration of Independence in 1776 and the French Proclamation of the Rights of Man in 1789 was definitely hostile. During the eighteenth and nineteenth centuries the church, especially in Europe, struggled to maintain its position of privilege vis-à-vis secular society, and as a consequence formed an alliance with the conservatism of the *ancien régime.* Thus, it could not "claim for itself a significant place in either the theoretical or the practical struggle for human rights in the eighteenth and nineteenth centuries."[14]

The real beginning of official Catholic rights teaching occurred under

Pope Leo XIII in his encyclical letter *Rerum Novarum* (1891). Interestingly enough, this document reflected an emphasis on the socioeconomic rights of a just wage and the ownership of property, while devoting little attention to what are known today as civil and political rights. Although these ideas were developed and amplified by Pope Pius XI (1922-1939) and Pope Pius XII (1939-1958), the church's great learning experience regarding rights revolved around the shattering experience of the Second World War and the overwhelming demonic power of totalitarianism and genocide, as exemplified above all in the Nazi regime under Adolf Hitler. The Universal Declaration of Human Rights in 1948 was the major consequence of intense worldwide reflection on this same catastrophic experience. And over the next decade the church came to see the lasting value of the Declaration as a protector of the human dignity of man and woman, and as a strong universal foundation for the inalienability and inviolability of all human rights.

In 1958, John XXIII became pope and in 1963 published his epoch-making letter, *Peace on Earth*, which is deeply indebted to the Universal Declaration and which must be considered the Magna Carta of human rights teaching and practice in the worldwide Catholic Church. This tradition has been carried on with great vigor and amplitude by the present pope, John Paul II, and his attitude to the Universal Declaration is evident in this text from his address to the United Nations in October of 1979:

> The Universal Declaration of Human Rights—with its collection of many declarations and conventions on highly important aspects of human rights in favor of children, of women, of equality between races, and especially the two international covenants on economic, social, and cultural rights and on civil and political rights—must remain the basic value in the United Nations, with which the consciences of its members must be confronted and from which they must draw continual inspiration.[15]

In this context, I would like to return to the text of Pope John XXIII mentioned at the beginning of this chapter regarding human dignity, from which proceed inviolable and inalienable human rights, as well as the obligation from Christian revelation to esteem this dignity and human rights "far more highly" than those who act on the basis of human reason alone. The key question which is at the heart of human rights in the church today is this: precisely how, in what concrete procedures and attitudes, does the church promote and protect the human rights of its own members? If these procedures and attitudes appear in some cases to be deficient, a corollary question would be: what should be the ones which correspond to the far higher esteem which the church proclaims for human dignity and human rights? This is the most serious issue regarding human rights that the church faces now and for the foreseeable future, and it affects both the church's inner life and exterior mission: "The tension between what a sound human rights theory *seems to demand* and what the church *does* may produce problems of governability within the church and a reaction of incredulity in the face of its teaching."[16]

In elaborating answers to these questions, I am going to focus on the work of the Brazilian liberation theologian, Leonardo Boff. His basic thesis consists in a rephrasal of the words of John XXIII: "The Church has developed an understanding of the human person that highlights his or her inviolable dignity and sacredness. This anthropological reality forms the basis for inalienable rights that establish unquestionable duties of respect that are so radical that human causes become God's causes."[17] Boff first discusses various violations of human rights within the church, focusing above all on discrimination against women.[18] But his major contribution is an analysis of the *structural* causes for the violation of rights which is also diachronic, thus moving beyond consideration of individual lapses or malice regarding human rights to the real structures of domination.[19] There are three levels (the author uses the rather odd term "collisions") of causality that are considered.

The first level is "sociohistorical," concerned with the power structure in the church and its historical evolution. Boff believes that, sociologically speaking, the structure is authoritarian, which means that "those in power exclude the free and spontaneous acknowledgment by their subordinates of that authority";[20] thus, the decision-making axis runs from pope to bishop to priest, excluding religious and laity. Theologically speaking, Boff's view is that the authority of Christ is present in the entire church, while its organic differentiation in the various members of the church, including laity, is the result of diverse cultural borrowing.

Then follows an historical summary of the church's political evolution which is of profound importance as a precedent for structural change today. Like all societies, the early Christian communities experienced powerful needs to organize, with predictable consequences: "They inevitably took social and political models from the surrounding world in which to incarnate their authority from God and Christ. The power structure in the Church today is indebted to centuries-old patterns, and two patterns are worth noting in particular: the experience with Roman power and the feudal structure. The Church assumed customs, titles, expressions, and symbols from them."[21]

Thus, at one point in history, the church incarnated itself along the lines of hierarchical and authoritarian secular models, imperial and feudal. One can say that this may have been a legitimate adaptation in its time, but one must also confront the fact that this structure today is in direct and irreconcilable conflict with both the global consciousness of human rights and the church's own unequivocal and often reiterated teaching, namely, that human rights are universal, inviolable and inalienable, proceeding not from church dogmas or law, but from the very nature of human persons.

My own view regarding this impasse is that the church should continue its previous process of inculturation, incorporating models and procedures from Western democracies and even socialist states that have proven effective in fostering and protecting human rights. To the oft-repeated assertion that the church is not a democracy, this brief historical analysis should illustrate that the church *by nature* is also not a Roman empire, nor a medieval fiefdom, nor a European monarchy. Yet elements of all of these now antiquated societies are at present the most conspicuous symbols of the church's own social organization; the issue is whether the church can continue its historical evolution in a positive direction or remain fixed in the obsolete trappings of the past. Or, as Norbert Greinacher has expressed it, "instead of continuing to run the risk of being one of the few surviving relics of feudalism in a democratic environment, the Church may become herself democratic in an exemplary way and thus be able to carry out her critical function in society."[22] It should also be stressed that abundant work has already been done on this topic in both dogmatic and scriptural areas.[23]

On a second level, "the analytical collision," Boff analyzes the church's concept of its own authority and identity as the principal if not exclusive bearer of God's revelation to the world, understood doctrinally as the collection of absolute and infallible truths necessary for salvation. But the bearer of absolute truths cannot tolerate other truths, thus giving rise to an intolerance and dogmatism that gravely affect human rights. Boff then concludes: "As long as this type of dogmatic and doctrinaire understanding of revelation and salvation continues, there inevitably will be repression of the freedom of thought within the Church. This repression will be carried out with the clean conscience of one fulfilling a sacred duty of preserving the divine right of revelation to which every human right must give way."

Finally, Boff adverts to a deeper and more structural collision which is concerned "not with what is thought and stated but rather with the actions that have marked daily life." Here he utilizes an industrial model for the church where one group, the clergy, holds the means of religious and symbolic production, while another group, the laity, functions as consumers of these good and services, without any capacity for production or participation in decision-making. Boff concludes that theology aside, the underlying conflict is one of the power of some over others, a power that will not abdicate its privileges and rights, at odds with the inviolable rights of human persons (participation, symbolic production, free expression, etc.) . . . There is nothing left but the acceptance of the fact that although the hierarchy recognizes certain rights they cannot be exercised because they do not fit into the ecclesial organization. The rights of the individual lose their inalienable quality and are thus violated.[24]

The author stresses that he is not questioning the legitimacy of authority in the church, but the imbalance of power among its members, together with a theology that justifies and reinforces its power by attributing divine origin to the historical exercise of that power.

Let us recall again the explicit teaching of Pope John XXIII, that human rights flow directly from the very nature of the human person and are therefore universal, inviolable and inalienable. Any *religious* justification for their violation, then, can in no way be considered authentic Christian theology, but rather the perversion of that discipline into an ideology of power.

This message was reechoed by Pope John Paul II in his visit to Filipino President Ferdinand Marcos at Malacanang Palace, Manila, on February 17, 1981. After first stressing that "the challenge that faces each nation, and more particularly a Christian nation, is *a challenge to its own internal life,*"[25] the pontiff continues as follows:

Even in exceptional situations that may at times arise, one can never justify any violation of the fundamental dignity of the human person or of the basic rights that safeguard this dignity. Legitimate concern for the security of a nation, as demanded by the common good, could lead to the temptation of subjugating to the State the human being and his or her dignity and rights. Any apparent conflict between the exigencies of security and of the citizens' basic rights must be resolved according to the fundamental principle—upheld always by the Church—that social organization exists only for the service of man and for the protection of his dignity, and that it cannot claim to serve the common good when human rights are not safeguarded.[26]

Clearly, these admonitions on the inviolability of human rights apply also in every respect to the "social organization" that is the church. That is, human rights as institutions of freedom are essential for all societies and all human beings.

Boff's prescriptions for change reject idealist temptations of raising consciousness in order to change structures. In his view, "it is not new ideas but new and different practices (supported by theory) that will modify ecclesial reality."[27] As is well known, he sees this practice as incarnated above all in the ecclesial base communities, which began and have especially flourished in his native Brazil and which have led to what he calls a true ecclesiogenesis.[28] This new experience of church, since it is better able to fulfill the requirements of human rights, also leads to a truly evangelical understanding of authority, based on traditions of equality, fraternity, and service, and of faith, which is primarily one's total adherence to the living God and not merely the acceptance of the propositions of a creed. Boff ends with a concise summary which I believe encapsulates the major challenge that human rights will represent to the Catholic church in the next few decades:

> The Church recognizes the unfathomable dignity of the human person and so can be the conscience of the world with respect to human rights. But proclamation itself is not enough. The Church will only be heard if it gives witness by its practices, if it is the first to respect and promote human rights within its own reality. Otherwise, one would be right to criticize a Church that sees the speck in the eyes of another while ignoring the beam in its own: Hypocrite, remove the beam from your own eye and then try to remove the speck from your neighbor's eye (see Matt 7:3-5).[29]

Certainly a growing number of voices in the church in the United States are raising and will continue to raise the issue of freedom and human rights within the church. Many of these are the voices of women who speak from within a long history of leadership in and service to the church and often from a profound experience of suffering within the church.

Sydney Callahan, for instance, has written concerning the activities of the Association for the Rights of Catholics in the Church. She insists that this organization is not merely imitating the secular pursuit of individual political rights, which she concedes may have been overemphasized in our society as a way of advancing moral concerns and social reforms. Instead of this, Callahan emphasizes a truly evangelical and deeply spiritual outlook which succinctly summarizes much of the discussion in the last section of this chapter. "When the concept of rights is used within the Catholic context," she declares, "rights are grounded in a religious vision of God's love and justice incarnate in Jesus Christ. Such a consciousness of our rights is necessary for structural change and the spiritual transformation of the church."[30]

Chapter 8
The Vatican and Liberation Theology

For a number of years, I have kept a list of themes in Scripture and tradition that for various reasons appear to be rarely employed in the ordinary teaching and preaching of the Catholic church. A high position on that list has long been occupied by the topic of "Christian freedom," as epitomized in the ringing words of St. Paul: "For freedom Christ has set us free; stand fast therefore and do not submit again to a yoke of slavery" (Gal 5:1). Even when Paul's essential corollary is immediately added: "Only do not use your freedom as an opportunity for the flesh, but through love be servants of one another" (Gal 5:13), the freedom motif is usually lost among a host of exhortations to obedience or similar virtues. We have also noted the church's sad record of opposition to human rights and their correlative freedoms throughout the eighteenth, nineteenth, and much of the twentieth century.

Therefore, it might have been expected that the publication from the Vatican Congregation on the Doctrine of the Faith of its *Instruction of Christian Freedom and Liberation*[1] would have been received enthusiastically and loudly applauded by theologians, who would be well aware of the profound importance of these themes in Christian Scripture and tradition, as well as in the dominant philosophical currents of this century. And as a matter of fact, a rousing welcome and widespread discussion of the document did take place throughout Latin America and, to a lesser degree, in the rest of the Third World. But in the United States very little attention has been given to the document thus far, except for brief articles or editorials in religious journals, a situation which is very puzzling in a country which so cherishes the ideals of liberation and freedom, and which considers itself to be the world leader in the pursuit of those ideals.

Despite the lack of attention the document received in the United States, it must be emphasized that it presents a well-organized, forceful, and often eloquent synthesis of a Christian theology of freedom. And even more importantly, it provides a formal Vatican endorsement (with all the necessary caveats and provisos) of this theology of freedom, not merely for Latin America or other parts of the Third World, but for the universal Catholic Church. This is pointed out with utmost clarity in the introduction, which indicates its purpose of presenting the "principal theoretical and practical aspects" of the theme of freedom and liberation and then goes on to insist: "As regards applications to different local situations, *it is for the local churches,* in communion with one another and with the See of Peter, *to make direct provisions for them*" (no. 3, my italics). Thus, the publication of *Christian Freedom and Liberation* is not meant only for Latin America (the term "liberation theology" is never used); rather, it is a theological event of profound importance and with far-reaching implications for Christian churches in every part of the world.

Introduction to the Document

The text of the *Instruction on Christian Freedom and Liberation* may be found in the appendix of this volume. At this point, I provide some introductory remarks and then a rather brief commentary on the text. In the succeeding sections of this chapter, I present a more synthetic analysis, and conclude with some reflections on its importance within the corpus of Catholic social thought.

Concerning the general method of the work, it has been asserted in the press that it actually represents a synthesis of the teaching of Pope John Paul II. There is some truth to this observation, but only in the sense that the pope has thoroughly assimilated Catholic social and political thought, especially of the past twenty-five years, beginning with Pope John XXIII's *Mater et Magistra* ("Christianity and Social Progress") in 1961 and including the Second Vatican Council's documents as well as the prolific writings of Pope Paul VI. The present pontiff's adoption of the names of these two popes in assuming the papacy was consequently much more than a merely symbolic gesture, since it was an expression of his genuine commitment to continue and to develop their astonishingly profound corpus on social, political, and economic issues. John Paul's major contribution to Catholic social thought, *Laborem Exercens* ("On Human Labor," 1981),[2] is also his most significant contribution to the instruction and one of the most original aspects of what must be called the document's major accomplishment: its thoroughgoing integration of the themes of freedom and liberation into the mainstream of Catholic social thought. Because of the importance of the latter accomplishment, a major disappointment with the instruction is that it was not issued as an encyclical letter, which would have provided even greater impact on the world theological scene.

Some warnings have been raised that the assimilation of liberation thinking into official or mainstream Catholic thought would blunt its cutting edge, and that it would be swiftly coopted, domesticated, and forgotten. I do not find this argument convincing, for the many liberation theologians I have met have by now many years of experience in resisting such pressures and appear to be expert in preventing what we in the United States call "hostile takeovers." Besides, the text I have quoted above on the need for applications of liberation themes by local churches seems to me to provide Latin American and other Third World theologians with all the carte blanche they need to continue on the paths they have already chosen.

It is also helpful to note carefully in this introduction the Vatican congregation's own understanding of its theological method, which I found to be both interesting and extremely challenging. In a chapter entitled "Nature of the Social Doctrine of the Church," the document asserts that its teaching develops "by using the resources of human wisdom and the sciences," that it is "essentially orientated toward action," that it "develops in accordance with the changing circumstances of history," and it "also involves contingent judgments." All this provides convincing evidence of a method solidly based on historical consciousness and human experience (as well as on the data of Scripture, tradition, and science) and the jettisoning of a methodology of essentialist or a priori assumptions that has characterized some church teaching in the past. Finally, an assertion is made which could be interpreted as an endorsement of the pioneering approach of the U.S. Catholic bishops in their pastoral letters on peace and on the economy:[3] "Far from constituting a closed system, [this teaching] remains constantly open to the new questions which continually arise; *it requires the contribution of all charisms, experiences, and skills*" (no. 72, my italics). All of the foregoing characteristics, and especially the italicized ones, appear to me to break new ground in the formation process of Catholic social thought, and I happily take this opportunity to make my own "contribution" in the following positive and negative reflections on the contents of the instruction.

Commentary on the Instruction

Turning to the text itself, the document may be conveniently divided into two major sections, the first consisting of the first three chapters and emphasizing historical, theoretical, and scriptural reflections on freedom, liberation and sin, while the second section is concerned with the integration of theoretical and practical issues regarding the liberating mission of the church (chap. 4), and a Christian practice of liberation (chap. 5). It must be frankly acknowledged that this long document (over eighteen thousand words) is at times tedious and repetitive, but there is nevertheless no doubt that it richly rewards a careful reading and study.

It is helpful to recall the remarks in chapter 2 that the instruction refers to the gospel of Jesus Christ as "by its very nature a message of freedom and liberation" (no.1) and refers to the theme of freedom and liberation as "at the heart of the Christian message" (no. 2). There I noted that it would be difficult to conceive of any higher accolade for a theological position than to refer to it as the "heart" or "very nature" of the gospel message that the church exists to transmit.

Developing this, I would stress that these strong statements at the beginning are not merely peripheral, but continue to be integrated into the entire document. For example, the excellent chapter discussing the scriptural background of liberation and Christian freedom begins as follows:

" . . . The *divine promises of liberation* and their victorious fulfillment in Christ's death and resurrection are the basis of the 'joyful hope' from which the Christian community draws the strength to act resolutely and effectively in the service of love, justice and peace. *The Gospel is a message of freedom and a liberating force* which fulfills the hope of Israel based upon the words of the prophets" (no. 43, italics mine). Further on, Yahweh, who chose Israel and intervened on her behalf, is referred to as the *goel*, that is, the *"liberator,* redeemer, and savior of his people." Especially significant in these texts is the further description of the gospel as "a force of liberation" and the reference to Yahweh as "liberator."

The first two chapters of the instruction are concerned with a history and analysis of freedom, liberation and sin. Frankly, they are the least illuminating parts of the document for several reasons. The first of those reasons is a certain triumphalism with regard to the history of freedom that pervades these chapters. For example, the document asserts that:

> . . . the quest for freedom and the aspiration to liberation, which are among the principal signs of the times in the modern world, have their first source in the Christian heritage. This remains true even in places where they assume erroneous forms and even oppose the Christian view of man and his destiny. Without this reference to the Gospel, the history of the recent centuries in the West cannot be understood (no. 5).

In response to this, one can only ask: what about the embarrassingly frequent and vehement denunciations of freedom, including religious freedom, made by religious authorities invoking the gospel throughout the eighteenth and nineteenth centuries? Why was a titanic struggle necessary during the Second Vatican Council for the acceptance of the principle of religious freedom, a principle accepted by secular governments centuries before the Council? There is a basic refusal in these chapters to acknowledge the church's own sinfulness and errors; in other words, there is a glaring *absence* of truth here, even though appeal is made to the words of Jesus, "The truth will make you free" (Jn 8:32), to "enlighten and guide all theological reflection and all pastoral decisions in this area" (no. 3). Once again, without facing the truth, that is, the church's adamant resistance to movements for freedom and liberation over centuries, there is no possibility for repentance, and thus no response to the basic call of Jesus Christ for conversion, a change of mind and heart.

In the second place, although the document aspires to present a viewpoint that is acceptable to the universal church, it lapses a number of times into a kind of Eurocentrism; a corollary of this is that it talks *about* the poor, while there is little evidence of any deeply felt and passionately committed solidarity *with* the poor. The tone of Eurocentrism that seems so pervasive is perhaps best described by a theologian who lives outside the ambience of Europe or the United States. Here is the description of Pablo Richard, writing from turbulent and war-torn Central America:

> The "climate" of the document is the climate one breathes in Germany, France, Switzerland, or northern Italy. A continent that is old, tired, frightened by the immoralities of an empire that is crumbling away; a Europe that is without youth and without a future; a Europe that is sad and pessimistic, which still looks at the rest of the world from the standpoint of its own experience. The Third World is still a periphery, an unknown horizon, a strange land.
>
> The "climate" that one breathes in Latin America, Africa, or Asia is very different. We are poor, very poor, but we live with happiness and hope; we have youth and a future; we have a cause for which to struggle; we have little, but with that little we are certain that we can construct a world that is both different and better.[4]

The tone in these chapters is also condescending and subtly disguises the desperate impoverishment of hundreds of millions of human beings by waxing lyrical about the "liberating joy" and "emancipation from the dominating claims of the learned" that flourish among the poor because of their knowledge of God (no. 21). I was able to find only one text that seemed to express the yearning of the masses of the Third World for their full liberation: "It remains true that one of the major phenomena of our time, of continental proportions, is the awakening of the consciousness of people who, bent beneath the weight of age-old poverty, aspire to live in dignity and justice and are prepared to fight for their freedom" (no. 17).

The pessimism that Richard mentions is evident throughout chapters 1 and 2, as in this text: "God calls man to be free. In each person there lives a desire to be free. And yet this desire *almost always* tends toward slavery and oppression" (no. 37, italics mine). One wonders what kind of belief the author of these sentences has in the redemptive power of Christ's life, death and resurrection or in the omnipresence of the grace of God in all human beings, or in the oft-quoted teaching of Paul: "Law came in to increase the trespass; but where sin increased, grace abounded all the more" (Rom 5:20).

One other evidence of a Eurocentric attitude lies in the document's narrative of the history of freedom which, it turns out, is a history of freedom in Europe. Thus, the history of modern times begins with the Renaissance, when human beings sought freedom of thought and action in a return to the philosophy of antiquity, as well as control of the laws of nature through the natural sciences. Then Luther appeared to renew the struggle for freedom by throwing off the yoke of the law, which was present above all in the church of his time. After this, the apex of the trajectory of freedom is achieved: " . . . it was above all in the age of the Enlightenment and at the French Revolution that the call to freedom rang out with full force" (no. 6). We might ask what influence the North American Revolution had in this version of history, but the more important question concerns the vast majority of human beings who had begun to endure a process of subjugation and enslavement by Europeans three hundred years before the French Revolution, a process which continued until far into the twentieth century. And it was only after the Second World War that most of the independent nations that now exist achieved their liberation through violent or nonviolent struggle against the "enlightened" nations of Europe. This, and not the French Revolution, is the epoch when the call to freedom rang out with full force for all of mankind.

A refreshing change from this chauvinistic world view occurs when we arrive at chapter 3, which contains a fine, brief survey of liberation themes in the entire Bible. Fortunately, it does not repeat familiar criticisms that liberation theology overemphasizes the Exodus or "reduces" it to a political event. Rather, it states the simple facts that the Exodus is "the liberating action of Yahweh that serves as model and reference for all others" and that it "has a meaning which is both religious and political" (no. 44).

Throughout the survey, the two axes that predominate are social injustice (although the expression "social sin" is not used) and its correlative, the struggle to bring justice to Israel, especially to "the poor, the needy, the widow, and the orphan," who "have a right to justice according to the juridical ordinances of the people of God" (no. 45; this reality could be designated as a situation of "social grace"). The prophets also "vigorously condemn injustice done to the poor: They make themselves spokesmen for the poor," while "Yahweh is the supreme refuge of the little ones and the oppressed, and the Messiah will have the mission of taking up their defense" (no. 46). Both here and at the conclusion of the instruction (no. 97), the role of Mary as model of Christian hope and faith, with a special relationship to the poor, is presented well and integrated gracefully into the biblical history.

In the New Testament, Jesus as "the Son of God, who has made himself poor for love of us, wishes to be recognized in the poor, in those who suffer or are persecuted: 'As you did it to one of the least of my brethren, you did it to me'." The best section here discusses many profound aspects of the new commandment of love of neighbor, as in this succinct passage: "Fraternal love is the touchstone of love of God: 'He who does not love his brother whom he has seen cannot love God whom he has not seen' (1 Jn 4:20). St. Paul also strongly emphasizes the link between sharing in the sacrament of the body and blood of Christ and sharing with one's neighbor who is in need" (no. 56). But in general, the tone of this section is rather idyllic and peaceful so that one is abruptly startled by an intrusive sentence that brings one sharply back to the present: "The evil inequities and oppression of every kind which afflict millions of men and women totally openly contradict Christ's Gospel and cannot leave the conscience of any Christian indifferent" (no. 57).

New Contributions to Catholic Social Thought

In chapters 4 and 5, the instruction goes beyond repeating what is already contained in other church documents, and opens up some new directions for Catholic thought, some ripples, to use Murray's term, that are likely to run far. In chapter 4, these include above all the endorsement for the entire church of a preferential option for the poor, a conditioned but genuine approval of the basic Christian communities, and the restatement of the church's ultimate purpose as "a liberating mission."

It should first be emphasized with a certain sadness, however, that a great opportunity has been lost in nos. 61-65, which discuss the important issue of the "integral salvation of the world." The failure here is a false ecclesiology, which was rejected by the Second Vatican Council but which continues to surface in some ecclesiastical documents. The Council declared that "the church" referred to the entire people of God, and countless teachers and preachers have labored mightily over the last two decades to convince the laity that *they are the church* and should accept full adult responsibility in and for the church. Thus, and to make this point very emphatically, the notion that the *church is the hierarchy* must be abandoned once and for all, since it directly contradicts the teaching of the Second Vatican Council.

Although this is not asserted explicitly, it is understood very clearly throughout nos. 61-65. For example, note the phrasing of this text, which concerns the important issue of the church's role in the promotion of justice: "Therefore, when the church speaks about the promotion of justice in human societies or when *she urges the faithful laity* to work in this sphere according to their own vocation, she is not going beyond her mission. She is, however, concerned that this mission should not be absorbed by preoccupations concerning the temporal order or reduced to such preoccupations" (no. 64, italics mine). Clearly, the "church" that is urging the laity here is the hierarchy (or perhaps the Congregation for the Doctrine of the Faith). Unless the laity are "preoccupied" by secular concerns, they will not achieve the goal of attaining greater justice in the varied institutions of society; but they are not motivated and encouraged by this document to do precisely that, and thus to fulfill their "liberating mission" in the church. The hierarchy's responsibilities are mainly preaching and teaching regarding justice; but the mission of the laity is praxis, actual decisions and wholehearted participation in the secular arenas which are the only places where justice will be achieved, and not merely preached. It is ironical that chapter 5 is concerned with a "Christian practice of liberation," since chapter 4 undermines a truly efficacious practice by centering on the hierarchy instead of the overwhelming majority of Christians who are laity.

But chapter 4 does make a very important contribution: on the level of the universal church, it strongly advocates a preferential option for the poor, and goes into some detail in elaborating the theological meaning of this commitment. It is noteworthy that both works of charity and structural changes are considered to be essential to the option:

> . . . Those who are oppressed by poverty are the object of a love of preference on the part of the church, which since her origin and in spite of the failings of many of her members, has not ceased to work for their relief, defense and liberation. In addition, through her social doctrine which she strives to apply, she has sought to promote structural changes in society so as to secure conditions of life worthy of the human person (no. 68).

Regarding the commitment to the poor, moreover, an agitated controversy erupted in various press reports concerning the phrase "a love of preference for the poor"; some accounts held that this was replacing the expression "preferential option for the poor," which had come into common usage through the Latin American Bishops' Conference. Supposedly, this was done to avoid the potentially divisive effects implied in a "preferential option." However, the phrase "special option for the poor" is used no less than three times in the pertinent section (no. 68), which clearly refutes the charge that it was being deliberately jettisoned. We may only speculate that the "love of preference" was also used in order to emphasize the Christian motivation of the option.

Another area in this chapter that created controversy centered around the attitude of the instruction with regard to basic Christian communities, which are very widespread in Latin America, the Philippines and many other parts of the Third World. The text states quite approvingly that these small worshiping communities are "a source of great hope," "a real expression of communion" and "a treasure to the whole church," as long as they live in unity with the local and universal church (no. 69). My own experience with Latin America's basic Christian communities has convinced me that they simply did not come into existence without the commitment of the services (e.g., for training lay leaders) and resources (e.g., simple teaching materials, explanations of Scripture) of the local church. Also, their extraordinarily keen sense of belonging to the worldwide church is demonstrated dramatically by their many prayers for that church during worship meetings. As regards the issue of unity, it is abundantly clear that this goal will require a constant commitment and ongoing effort on both sides, people *and* bishops, in order to construct "a still deeper communion" (no. 69).

Chapter 5, which concludes the instruction, has a subtitle that calls for "a Christian Practice of Liberation," an expression which to my knowledge is used here for the first time in official church documents. In a sense, the chapter constitutes a mini-instruction on its own, since it tries, and succeeds for the most part, in integrating the practice of liberation with the whole structure of Catholic social doctrine. Because of the wide range of issues, it will be necessary to select those which appear of greater importance.

The document has some difficulty and confusion relating the dignity and rights of the individual person and the need for institutions and structures, as may be seen in the following text:

> The priority given to structures and technical organization over the person and the requirements of his dignity is the expression of a materialistic anthropology and is contrary to the construction of a just social order.
> On the other hand, the recognized priority of freedom and of conversion

of heart in no way eliminates the need for unjust structures to be changed. It is therefore perfectly legitimate that those who suffer oppression on the part of the wealthy or the politically powerful should take action through morally licit means, in order to secure structures and institutions in which their rights will be truly respected (no. 75).

The instruction complicates the matter further by going on to assert that the structures established for people's good are of themselves incapable of securing and guaranteeing that good. Finally, the solution to this dialectic is sought in a via media approach: "It is therefore necessary to work simultaneously for the conversion of hearts and for the improvement of structures."

However, I believe that this approach leads to a major weakness in this chapter with regard to its treatment of another central notion of liberation theology, and that is the concept of "social sin." The document first asserts that "the sin which is at the root of unjust situations is *in a true and immediate sense*, a voluntary act which has its source in the freedom of individuals" (no. 75, my italics). But this statement is immediately followed by what appears to be a non sequitur: "Only *in a derived and secondary* sense is [sin] applicable to structures, and only in this sense can one speak of 'social sin'" (no. 75, my italics). But is it not clear, as in the case of apartheid in South Africa, that though the structures were the creation of individual sinful acts and are continued in existence by individual human acts, nevertheless the oppression and suffering they inflict upon human persons for generations upon generations is immeasurably greater than any individual act of sin? The best depiction I have found of the profound primary evil of social sin is the following text of Laurenti Magesa of Zambia in the context of an African liberation theology:

> The worst type of sin, in fact the only "mortal sin" which has enslaved man for the greater part of his history, is the institutionalized sin. Under the institution, vice appears to be, or is actually turned into, virtue. Apathy toward evil is thus engendered; recognition of sin becomes totally effaced; sinful institutions become absolutized, almost idolized, and sin becomes absolutely mortal . . . recognition of evil, and therefore repentance for sin, is made practically impossible when sin is idolized as an institution.[5]

With that in mind, I find it impossible to understand why such "social sin" cannot be called sin in a very true and extremely immediate sense.

Although it is not an important element in this chapter, the question of violence became an issue in certain of the media, which proclaimed that the Vatican was fomenting violent revolutions by Catholics throughout the world. That this charge is completely false may be easily seen from a consideration of the texts involved. The instruction does hold that situations of grave injustice require far-reaching reforms and the suppression of unjustifiable privileges. It then goes on to insist that the new social order must be marked by justice and a morality of means. It then continues:

> These principles must be especially applied in the extreme case where there is recourse to armed struggle, which the church's magisterium admits as a last resort to put an end to an obvious and prolonged tyranny which is gravely damaging the fundamental rights of individuals and the common good. Nevertheless, the concrete application of this means cannot be contemplated until there has been a very rigorous analysis of the situation (no. 79).

These principles make up a very compact summary of traditional Catholic just war theory, which the church has held for centuries and continues to hold in all recent documents of the magisterium; thus there is no question here of an incitement to violence. The instruction also shows a preference for nonviolent methods which are considered more conformable to morality and "having no less prospects for success" in achieving social change (no. 79).

The most outstanding feature of this chapter—and the most significant contribution of the entire instruction—is the integration of Pope John Paul's groundbreaking encyclical *Laborem Exercens* into a liberation context: "Thus the solution of most of the serious problems related to poverty is to be found in a true civilization of work. In a sense, work is the key to the whole social question. It is therefore in the domain of work that priority must be given to the *action of liberation in freedom*" (no. 83, my italics). Since this part of the instruction is already a digest of the entire encyclical, it would be impossible to summarize it again, but it seems worthwhile to reiterate certain familiar principles:

> The person of the worker is the principle, subject and purpose of work. . . . Every person has a right to work and this right must be recognized in a practical way by an effective commitment to solving the tragic problem of unemployment. . . . The creation of jobs is a primary social task facing individuals and private enterprise, as well as the state. . . . The right to private property is inconceivable without responsibilities to the common good (nos. 84-87).

There is much more that deserves careful study in the text, but what is most important is its overarching meaning: The instruction places human labor—the key to the whole social question—at the heart of the process of liberation in every nation and in every culture, and thus provides an inner dynamism for a truly universal liberating theology.

A few other general reflections on the instruction may be added here. First of all, it has probably occurred to some readers that certain issues which they consider to be absolutely crucial to human liberation have received no mention at all so far. At least this did occur to me, and my response is to reemphasize the importance of the first text I quoted in this article, wherein local churches are told to apply the theory and practice of the instruction to their different local situations.

Thus, in our own local U.S. situation as a military and economic superpower, I think the application would be to reflect and act even more energetically and courageously about the threat of nuclear weapons and the ending of an insane arms race, to increase the urgency of our reflection on the U.S. economy and its impact, especially on the poor, both at home and abroad, and perhaps to launch a third pastoral that would begin serious reflections on our increasingly belligerent and militaristic foreign policy.

The liberation of women is not alluded to in the document, but, according to the argument above, it should encourage the many talented and dedicated U.S. women who are world leaders in creating a feminist liberating theology. Neither is there mention in the text of the deep roots of racial discrimination and oppression, but it could strengthen this country's many followers of the tradition of Martin Luther King, Jr., who are far advanced in the development of a black theology of liberation, which in turn serves as a model for other minority communities.

The instruction raises a final and very important question that goes to the heart of the theological discipline itself. If my assertion is true—namely, that a *universal significance* has been accorded to a liberating theology—what effect will this have on our reigning centers of theology, that is, the U.S. universities and seminaries that are now busily preparing the next generation of church leaders? In answering this question, it is of primary importance to stress that the implied problem will not be solved by adding a course or two on liberation theology to an already established curriculum. For the key elements of any liberating theology, as the Uruguayan Jesuit Juan Luis Segundo has insisted in all his published work, is not its liberating *content* but its liberating *method*. This method, which is explicitly intellectual in the classical sense of "faith seeking *intellectum*," includes a critique of ideology, which critique exposes the alienating or oppressive ideas that legitimate domination in any given society, and a hermeneutical critique, which uncovers the same mechanisms of alienation and legitimation in the interpretation of Scripture and the articulation of theology.

Clearly, then, such a theological method is not restricted to systematic theology, although as a method it should certainly affect every treatise in that field. But it also applies to the exegesis of Scripture, to the methods and subjects of moral theology, to church history and the history of dogma and, perhaps most of all, to the usually rarefied realms of spirituality, worship and sacramental theology and practice. In brief, if liberating theology is taken seriously, as the instruction proposes, it must necessarily become central to the theological enterprise, and not remain the fringe phenomenon it is at present. Such a change should not be considered impossible, for to many in the younger generation of theologians it has already become the dominant theological movement for the 1990s and beyond.

Concluding Remarks

Some readers may be puzzled by the fact that this book concludes with a detailed study of a document from the Vatican Congregation for the Doctrine of the Faith. In defense of this, I reiterate my view in this chapter that it is a well-organized, forceful, and often eloquent synthesis of a Christian theology of freedom, and that it is the first official document in the history of the Catholic church that integrates the themes of freedom and liberation within the corpus of Catholic social thought, including the important social writings of Pope John Paul II.

But there is yet another reason for concluding in this way. I began this book with a discussion of another official document, the *Declaration on Religious Freedom* of Vatican II. The main author of that statement, John Courtney Murray, admitted that it was only concerned "with the minor issue of religious freedom," but that "inevitably, a second great argument will be set afoot—now on the theological meaning of Christian freedom." That prophecy, I believe, has been at least partially fulfilled in the instruction on freedom and liberation.

Like the text on religious freedom, the Vatican instruction has also now been flung into that pool whose shores are as wide as the universal church and whose borders are as broad as the inhabited universe. In solidarity with all those—in my church community and outside it—who labor and struggle for the liberation and freedom of the human family, my most passionate hope is that these ripples of freedom will also run far.

Epilogue
Structures of Sin and Grace

"Without going into analysis of figures and statistics, it is sufficient to face squarely the reality of an innumerable multitude of people—children, adults and the elderly—in other words, real and unique human persons who are suffering under the intolerable burden of poverty. . . . Before these tragedies of total indigence and need in which so many of our brothers and sisters are living, it is the Lord Jesus himself who comes to question us (cf. Mt. 24:31-46)." This piercing image of Pope John Paul II recapitulates profoundly but succinctly the dramatic challenge contained in his recent encyclical *On Social Concerns (Sollicitudo Rei Socialis)*, issued February 19, 1988.[1] For all those struggling for social justice, this publication constituted an event of great importance, since it was the first instance in which the pope has presented a synthetic analysis of his sociocultural and political thought, and since he has become in the decade of his pontificate one of the major actors and most profound thinkers on the world scene.

This book had been substantially completed when the letter was published, but it immediately impressed me as related to many of the issues I have raised and thus as an excellent vehicle for synthesizing and integrating many of my ideas in this concluding epilogue. As I noted in chapter 8, an open and respectful dialogue with the thought of the magisterium is an essential ingredient in the writing of a theological reflection that calls itself Roman Catholic.

As a first step, then, I analyze what I consider to be a very close relationship between Pope John Paul's thought and the instruction *On Christian Freedom and Liberation* that was discussed in chapter 8. Then I present some reflections on the key doctrines of the letter, concentrating on those that represent original advances or more profound articulations that contribute to the development of the tradition of Catholic social thought. Third, I argue that the major overall accomplishment of the encyclical has been the pope's creative portrait of a new type of spirituality, that is to say, a spirituality for the "world church" that was discussed in chapter 2 of this book. And finally, I conclude with a general evaluation of the encyclical along with some suggestions for the future development of Catholic social thought and praxis.

Solidarity and Liberation

The *Instruction on Christian Freedom and Liberation* ended with a section entitled: "The Social Doctrine of the Church: For a Christian Practice of Liberation." To my knowledge, this was the first time in the teaching of the magisterium that this very important link between social teaching and a liberating practice was explicitly mentioned. The consequences of this linkage were also expressed with clarity and precision in the following text: "Being essentially orientated toward action, this teaching develops in accordance with the changing circumstances of history. This is why, together with principles that are always valid, it also involves contingent judgments. Far from constituting a closed system, it remains constantly open to the new questions which constantly arise; it requires the contribution of all charisms, experiences and skills" (no. 72). Immediately after this it is asserted, apparently as a consequence, that there is a tripartite structure to the church's social teaching: it offers a set of principles for reflection, criteria for judgment and directives for action "so that the profound changes demanded by situations of poverty and injustice may be brought about."

In his encyclical, the pope endorses the above description of the social doctrine of the church no less than three different times (nos. 6, 20, and 72), clearly emphasizing it as his own approach. In the final reference he also expresses the need for "the contribution of all charisms, experiences and skills" mentioned above from a different perspective: "The teaching and spreading of her social doctrine are part of the church's evangelizing mission. And since it is a doctrine aimed at guiding people's behavior, it consequently gives rise to a 'commitment to justice,' *according to each individual's role, vocation and circumstances.*" In both documents, then, the *whole people of God* are included in both the discernment and practice of Catholic social teaching. Thus, I repeat my assertion in chapter 8 that this is an extremely important development in the understanding of Christian freedom, since it calls upon all members of the church community to act together for the creation in justice and love of the kingdom of God.

Let me also note that Pope John Paul in his encyclical makes *nine* distinct references to the instruction on Christian freedom and liberation, more citations than from any other magisterial document except for *The Progress of Peoples*, which he is commemorating, and the pivotal document of Vatican II, *The Pastoral Constitution on the Church in the Modern World*. This fact lends credence to my speculation in chapter 8 that Pope John Paul took a very personal interest in the composition of the instruction, and that he has firmly established its insights in his own thought.

Furthermore, the pontiff himself explicitly presents his views on the themes of freedom and liberation in the conclusion to *Sollicitudo Rei Socialis*. There he takes note of the fact that in the period following the publication of *The Progress of Peoples* (1967) "a new way of confronting the problems of poverty and underdevelopment has spread in some areas of the world, especially in Latin America" (no. 46). Although the pope does not use the words "liberation theology" to characterize this new approach, he is obviously referring to it when he asserts that "this approach makes liberation the fundamental category and the first principle of action" and that this "aspiration to freedom from all forms of slavery affecting the individual and society is something noble and legitimate."

After pointing out that the concepts of liberation and development are intimately linked together, the letter goes on to insist that a purely *economic* form of development is not capable of liberating human beings, since it does not include the cultural, transcendent and religious dimensions of the person and society, and consequently results in an even more profound enslavement than that which existed previously. He then sketches the outline of an authentic form of liberation by (1) citing three references from the instruction on Christian freedom and liberation to the effect that sin is the principal obstacle to liberation, (2) quoting St. Paul's teaching (Gal 5:1) that the freedom for which Christ has set us free is basically a call to the service of others, and finally (3) insisting that liberation/development are concretely expressed in the exercise of solidarity, which the pope defines as the love and service of the neighbor, especially the poorest.

In the next section (no. 47), Pope John Paul stresses the fact that despite the many negative aspects of the present world situation, the church must strongly affirm that the obstacles that lie in the way of development can be overcome and that she must also "affirm her confidence in a true liberation." He provides theological justification for such confidence by referring to what must be regarded as a central theological axis of liberation theology: "Ultimately, this confidence and this possibility are based on the church's awareness of the divine promise guaranteeing that our present history does not remain closed in upon itself but is open to the kingdom of God." Along with this, he reinforces the centrality of confidence by stressing the fundamental goodness of creation in the book of Genesis, the universality of the redemptive action of Christ, and the efficacious action of the Holy Spirit that extends to the entire world.

It is well known that liberation theology is characterized by a sense of distress and urgency because of the enormity of the impoverishment that infects the entire Latin American continent. The pontiff also manifests a similar passion as he vigorously repudiates all the attitudes that are diametrically opposed to confidence, including despair, pessimism and inertia as well as fear, indecision and basic cowardice. His own sense of distress and urgency is also obvious in a ringing challenge that splendidly encapsulates the basic message of the letter:

> We are all called, indeed obliged, to face the tremendous challenge of the last decade of the second millennium, also because of the dangers that threaten everyone: a world economic crisis, a war without frontiers, without winners or losers. In the face of such a threat, the distinction between rich individuals and countries and poor individuals and countries will have little value, except that a greater responsibility rests on those who have more and can do more (no. 47).

Finally, the pontiff clearly moves closer to the approach of liberation theology in his reflections on Marian devotion in the very last paragraphs of the encyclical (no. 49). For example, in the conclusion to the instruction on freedom and liberation, the Magnificat is mentioned only in very general terms. In the encyclical, however, the pope notes quite openly the more controversial parts of that prayer, namely, the praise of God because "he has put down the mighty from their thrones and exalted those of low degree; he has filled the hungry with good things, and the rich he has sent empty away" (Lk 1:52-53). And he concludes this by emphasizing that Mary's "maternal concern extends to the personal and social aspect of people's life on earth."

Furthermore, the pope appears to sense that he is expanding and enlarging what has been the traditional devotion to Mary for centuries. For, after approving "Christian piety through the ages," when the prayer of the devout was principally concerned with difficult individual situations, he moves on to a new devotional stress that is more harmonious with the entire tenor of the letter: "But we also present to her social situations and the international crisis itself, in their worrying aspects of poverty, unemployment, shortage of food, the arms race, contempt for human rights and situations of dangers or conflict, partial or total."

In the next section, I am going to discuss other aspects of the encyclical, some of which also manifest a clear relationship to the themes of liberation theology. What has been said so far should serve as one more convincing refutation of the canard assiduously promoted by certain circles in the

United States, that the pope or the Vatican or both have officially condemned the theology of liberation. The reality is exactly the opposite: Pope John Paul has been deeply and broadly influenced by liberation theology, more than by any other contemporary development, in the ongoing evolution and articulation of his social vision and praxis.

New Developments in the Letter

In chapter 8 I expressed my disagreement on a theological level with the description of social sin in the instruction on freedom and liberation. That document had asserted that "the sin which is at the root of unjust situations is, *in a true and immediate sense,* a voluntary act which has its source in the freedom of individuals," whereas "only in a derived and secondary sense is [sin] applicable to structures, and only in this sense can one speak of 'social sin'" (no. 75, my italics).

In his encyclical, however, Pope John Paul has for whatever reason completely removed the ambiguity surrounding the above distinction and employed a dialectical definition of sin that is for all practical purposes identical with that of liberation theology. In speaking of the two superpowers and their forms of imperialism, the pontiff refers to their mutual domination as "structures of sin" (no. 36). He then proceeds to describe the relationship of these structures to personal sins by emphasizing that the structures "are rooted in personal sin and thus always linked to the concrete acts of individuals who introduce these structures, consolidate them and make them difficult to remove. And thus they grow stronger, spread and become the source of other sins, and so influence people's behavior." Shortly afterward, he refers to the structures as "influences and obstacles which go far beyond the actions and brief lifespan of an individual," thus creating a mechanism which continues to involve "interference in the process of the development of peoples, the delay or slowness of which must be judged also in this light."

Even further light on the pope's understanding of sinful structures may be found in a footnote referring to his apostolic exhortation *Reconciliatio et Paenitentia* (note 65). Here John Paul uses the expression "social sin," which is also preferred in liberation theology, and describes it as "the accumulation and concentration of many personal sins." Of special interest is his specification of the different kinds of personal sins involved:

> It is a case of the very personal sins of those who cause or support evil or exploit it; of those who are in a position to avoid, eliminate or at least limit certain social evils but who fail to do so out of laziness, fear or the conspiracy of

silence, through secret complicity or indifference; of those who take refuge in
the supposed impossibility of changing the world and also of those who side-
step the effort and sacrifice required, producing specious reasons of a
higher order.

A second development of major importance concerned the pope's
charge of "imperialism" against both the United States and the Soviet
Union—an imperialism which they were alleged to have practiced throughout the postwar period and which continued to be a major cause of the underdevelopment of the nations of the Third World and thus of the suffering
of the poor. With this approach, Pope John Paul moved decisively beyond
the discussion of social problems, as in his encyclical on labor, *Laborem Exercens,* and moved boldly into the dangerous arena of politics and the root
geopolitical causes of underdevelopment. In the United States, this produced an immediate furor as a number of conservative pundits and jour-
nalists attacked the pope ferociously for his temerity in alleging a "moral
equivalence" between the United States and the Soviet Union and thus providing a "stunning unexpected boon" for the USSR.

Actually, the "moral equivalence" argument is at present a favorite
but transparent ideology of the American right, which uses it to ward off
any criticism of American policy while propping up its manichaean version
of the Soviet "evil empire." The encyclical, in my view, does not provide a
boon to either side. Rather, it is a direct challenge, a *j'accuse* against both
sides, summoning them to a crucial conversion or, in secular terms, to a
profound transformation in their attitudes toward and their relationships
with the nations of the Third and Fourth Worlds.

This question of geopolitics is an immense complex of issues which I
cannot even begin to analyze in this context. I do, nevertheless, believe that
the pope's political analysis is certainly arguable and in my opinion substantially correct. I agree fully with his assertion that for more than forty
years *both* superpowers have become so obsessed with their own security
and so committed to political, ideological, and military struggle with each
other (using such ideologies as "containment" as opposed to the enemy's
"expansionism") that the poor nations have been routinely treated with
contempt as mere expendable pawns on the all-important, gigantic East-
West chessboard. It is also difficult to deny that this struggle over the past
four decades has resulted in an unparalleled and continuing waste of the
limited resources of capital, manpower, and scientific research for the sake
of ever more lethal nuclear and conventional weapons systems for the superpowers, along with a parallel arming to the teeth of their own allies,
satellites, and puppets. At the same time, the real and desperate needs of
the developing nations have been virtually ignored unless, of course, they

have been chosen to play some bit part on the world stage of the superpowers.

Here I would like to touch upon other advances in the teaching of the encyclical which are significant but not of the same importance as the ones I have just discussed. An emphasis on ecological issues is one of these, and Pope John Paul allots it more emphasis than is to be found in other papal documents of the modern era. He considers it to be part of the moral character proper to authentic development, and emphasizes harmony with all of animate and inanimate nature, an urgent awareness that natural resources are limited and often nonrenewable, and great caution with regard to a haphazard industrialization that leads to environmental pollution with consequent deleterious effects on the health of inhabitants of the area. Some reports in the Catholic press proclaimed that the ecology was the most important issue in the encyclical, but this reflects special pleading rather than a careful reading of the document.

I believe, furthermore, that Pope John Paul was more explicit on a number of sensitive political issues than his predecessor Paul VI had been in *The Progress of Peoples*. For one thing, he stresses in various ways the responsibility of the poor nations themselves, noting that the "development of peoples begins and is most appropriately accomplished in the dedication of each people to its own development, in collaboration with others" (no. 44). In the same section, the pope definitely shows a preference for certain forms of government when he stresses (emphasis in the text) that "the *necessary condition and sure guarantee*" of all forms of development lie precisely in the "free and responsible participation of all citizens in public affairs, in the rule of law and in respect for and promotion of human rights." And his preference is made very explicit when he calls for political reforms "in order to replace corrupt, dictatorial, and authoritarian forms of government by democratic and participatory ones." All of the above are subsumed by the pope under the new metaphor of the "political health" of the community.

Another novelty in the letter is the coining of the phrase "superdevelopment" to express the shadow side of underdevelopment and the form of enslavement peculiar to the developed world vis-à-vis the Third and Fourth Worlds. Although the phrase is prima facie similar to the now familiar terminology of "the consumer society," it does connote certain nuances of its own. "This superdevelopment," states the pontiff, "which consists in an excessive availability of every kind of material goods for the benefit of certain social classes, easily makes people slaves of 'possession' and of immediate gratification, with no other horizon other than the multiplication of the things already owned with others still better" (no. 28).

Pope John Paul then continues, stating that "all of us," obviously referring to all in the West including himself, have firsthand experience of the baneful consequences of this blind submission to a form of pure consumerism. The consequences are seen to be double-edged, including "in the first place a crass materialism, and at the same time a radical dissatisfaction because one quickly learns—unless one is shielded from the flood of publicity and ceaseless and tempting offer of products—that the more one possesses the more one wants, while deeper aspirations remain unsatisfied and perhaps even stifled" (no. 28). Aside from the name of "superdevelopment" itself then, the theme of the dangers of the consumer society is a familiar refrain in the teaching of all the modern popes, including the present one. The fact that they are familiar, however, should not blind us to the need of constant vigilance against the myriad forms of "consumer atheism" which erode religious faith like a malignant and invisible gas, with considerably more effect than the crude instruments of repression of religion that are wielded in some officially atheistic societies.

Other economic insights in the encyclical include the new concept of a "right of economic initiative" (no. 15). If this right is denied in the name of an alleged "equality" of everyone in society, the pontiff asserts, it will destroy "the spirit of initiative, that is to say, the creative subjectivity of the citizen." Some have held that this is not necessarily an objection against socialism. The pope, however, appears to have socialism in mind, for he refers to the "bureaucratic apparatus, which is the only 'ordering' and 'decision-making' body—if not also the 'owner'—of the means of production, puts everyone in a position of almost absolute dependence, which is *similar to the traditional dependence of the worker proletarians in capitalism*" (no. 15, my italics).

Finally, in the context of the encyclical's very strong stress on the option or love of preference for the poor, John Paul evenhandedly criticizes capitalist economies also, for he places great emphasis on what he calls the "characteristic principle of Christian social doctrine: The goods of this world are originally meant for all" (no. 42). He also underlines a teaching which he had addressed to the Latin American bishops at Puebla, Mexico, in 1979, and which he now endorses in the letter for the world church. This concerns the understanding of private property under the rubric of a "social mortgage," that is, it "has an intrinsically social function based upon and justified precisely by the principle of the universal destination of goods."

A New Spirituality

Now I want to move beyond individual teachings in the letter and emphasize its major underlying purpose, which I believe is also its greatest lasting achievement. Recalling Karl Rahner's article on the world church, I believe that John Paul's principal originality has been to articulate as clearly as possible and to commend to all religious people, as well as to all persons of good will, one overriding concern: the urgent need today for a *new spirituality for the world church.* This, I would hold, is far more important in the long run than his social analysis, although that analysis is certainly arguable and in my opinion basically correct.

From this it follows that the primary originality of the encyclical is not to be discovered in the first four parts (nos. 1-34). There, Pope John Paul repeats and emphasizes the principle contributions of the encyclical *The Progress of Peoples,* published twenty years earlier by his predecessor Paul VI. He also insists that the gap between rich and poor nations has not only continued but has become considerably wider in the two intervening decades. And John Paul is radical (in the sense of probing the *roots* of this catastrophic situation), for he unambiguously identifies the numerous causes which have created and continue to maintain this situation and which range from the corruption and incompetence of Third World rulers to the new forms of imperialism and colonialism created by the superpowers during the past forty years of the cold war.

The heart of the pope's message, however, may be found most clearly and profoundly in the theological reading of the modern situation and subsequent guidelines that he provides in the fourth and fifth parts of the letter (nos. 35-45). Here, he asserts in clear and more vigorous terms than have appeared in any previous papal utterance that this exhaustive list of causes of the world's misery must be understood as "structures of sin." These "negative factors" or "influences and obstacles which go far beyond the brief lifespan of an individual" are not, however, beyond the scope of human causality and responsibility, for they are "rooted in personal sin and thus always linked to the concrete acts of individuals who introduce these structures, consolidate them and make them difficult to remove. And thus they grow stronger, spread, and become the source of other sins, and so influence people's behavior" (no. 36).

John Paul goes on to identify and to emphasize the importance of two sinful attitudes that contribute to the creation of structures of sin, namely, "the all consuming desire for profit" and "the thirst for power, with the intention of imposing one's will upon others," adding the deadly modifier, "at any price," to each of these attitudes. Some commentators have mistakenly concluded that the first of these vices was directed against the United States and capitalism, while the second was intended for the Soviet Union and Communism. But the pope clearly indicates that while these attitudes can exist independently of one another "in today's world both are indissolubly united, with one or the other predominating." It should also be noted that

John Paul injects a subtle but unmistakable element of ideology-criticism with regard to certain forms of imperialism (presumably those mentioned earlier), for he points out that "hidden behind certain decisions, apparently inspired only by economics or politics, are real forms of idolatry: of money, ideology, class, technology" (no. 37).

The letter's detailed analyses of the structures of sin have led to the charge that a negative and pessimistic tone pervades the entire document. Perhaps anticipating this, John Paul is careful to point out that, although the condemnation of evil and injustice is part of evangelization, "it should be made clear that proclamation is always more important than condemnation, and the latter cannot ignore the former, which gives it solidity and the force of higher motivation" (no. 41). The realistic diagnosis, therefore, of the causes of the sinful structures provides an essential prelude to the more positive task of choosing a path toward the necessary conversion and renewal of the structures. Moreover, since the latter "change of behavior or mentality or mode of existence" applies not only to personal conversion but also to changes in whole nations and blocs, it seems to me that we should logically speak here of the need to create or reform "structures of grace," although John Paul does not employ that term.

It is precisely at this point that the pope presents in a most succinct and forceful manner a very positive analysis of the "spirituality for the world church" that I referred to earlier. It is extremely important to note from the start that this spirituality is not intended to be restricted to church members, but rather is to be shared and communicated to all human beings. Thus, the pontiff first appeals to the moral values of men and women of faith, based on the demand of God's will; but then he immediately shifts his vision to the entire world, in what I believe is the most important text and indeed an apt summary of the entire encyclical:

> Thus one would hope that all those who, to some degree or other, are responsible for ensuring a "more human life" for their fellow human beings, whether or not they are inspired by religious faith, will become fully aware of the urgent need to change the spiritual attitudes which define each individual's relationship with self, with neighbor, with even the remotest human communities and with nature itself; and all of this in view of higher values such as the common good or, to quote the felicitous expression of the encyclical *Populorum Progressio*, the full development "of the whole human being and of all people" (no. 38).

Again, although the pope does not use the term, he is calling for a gigantic effort at what the Latin American church calls conscientization or consciousness-raising, but one which he applies to the entire planet.

The pontiff's detailed analysis of this "geospirituality" is quite complex, and can only be discussed very schematically here. He begins by emphasizing the moral virtues that are open to all human beings, placing major emphasis on "the growing awareness of interdependence among individuals and nations," as well as the proper response to this awareness through the correlative social attitude or virtue of *solidarity*, which is the pivotal virtue in his spirituality. This virtue (which was also used by Pope Paul VI in *The Progress of Peoples*) transcends feelings of vague compassion or distress, and is rather a "firm and persevering determination to commit oneself to the . . . good of all and of each individual because we are really responsible for all" (no. 38). The encyclical does not leave this commitment on a general level, but sees it as intimately linked with and leading to genuine peace and development. World peace, then, requires that the world's leaders abandon "the politics of blocs" in favor of "the sacrifice of all forms of economic, military, or political imperialism and the transformation of mutual distrust into collaboration" (no. 39).

With regard to its relationship to Christianity, solidarity is considered to share many points of contact with charity, the distinguishing mark of Christ's disciples. Indeed, in the light of the whole encyclical and of what has been said here so far, it would seem logical to draw the necessary conclusion and state flatly that solidarity constitutes *the privileged expression* of Christian charity in the contemporary world. It is also closely linked to the Christian ideal of unity or "communion," a unity which reflects the intimate life of the Trinity and discloses "a new model of the unity of the human race, which must ultimately inspire our solidarity" (no. 40).

A number of other nuances and clarifications regarding a spirituality for the world church are explored in the encyclical. Meriting special mention is the extensive analysis and emphasis that the pope gives to the option or love of preference for the poor (terms he uses interchangeably) as a specific expression of solidarity, insisting that this preferential love must "embrace the immense multitudes of the hungry, the needy, the homeless, those without medical care and, above all, those without hope for a better future" (no. 42). It is clear from this and other texts that the spirituality John Paul envisions as necessary for *all members* of the world church (and all persons of good will) must include as an essential element an option or commitment to the poor. Considering also the declarations of the Latin American and North American bishops, the option must constitute the keystone of any contemporary spirituality.

Final Evaluation and Conclusions

The encyclical letter, *On Social Concerns* must certainly be considered the most significant work that Pope John Paul has produced in the extremely prolific first decade of his pontificate. I believe it will rank along with Pope John XXIII's *Peace on Earth* (1963) and Pope Paul VI's *The Progress of Peoples* (1967) as the most important encyclicals of the modern papacy. My reasons for this have been outlined here, although a great deal more could be fruitfully analyzed in this very complex and profound document.

My basically positive evaluation of the many incisive and creative contributions of the encyclical should also be abundantly clear throughout this epilogue. Now I want to proceed further and present my suggestions for developing and going beyond the framework of the encyclical. My remarks will be concerned first of all with the world church and next with the local church, which in my case is the Catholic Church in the United States. Given such a vast panorama, it is obvious that only a broad sketch is possible at this point.

First of all, my comments should not be understood as disagreement with the thrust of the document, but rather as reflecting a sense of disappointment that it did not proceed more boldly along certain promising terrain. Also, considering the pope's repeated stress that Catholic social doctrine offers principles for reflection, criteria for judgment, and directives for action, I was surprised to find so little attention given to the third category regarding praxis or, to be more specific, to the actual *implementation* of the multitude of ideas that are expressed so eloquently in the letter.

To begin with one example, the pope places great emphasis throughout the letter on the importance of a spirituality focused on solidarity and consequently on the absolute necessity of a decisive option or love of preference for the poor. Yet there is comparatively little said about solidarity by and among the poor themselves and their need to organize and act *on their own initiative.* For instance, in no. 39 there is reference to "positive signs" such as "the growing awareness of the solidarity of the poor among themselves, their efforts to support one another and their public demonstrations on the social scene..." In response to this, the letter continues, "the church feels called to take her stand beside the poor, to discern the justice of their requests and to help satisfy them, without losing sight of the good of groups in the context of the common good."

There is a clear tone of paternalism in this response, as if the poor were incapable of discerning the glaring causes of injustice in every moment of their lives and also of perceiving the struggle they must undertake in order to achieve some measure of justice for themselves. It is also unclear what the "good of groups" means in this context, but surely for the poor it means solidarity with their own group and opposition to the "group" of oppressors who will continue to dominate them unless forced to do otherwise.

If we also take into consideration the very careful reading of "the signs of the times" as regards the realm of political economy and geopolitics that is to be found throughout the letter, we can only be puzzled that the same type of analysis has not been attempted regarding the "signs of the times" that are occurring within the church itself, and especially among the poor within the church. Without reviewing the entire argument of this book, does not the spiritual and social renaissance of half the Catholic Church that flourishes in Latin America provide abundant examples of new methods of theologizing, processes for reflection and action, methods for organizing the grassroots church, and ways of defending basic rights that provide vivid models for the entire church on how concretely and practically to *empower* the poor, and not merely to maintain them as objects of our assistance and good will? My answer is obviously yes, and I would make the theological conclusion that this social charism of the Latin American church is clearly to provide at this juncture of history the "structures of grace" that are so urgently needed for the church of the future, that is to say, for the church of the poor. Thus, the purpose of every chapter of this book has been to describe, analyze, and evaluate these structures of grace, so they may serve as possible models, examples, and paradigms for the rest of the world church.

My concluding remarks are directed to my own local church in the United States. Let me begin by stating that the leadership of the Catholic Church in this country has in the past decade pioneered in the creation of an indigenous American structure of grace that deserves the highest praise. I am referring to the process of dialogue and consultation that marked the bishops' pastoral letter on peace in the nuclear age (1983) and on the U.S. economy (1986), and thus provided a unique form of conscientization on those issues for what has become an increasingly educated and adult laity.

I believe that Archbishop Rembert Weakland of Milwaukee has responded brilliantly to the criticisms from many different sectors and interested groups against the bishops' intrusion into these supposedly sacrosanct "secular" domains. The archbishop first discloses the theological underpinning of the critique from ecclesiastical sources: "Underneath this criticism is a definite concept of ecclesiology. Its proponents see a strongly hierarchical model of church, where the faithful are taught by the bishops, who are in possession of the gifts of the Spirit needed for such authoritative teaching." He then follows this up with an equally splendid description of the theology of the bishops: "The model adopted by the U.S. conference believes that the Holy Spirit resides in all members of the church and that the hierarchy must listen to what the Spirit is saying to the whole church. This does not deny the teaching role of the hierarchy, but enhances it. It does not weaken the magisterium, but ultimately strengthens it. Discernment, not just innovation or self-reliance, becomes a part of the teaching process."[2]

I do think, however, that there is also room for development and going beyond the framework of the pastoral letters of the U.S. bishops. Although much of the criticism of the letters was ideological or self-interested, the views of others were more constructive and to the mark. One of these, the political economist William Tabb, admits to "genuine, if qualified, enthusiasm for what they have done" but also points to "a sharp disjuncture in the document between the theological section on Catholic social teaching and the other sections on economic policy. The former offers a strong and clear moral argument; the latter are limited and inadequate responses." Thus, he concludes, "the bishops' critique and goals are admirable, while the methods proposed for achieving them are totally inadequate and there is no *systemic* analysis of the way in which the U.S. economy works."[3]

Pope John Paul's letter points to a way in which the bishops could achieve a more causal and systemic analysis in both pastorals (or in the recurrent updates of the pastorals that are planned). In his discussion of development, the pope also is searching for the causes of underdevelopment: "If at this point we examine the reasons for this serious delay in the process of development, a delay which has occurred contrary to the indications of the encyclical *Populorum Progressio*, which had raised such great hopes, our attention is especially drawn to the *political causes* of today's situation" (no. 20, my italics). He then proceeds from politics to geopolitics, and assigns a major role to the continuing opposition between East and West discussed earlier.

My proposal flows from this diagnosis of Pope John Paul. Basically, it is to suggest that the most urgent need of the U.S. church at the present time is to respond to the pope's leadership and to initiate a process for the moral evaluation of U.S. foreign policy or U.S. geopolitics that will include both the East-West and North-South dimensions. Such a study will furnish the necessary depth and breadth for a genuinely causal or systemic analysis of both nuclear war and the U.S. economy. It could also follow the pope's lead by dividing its treatment into "principles for reflection, criteria for judgment, and directives for action."

In this way, the U.S. church could make another valuable contribution to the theology of the world church from its unique position as a major actor in the First World. I have tried to show in this book that the world church has also been enriched and revitalized by the theology and praxis of the Third World, especially the liberation theology of Latin America. And finally, in the person of Karol Wojtyla a very powerful prophetic voice has arisen from the heart of the Second World, with a radically new vantage point to interpret the contemporary situation of humanity. From that perspective he calls not so much for agreement as for profound and far-reaching changes in the thinking and acting of the human family. On the family's response to that challenge depend the lives and well-being of billions of human beings.

Appendix
The Congregation for the Doctrine of the Faith Instruction on Christian Freedom and Liberation

Introduction

1. Awareness of man's freedom and dignity, together with the affirmation of the inalienable rights of individuals and peoples, is one of the major characteristics of our time. But freedom demands conditions of an economic, social, political and cultural kind which make possible its full exercise. A clear perception of the obstacles which hinder its development and which offend human dignity is at the source of the powerful aspirations to liberation which are at work in our world.

The church of Christ makes these aspirations her own, while exercising discernment in the light of the gospel, which is by its very nature a message of freedom and liberation. Indeed, on both the theoretical and practical levels, these aspirations sometimes assume expressions which are not always in conformity with the truth concerning man as it is manifested in the light of his creation and redemption. For this reason the Congregation for the Doctrine of the Faith has considered it necessary to draw attention to "deviations, or risks of deviation, damaging to the faith and to Christian living."[1] Far from being outmoded, these warnings appear ever more timely and relevant.

2. The instruction *Libertatis Nuntius*, on certain aspects of the theology of liberation, stated the intention of the congregation to publish a second document which would highlight the main elements of the Christian doctrine on freedom and liberation. The present instruction responds to that intention. Between the two documents there exists an organic relationship. They are to be read in the light of each other.

With regard to their theme, which is at the heart of the gospel message, the church's magisterium has expressed itself on many occasions.[2] The present document limits itself to indicating its principal theoretical and practical aspects. As regards applications to different local situations, it is for the local churches, in communion with one another and with the See of Peter, to make direct provision for them.[3]

The theme of freedom and liberation has an obvious ecumenical dimension. It belongs in fact to the traditional patrimony of the churches and ecclesial communities. Thus the present document can assist the testimony and action of all Christ's disciples, called to respond to the great challenges of our times.

3. The words of Jesus, "The truth will make you free" (Jn 8:32), must enlighten and guide all theological reflection and all pastoral decisions in this area.

This truth which comes from God has its center in Jesus Christ, the savior of the world.[4] From him, who is "the way, and the truth, and the life" (Jn 14:6), the church receives all that she has to offer to mankind. Through the mystery of the incarnate word and redeemer of the world, she possesses the truth regarding the Father and his love for us, and also the truth concerning man and his freedom.

Through his cross and resurrection, Christ has brought about our redemption, which is liberation in the strongest sense of the word since it has freed us from the most radical evil, namely sin and the power of death. When the church, taught by her Lord, raises to the Father her prayer "Deliver us from evil," she asks that the mystery of salvation may act with power in our daily lives. The church knows that the redeeming cross is truly the source of light and life and the center of history. The charity which burns in her impels her to proclaim the Good News and to distribute its life-giving fruits through the sacraments. It is from Christ the redeemer that her thought and action originate when, as she contemplates the tragedies affecting the world, she reflects on the meaning of liberation and true freedom and on the paths leading to them.

Truth, beginning with the truth about redemption which is at the heart of the mystery of faith, is thus the root and the rule of freedom, the foundation and the measure of all liberating action.

4. Man's moral conscience is under an obligation to be open to the fullness of truth; he must seek it out and readily accept it when it presents itself to him.

According to the command of Christ the Lord,[5] the truth of the Gospel must be presented to all people, and they have a right to have it presented to them. Its proclamation, in the power of the Spirit, includes full respect for the freedom of each individual and the exclusion of every form of constraint or pressure.[6]

The Holy Spirit guides the church and the disciples of Jesus Christ "into the full truth" (Jn 16:13). The Spirit directs the course of the centuries and "renews the face of the earth" (Ps 104:30). It is he who is present in the maturing of a more respectful awareness of the dignity of the human person.[7] The Holy Spirit is at the root of courage, boldness and heroism: "Where the Spirit of the Lord is, there is freedom" (2 Cor 3:17).

Chapter 1
The State of Freedom in the World Today

I. Achievements and Dangers
of the Modern Liberation Process

5. By revealing to man his condition as a free person called to enter into communion with God, the gospel of Jesus Christ has evoked an awareness of the hitherto unsuspected depths of human freedom.

Thus the quest for freedom and the aspiration to liberation, which are among the principal signs of the times in the modern world, have their first source in the Christian heritage. This remains true even in places where they assume erroneous forms and even oppose the Christian view of man and his destiny. Without this reference to the Gospel, the history of the recent centuries in the West cannot be understood.

6. Thus it is that from the dawn of modern times at the Renaissance it was thought that by a return to antiquity in philosophy and through the natural sciences man would be able to gain freedom of thought and action, thanks to his knowledge and control of the laws of nature.

Luther, for his part, basing himself on his reading of St. Paul, sought to renew the struggle for freedom from the yoke of the law, which he saw as represented by the church of his time.

But it was above all in the age of the Enlightenment and at the French Revolution that the call to freedom rang out with full force. Since that time, many have regarded future history as an irresistible process of liberation inevitably leading to an age in which man, totally free at last, will enjoy happiness on this earth.

7. Within the perspective of such an ideology of progress, man sought to become master of nature. The servitude which he had experienced up to that point was based on ignorance and prejudice. By wresting from nature its secrets, man would subject it to his own service. The conquest of freedom thus constituted the goal pursued through the development of science and technology. The efforts expended have led to remarkable successes. While man is not immune from natural disasters, many natural dangers have been removed. A growing number of individuals is ensured adequate nourishment. New means of transport and trade facilitate the exchange of food resources, raw materials, labor and technical skills, so that a life of dignity with freedom from poverty can be reasonably envisaged for mankind.

8. The modern liberation movement had set itself a political and social objective. It was to put an end to the domination of man by man and to promote the equality and brotherhood of all. It cannot be denied that in this sphere, too, positive results have been obtained. Legal slavery and bondage have been abolished. The right of all to share in the benefits of culture has made significant progress. In many countries the law recognizes the equality of men and women, the participation of all citizens in political life and equal rights for all. Racism is rejected as contrary to law and justice. The formulation of human rights implies a clearer awareness of the dignity of all human beings. By comparison with previous systems of domination, the advances of freedom and equality in many societies are undeniable.

9. Finally and above all, the modern liberation movement was supposed to bring man inner freedom in the form of freedom of thought and freedom of decision. It sought to free man from superstition and atavistic fears, regarded as so many obstacles to his development. It proposed to give man the courage and boldness to use his reason without being held back by fear before the frontiers of the unknown. Thus, notably in the historical and human sciences, there developed a new notion of man, professedly to help him gain a better self-understanding in matters concerning his personal growth or the fundamental conditions for the formation of the community.

10. With regard to the conquest of nature, or social and political life, or man's self-mastery on both the individual and collective level, anyone can see that the progress achieved is far from fulfilling the original ambitions. It is also obvious that new dangers, new forms of servitude and new terrors have arisen at the very time that the modern liberation movement was spreading. This is a sign that serious ambiguities concerning the very meaning of freedom have from the very beginning plagued this movement from within.

11. So it is that the more man freed himself from the dangers of nature, the more he experienced a growing fear confronting him. As technology gains an ever greater control of nature, it threatens to destroy the very foundations of our future in such a way that mankind living today becomes the enemy of the generations to come. By using blind power to subjugate the forces of nature, are we not on the way to destroying the freedom of the men and women of tomorrow? What forces can protect man from the slavery of his own domination? A wholly new capacity for freedom and liberation, demanding an entirely renewed process of liberation, becomes necessary.

12. The liberating force of scientific knowledge is objectively expressed in the great achievements of technology. Whoever possesses technology has power over the earth and men. As a result of this, hitherto unknown forms of inequality have arisen between those who possess knowledge and those who are simple users of technology. The new technological power is linked to economic power and leads to a concentration of it. Thus, within nations and between nations, relationships of dependence have grown up which within the last 20 years have been the occasion for a new claim to liberation. How can the power of technology be prevented from becoming a power of oppression over human groups or entire peoples?

13. In the field of social and political achievements, one of the fundamental ambiguities of the affirmation of freedom in the age of the Enlightenment had to do with the concept of the subject of this freedom as an individual who is fully self-sufficient and whose finality is the satisfaction of his own interests in the enjoyment of earthly goods. The individualistic ideology inspired by this concept of man favored the unequal distribution of wealth at the beginning of the industrial era to the point that workers found themselves excluded from access to the essential goods which they had helped to produce and to which they had a right. Hence the birth of powerful liberation movements from the poverty caused by industrial society.

Certain Christians, both lay persons and pastors, have not failed to fight for a just recognition of the legitimate rights of workers. On many occasions the magisterium of the church has raised its voice in support of this cause.

But more often than not the just demands of the worker movement have led to new forms of servitude, being inspired by concepts which ignored the transcendental vocation of the human person and attributed to man a purely earthly destiny. These demands have sometimes been directed toward collectivist goals, which have then given rise to injustices just as grave as the ones which they were meant to eliminate.

14. Thus it is that our age has seen the birth of totalitarian systems and forms of tyranny which would not have been possible in the time before the technological leap forward. On the one hand, technical expertise has been applied to acts of genocide. On the other, various minorities try to hold in thrall whole nations by the practice of terrorism. Today control can penetrate into the innermost lives of individuals, and even the forms of dependence created by the early-warning systems can represent potential threats of oppression.

A false liberation from the constraints of society is sought in recourse to drugs, which have led many young people from all over the world to the point of self-destruction and brought whole families to sorrow and anguish.

15. The recognition of a juridical order as a guarantee of relationships within the great family of peoples is growing weaker and weaker. When confidence in the law no longer seems to offer sufficient protection, security and peace are sought in mutual threats, which become a danger for all humanity. The forces which ought to serve the development of freedom serve instead the increase of threats. The weapons of death drawn up against each other today are capable of destroying all human life on earth.

16. New relationships of inequality and oppression have been established between the nations endowed with power and those without it. The pursuit of one's own interest seems to be the rule for international relations, without the common good of humanity being taken into consideration.

The internal balance of the poor nations is upset by the importation of arms, which introduces among them a divisive element leading to the domination of one group over another. What powers could eliminate systematic recourse to arms and restore authority to law?

17. It is in the context of the inequality of power relationships that there have appeared movements for the emancipation of young nations, generally the poor ones, until recently subjected to colonial domination. But too often the people are frustrated in their hard-won independence by unscrupulous regimes or tyrannies which scoff at human rights with impunity. The people thus reduced to powerlessness merely have a change of masters.

It remains true that one of the major phenomena of our time, of continental proportions, is the awakening of the consciousness of people who, bent beneath the weight of age-old poverty, aspire to a life in dignity and justice and are prepared to fight for their freedom.

18. With reference to the modern liberation movement within man himself, it has to be stated that the effort to free thought and will from their limits has led some to consider that morality as such constitutes an irrational limit. It is for man, now resolved to become his own master, to go beyond it.

For many more, it is God himself who is the specific alienation of man. There is said to be a radical incompatibility between the affirmation of God and of human freedom. By rejecting belief in God, they say, man will become truly free.

19. Here is the root of the tragedies accompanying the modern history of freedom. Why does this history, in spite of great achievements which also remain always fragile, experience frequent relapses into alienation and see the appearance of new forms of slavery? Why do liberation movements which had roused great hopes result in regimes for which the citizens' freedom,[8] beginning with the first of these freedoms, which is religious freedom,[9] becomes enemy no. 1?

When man wishes to free himself from the moral law and become independent of God, far from gaining his freedom he destroys it. Escaping the measuring rod of truth, he falls prey to the arbitrary; fraternal relations between people are abolished and give place to terror, hatred and fear.

Because it has become contaminated by deadly errors about man's condition and his freedom, the deeply rooted modern liberation movement remains ambiguous. It is laden both with promises of true freedom and threats of deadly forms of bondage.

II. Freedom in the Experience of the People of God

20. It is because of her awareness of this deadly ambiguity that through her magisterium the church has raised her voice over the centuries to warn against aberrations that could easily bring enthusiasm for liberation to a bitter disillusionment. She has often been misunderstood in so doing. With the passage of time, however, it is possible to do greater justice to the church's point of view.

It is in the name of the truth about man, created in the image of God, that the church has intervened.[10] Yet she is accused of thereby setting herself up as an obstacle on the path to liberation. Her hierarchical constitution is said to be opposed to equality, her magisterium to be opposed to freedom of thought. It is true that there have been errors of judgment and serious omissions for which Christians have been responsible in the course of the centuries;[11] but these objections disregard the true nature of things. The diversity of charisms in the people of God, which are charisms of service, is not opposed to the equal dignity of persons and to their common vocation to holiness.

Freedom of thought, as a necessary condition for seeking the truth in all the fields of human knowledge, does not mean that human reason must cease to function in the light of the revelation which Christ entrusted to his church. By opening itself to divine truth, created reason experiences a blossoming and a perfection which are an eminent form of freedom. Moreover, the Second Vatican Council has recognized fully the legitimate autonomy of the sciences,[12] as well as of activities of a political nature.[13]

21. One of the principal errors that has seriously burdened the process of liberation since the age of the Enlightenment comes from the widely held conviction that it is the progress achieved in the fields of the sciences, technology and economics which should serve as a basis for achieving freedom. This was a misunderstanding of the depths of freedom and its needs.

The reality of the depth of freedom has always been known to the church, above all through the lives of a multitude of the faithful, especially among the little ones and the poor. In their faith, these latter know that they are the object of God's infinite love. Each of them can say: "I live by faith in the Son of God, who loved me and gave himself for me" (Gal 2:20). Such is the dignity which none of the powerful can take away from them; such is the liberating joy present in them. They know that to them too are addressed Jesus' words: "No longer do I call you servants, for the servant does not know what his master is doing; but I have called you friends, for all that I have heard from my Father I have made known to you" (Jn 2:20, 27). They are also aware of sharing in the highest knowledge to which humanity is called.[14] They know that they are loved by God, the same as all other people and more than all other people. They thus live in the freedom which flows from truth and love.

22. The same sense of faith, possessed by the people of God in its hope-filled devotion to the cross of Jesus, perceives the power contained in the mystery of Christ the redeemer. Therefore, far from despising or wishing to suppress the forms of popular piety which this devotion assumes, one should take and deepen all its meaning and implications.[15] Here we have a fact of fundamental theological and pastoral significance: it is the poor, the object of God's special love, who understand best, and as it were instinctively, that the most radical liberation, which is liberation from sin and death, is the liberation accomplished by the death and resurrection of Christ.

23. The power of this liberation penetrates and profoundly transforms man and his history in its present reality and animates his eschatological yearning. The first and fundamental meaning of liberation which thus manifests itself is the salvific one: Man is freed from the radical bondage of evil and sin.

In this experience of salvation, man discovers the true meaning of his freedom, since liberation is the restoration of freedom. It is also education in freedom, that is to say, education in the right use of freedom. Thus to the salvific dimension of liberation is linked its ethical dimension.

24. To different degrees, the sense of faith, which is at the origin of a radical experience of liberation and freedom, has imbued the culture and the customs of Christian peoples.

But today, because of the formidable challenges which humanity must face, it is in a wholly new way that it has become necessary and urgent that the love of God and freedom in truth and justice should mark relations between individuals and peoples and animate the life of cultures.

For where truth and love are missing, the process of liberation results in the death of a freedom which will have lost all support.

A new phase in the history of freedom is opening before us. The liberating capacities of science, technology, work, economics and political activity will only produce results if they find their inspiration and measure in the truth and love which are stronger than suffering: the truth and love revealed to men by Jesus Christ.

Chapter 2
Man's Vocation to Freedom and the Tragedy of Sin

I. Preliminary Approaches to Freedom

25. The spontaneous response to the question, What does being free mean, is this: A person is free when he is able to do whatever he wishes without being hindered by an exterior constraint and thus enjoys complete independence. The opposite of freedom would therefore be the dependence of our will upon the will of another.

But does man always know what he wants? Can he do everything he wants? Is closing in on oneself and cutting oneself off from the will of others in conformity with the nature of man? Often the desire of a particular moment is not what a person really wants. And in one and the same person there can exist contradictory wishes. But above all man comes up against the limits of his own nature: His desires are greater than his abilities. Thus the obstacle which opposes his will does not always come from outside, but from the limits of his own being. This is why, under pain of destroying himself, man must learn to harmonize his will with his nature.

26. Furthermore, every individual is oriented toward other people and needs their company. It is only by learning to unite his will to the others for the sake of true good that he will learn rectitude of will. It is thus harmony with the exigencies of human nature which makes the will itself human. This in fact requires the criterion of truth and a right relationship to the will of others. Truth and justice are therefore the measure of true freedom. By discarding this foundation and taking himself for God, man falls into deception, and instead of realizing himself he destroys himself.

Far from being achieved in total self-sufficiency and an absence of relationships, freedom only truly exists where reciprocal bonds, governed by truth and justice, link people to one another. But for such bonds to be possible, each person must live in the truth.

Freedom is not the liberty to do anything whatsoever. It is the freedom to do good, and in this alone happiness is to be found. The good is thus the goal of freedom. In consequence man becomes free to the extent that he comes to a knowledge of the truth and to the extent that this truth—and not any other forces—guides his will. Liberation for the sake of a knowledge of the truth which alone directs the will is the necessary condition for a freedom worthy of the name.

II. Freedom and Liberation

27. In other words freedom, which is interior mastery of one's own acts and self-determination, immediately entails a relationship with the ethical order. It finds its true meaning in the choice of moral good. It then manifests itself as emancipation from moral evil.

By his free action, man must tend toward the supreme good through lesser goods which conform to the exigencies of his nature and his divine vocation.

In exercising his freedom, he decides for himself and forms himself. In this sense man is his own cause. But he is this only as a creature and as God's image. This is the truth of his being, which shows by contrast how profoundly erroneous are the theories which think they exalt the freedom of man or his "historical praxis" by making this freedom the absolute principle of his being and becoming. These theories are expressions of atheism or tend toward atheism by their own logic. Indifferentism and deliberate agnosticism go in the same direction. It is the image of God in man which underlies the freedom and dignity of the human person.[16]

28. By creating man free, God imprinted on him his own image and likeness.[17] Man hears the call of his Creator in the inclination and aspiration of his own nature toward the good and still more in the word of revelation, which was proclaimed in a perfect manner in the Christ. It is thus revealed to man that God created him free so that by grace man could enter into friendship with God and share his life.

29. Man does not take his origin from his own individual or collective action, but from the gift of God who created him. This is the first confession of our faith, and it confirms the loftiest insights of human thought.

The freedom of man is a shared freedom. His capacity for self-realization is in no way suppressed by his dependence on God. It is precisely the characteristic of atheism to believe in an irreducible opposition between the causality of a divine freedom and that of man's freedom, as though the affirmation of God meant the negation of man or as though God's intervention in history rendered vain the endeavors of man. In reality, it is from God and in relationship with him that human freedom takes its meaning and consistency.

30. Man's history unfolds on the basis of the nature which he has received from God and in the free accomplishment of the purpose toward which the inclinations of his nature and of divine grace orient and direct him.

But man's freedom is finite and fallible. His desire may be drawn to an apparent good: In choosing a false good, he fails in his vocation to freedom. By his free will, man is master of his own life: He can act in a positive sense or in a destructive one.

By obeying the divine law inscribed in his conscience and received as an impulse of the Holy Spirit, man exercises true mastery over himself and thus realizes his royal vocation as a child of God. "By the service of God he reigns."[18] Authentic freedom is the "service of justice," while the choice of disobedience and evil is the "slavery of sin."[19]

31. This notion of freedom clarifies the scope of temporal liberation: It involves all the processes which aim at securing and guaranteeing the conditions needed for the exercise of an authentic human freedom.

Thus it is not liberation which in itself produces human freedom. Common sense, confirmed by Christian sense, knows that even when freedom is subject to forms of conditioning it is not thereby completely destroyed. People who undergo terrible constraints succeed in manifesting their freedom and taking steps to secure their own liberation. A process of liberation which has been achieved can only create better conditions for the effective exercise of freedom. Indeed, a liberation which does not take into account the personal freedom of those who fight for it is condemned in advance to defeat.

III. Freedom and Human Society

32. God did not create man as a "solitary being" but wished him to be a "social being."[20] Social life therefore is not exterior to man: He can only grow and realize his vocation in relation with others. Man belongs to different communities: the family and professional and political communities; and it is inside these communities that he must exercise his responsible freedom. A just social order offers man irreplaceable assistance in realizing his free personality. On the other hand, an unjust social order is a threat and an obstacle which can compromise his destiny.

In the social sphere, freedom is expressed and realized in actions, structures and institutions, thanks to which people communicate with one another and organize their common life. The blossoming of a free personality, which for every individual is a duty and a right, must be helped and not hindered by society.

Here we have an exigency of a moral nature, which has found its expression in the formulation of the rights of man. Some of these have as their object what are usually called "the freedoms," that is to say, ways of recognizing every human being's character as a person responsible for himself and his transcendent destiny, as well as the inviolability of his conscience.[21]

33. The social dimension of the human being also takes on another meaning: Only the vast numbers and rich diversity of people can express something of the infinite richness of God.

Finally, this dimension is meant to find its accomplishment in the body of Christ, which is the church. This is why social life, in the variety of its forms and to the extent that it is in conformity with the divine law, constitutes a reflection of the glory of God in the world.[22]

IV. Human Freedom and Dominion over Nature

34. As a consequence of his bodily dimension, man needs the resources of the material world for his personal and social fulfillment. In this vocation to exercise dominion over the earth by putting it at his service through work, one can see an aspect of the image of God.[23] But human intervention is not "creative"; it encounters a material nature which like itself has its origin in God the Creator and of which man has been constituted the "noble and wise guardian."[24]

35. Technical and economic transformations influence the organization of social life; they cannot help but affect to some extent cultural and even religious life.

However, by reason of his freedom man remains the master of his activity. The great and rapid transformations of the present age face him with a dramatic challenge: that of mastering and controlling by the use of his reason and freedom the forces which he puts to work in the service of the true purposes of human existence.

36. It is the task of freedom, then, when it is well ordered, to ensure that scientific and technical achievements, the quest for their effectiveness, and the products of work and the very structures of economic and social organization are not made to serve projects which would deprive them of their human purposes and turn them against man himself.

Scientific activity and technological activity each involve specific exigencies. But they only acquire their properly human meaning and value when they are subordinate to moral principles. These exigencies must be respected; but to wish to attribute to them an absolute and necessary autonomy not in conformity with the nature of things is to set out along a path which is ruinous for the authentic freedom of man.

V. Sin, the Source of Division and Oppression

37. God calls man to freedom. In each person there lives a desire to be free. And yet this desire almost always tends toward slavery and oppression. All commitment to liberation and freedom therefore presupposes that this tragic paradox has been faced.

Man's sin, that is to say his breaking away from God, is the radical reason for the tragedies which mark the history of freedom. In order to understand this, many of our contemporaries must first rediscover a sense of sin.

In man's desire for freedom there is hidden the temptation to deny his own nature. Insofar as he wishes to desire everything and to be able to do everything and thus forget that he is finite and a created being, he claims to be a god. "You will be like God" (Gn 3;5). These words of the serpent reveal the essence of man's temptation; they imply the perversion of the meaning of his own freedom. Such is the profound nature of sin: Man rejects the truth and places his own will above it. By wishing to free himself from God and be a god himself, he deceives himself and destroys himself. He becomes alienated from himself.

In this desire to be a god and to subject everything to his own good pleasure, there is hidden a perversion of the very idea of God. God is love and truth in the fullness of the mutual gift of the Divine Persons. It is true that man is called to be like God. But he becomes like God not in the arbitrariness of his own good pleasure but to the extent that he recognizes that truth and love are at the same time the principle and the purpose of his freedom.

38. By sinning, man lies to himself and separates himself from his own truth. But seeking total autonomy and self-sufficiency, he denies God and denies himself. Alienation from the truth of his being as a creature loved by God is the root of all other forms of alienation.

By denying or trying to deny God, who is his beginning and end, man profoundly disturbs his own order and interior balance and also those of society and even of visible creation.[25]

It is in their relationship to sin that Scripture regards all the different calamities which oppress man in his personal and social existence.

Scripture shows that the whole course of history has a mysterious link with the action of man who, from the beginning, has abused his freedom by setting himself up against God and by seeking to gain his ends without God.[26] Genesis indicates the consequences of this original sin in the painful nature of work and childbirth, in man's oppression of woman and in death. Human beings deprived of divine grace have thus inherited a common mortal nature, incapable of choosing what is good and inclined to covetousness.[27]

39. Idolatry is an extreme form of disorder produced by sin. The replacement of adoration of the living God by worship of created things falsifies the relationships between individuals and brings with it various kinds of oppression.

Culpable ignorance of God unleashes the passions, which are causes of imbalance and conflicts in the human heart. From this there inevitably come disorders which affect the sphere of family and society: sexual license, injustice and murder. It is thus that St. Paul describes the pagan world, carried away by idolatry to the worst aberrations which ruin the individual and society.[28]

Even before St. Paul the prophets and wise men of Israel saw in the misfortunes of the people a punishment for their sin of idolatry; and in the "heart full of evil" (Eccl 9:3),[29] they saw the source of man's radical slavery and of the forms of oppression which he makes his fellow men endure.

40. The Christian tradition, found in the fathers and doctors of the church, has made explicit this teaching of Scripture about sin. It sees sin as contempt for God (*contemptus Dei*). It is accompanied by a desire to escape from the dependent relationship of the servant to his Lord or still more of the child to its Father. By sinning, man seeks to free himself from God. In reality he makes himself a slave. For by rejecting God he destroys the momentum of his aspiration to the infinite and of his vocation to share in the divine life. This is why his heart is a prey to disquiet.

Sinful man who refuses to accept God is necessarily led to become attached in a false and destructive way to creatures. In this turning toward creatures (*conversio ad creaturam*) he focuses on the latter his unsatisfied desire for the infinite. But created goods are limited; and so his heart rushes from one to another, always searching for an impossible peace.

In fact, when man attributes to creatures an infinite importance, he loses the meaning of his created being. He claims to find his center and his unity in himself. Disordered love of self is the other side of contempt for God. Man then tries to rely on himself alone; he wishes to achieve fulfillment by himself and to be self-sufficient in his own immanence.[30]

41. This becomes more particularly obvious when the sinner thinks that he can only assert his own freedom by explicitly denying God. Dependence of the creature upon the Creator and the dependence of the moral conscience upon the divine law are regarded by him as an intolerable slavery. Thus he sees atheism as the true form of emancipation and of man's liberation, whereas religion or even the recognition of moral law constitute forms of alienation. Man then wishes to make independent decisions about what is good and what is evil, or decisions about values; and in a single step he rejects both the idea of God and the idea of sin. It is through the audacity of sin that he claims to become adult and free, and he claims this emancipation not only for himself but for the whole of humanity.

42. Having become his own center, sinful man tends to assert himself and to satisfy his desire for the infinite by the use of things: wealth, power and pleasure, despising other people and robbing them unjustly and treating them as objects or instruments. Thus he makes his own contribution to the creation of those very structures of exploitation and slavery which he claims to condemn.

Chapter 3
Liberation and Christian Freedom

43. Human history, marked as it is by the experience of sin, would drive us to despair if God had abandoned his creation to itself. But the divine promises of liberation and their victorious fulfillment in Christ's death and resurrection are the basis of the "joyful hope" from which the Christian community draws the strength to act resolutely and effectively in the service of love, justice and peace. The gospel is a message of freedom and a liberating force[31] which fulfills the hope of Israel based upon the words of the prophets. This hope relied upon the action of Yahweh, who even before he intervened as the *goel*,[32] liberator, redeemer and savior of his people, had freely chosen that people in Abraham.[33]

I. Liberation in the Old Testament

44. In the Old Testament the liberating action of Yahweh which serves as model and reference for all others is the Exodus from Egypt, "the house of bondage." When God rescues his people from hard economic, political and cultural slavery, he does so in order to make them, through the covenant on Sinai, "a kingdom of priests and a holy nation" (Ex 19:6). God wishes to be adored by people who are free. All the subsequent liberations of the people of Israel help to lead them to this full liberty that they can only find in communion with their God.

The major and fundamental event of the Exodus therefore has a meaning which is both religious and political. God sets his people free and gives them descendants, a land and a law, but within a covenant and for a covenant. One cannot therefore isolate the political aspect for its own sake; it has to be considered in the light of a plan of a religious nature within which it is integrated.[34]

45. In his plan of salvation God gave Israel its law. This contained, together with the universal moral precepts of the Decalogue, religious and civil norms which were to govern the life of the people chosen by God to be his witness among the nations.

Of this collection of laws, love of God above all things[35] and of neighbor as oneself[36] already constitute the center. But the justice which must govern relations between people and the law which is its juridical expression also belong to the sum and substance of the biblical law. The codes and the preaching of the prophets, as also the Psalms, constantly refer to both of them, very often together.[37] It is in this context that one should appreciate the biblical law's care for the poor, the needy, the widow and the orphan: They have a right to justice according to the juridical ordinances of the people of God.[38] Thus there already exist the ideal and the outline of a society centered upon worship of the Lord and based upon justice and law inspired by love.

46. Prophets constantly remind Israel of the demands made by the law of the covenant. They condemn man's hardened heart as the source of repeated transgressions, and they foretell a new covenant in which God will change hearts by writing on them the law of his Spirit.[39]

In proclaiming and preparing for this new age, the prophets vigorously condemn injustice done to the poor: They make themselves God's spokesmen for the poor. Yahweh is the supreme refuge of the little ones and the oppressed, and the Messiah will have the mission of taking up their defense.[40]

The situation of the poor is a situation contrary to the covenant. This is why the law of the covenant protects them by means of precepts which reflect the attitude of God himself when he liberated Israel from the slavery of Egypt.[41] Injustice to the little ones and the poor is a grave sin and one which destroys communion with God.

47. Whatever the forms of poverty, injustice and affliction they endure, the "just" and the "poor of Yahweh" offer up their supplications to him in the Psalms.[42] In their hearts they suffer the servitude to which the "stiff-necked" people are reduced because of their sins. They endure persecution, martyrdom and death; but they live in hope of deliverance. Above all, they place their trust in Yahweh, to whom they commend their cause.[43]

The "poor of Yahweh" know that communion with him[44] is the most precious treasure and the one in which man finds his true freedom.[45] For them, the most tragic misfortune is the loss of this communion. Hence their fight against injustice finds its deepest meaning and its effectiveness in their desire to be freed from the slavery of sin.

48. On the threshold of the New Testament, the "poor of Yahweh" make up the first fruits of a "people humble and lowly" who live in hope of the liberation of Israel.[46]

Mary, personifying this hope, crosses the threshold from the Old Testament. She proclaims with joy the coming of the Messiah and praises the Lord, who is preparing to set his people free.[47] In her hymn of praise to the divine mercy, the humble Virgin, to whom the people of the poor turn spontaneously and so confidently, sings of the mystery of salvation and its power to transform. The *sensus fidei*, which is so vivid among the little ones, is able to grasp at once all the salvific and ethical treasures of the Magnificat.[48]

II. Christological Significance of the Old Testament

49. The exodus, the covenant, the law, the voices of the prophets and the spirituality of the "poor of Yahweh" only achieve their full significance in Christ. The church reads the Old Testament in the light of Christ, who died and rose for us. She sees a prefiguring of herself in the people of God of the old covenant, made incarnate in the concrete body of a particular nation, politically and culturally constituted as such. This people was part of the fabric of history as Yahweh's witness before the nations until the fulfillment of the time of preparation and prefigurement. In the fullness of time which came with Christ, the children of Abraham were invited to enter, together with all the nations, into the church of Christ in order to form with them one people of God, spiritual and universal.[49]

III. Christian Liberation

50. Jesus proclaims the good news of the kingdom of God and calls people to conversion.[50] "The poor have the good news preached to them" (Mt 11:5). By quoting the expression of the prophet,[51] Jesus manifests his Messianic action in favor of those who await God's salvation.

Even more than this, the Son of God, who has made himself poor for love of us,[52] wishes to be recognized in the poor, in those who suffer or are persecuted:[53] "As you did it to one of the least of these my brethren, you did it to me."[54]

51. But it is above all by the power of his paschal mystery that Christ has set us free.[55] Through his perfect obedience on the cross and through the glory of his resurrection, the Lamb of God has taken away the sin of the world and opened for us the way to definitive liberation.

By means of our service and love, but also by the offering up of our trials and sufferings, we share in the one redeeming sacrifice of Christ, completing in ourselves "what is lacking in Christ's afflictions for the sake of his body, that is, the church" (Col 1:24), as we look forward to the resurrection of the dead.

52. The heart of the Christian experience of freedom is in justification by the grace received through faith and the church's sacraments. This grace frees us from sin and places us in communion with God. Through Christ's death and resurrection we are offered forgiveness. The experience of our reconciliation with the Father is the fruit of the Holy Spirit. God reveals himself to us as the Father of Mercy, before whom we can come with total confidence.

Having been reconciled with him[56] and receiving this peace of Christ which the world cannot give,[57] we are called to be peacemakers among all men.[58]

In Christ, we can conquer sin, and death no longer separates us from God; death will finally be destroyed at our resurrection, which will be like that of Jesus.[59] The "cosmos" itself, of which man is the center and summit, waits to be "set free from its bondage to decay and to share in the glorious freedom of the children of God" (Rom 8:21). Even now Satan has been checked; he who has the power of death has been reduced to impotence by the death of Christ.[60] Signs are given which are a foretaste of the glory to come.

53. The freedom brought by Christ in the Holy Spirit has restored to us the capacity, which sin had taken away from us, to love God above all things and remain in communion with him.

We are set free from disordered self-love, which is the source of contempt of neighbor and of human relationships based on domination.

Nevertheless, until the Risen One returns in glory, the mystery of iniquity is still at work in the world. St. Paul warns us of this: "For freedom Christ has set us free" (Gal 5:1). We must therefore persevere and fight in order not to fall once more under the yoke of slavery. Our existence is a spiritual struggle to live according to the gospel, and it is waged with the weapons of God.[61] But we have received the power and the certainty of our victory over evil, the victory of the love of Christ, whom nothing can resist.[62]

54. St. Paul proclaims the gift of the new law of the Spirit in opposition to the law of the flesh or of covetousness which draws man toward evil and makes him powerless to choose what is good.[63] This lack of harmony and this inner weakness do not abolish man's freedom and responsibility, but they do have a negative effect on their exercise for the sake of what is good. This is what causes the Apostle to say: "I do not do the good I want, but the evil I do not want is what I do" (Rom 7:19). Thus he rightly speaks of the "bondage of sin" and the "slavery of the law," for to sinful man the law, which he cannot make part of himself, seems oppressive.

However, St. Paul recognizes that the law still has value for man for the Christian, because it "is holy and what it commands is sacred, just and good" (Rom 7:12).[64] He reaffirms the Decalogue, while putting it into relationship with that charity which is its true fullness.[65] Furthermore, he knows well that a juridical order is necessary for the development of life in society.[66] But the new thing he proclaims is God's giving us his Son "so that the law's just demands might be satisfied in us" (Rom 8:1).

The Lord Jesus himself spelled out the precepts of the new law in the Sermon on the Mount. By the sacrifice he offered on the cross and again by his glorious resurrection, he conquered the power of sin and gained for us the grace of the Holy Spirit, which makes possible the perfect observance of God's law[67] and access to forgiveness if we fall again into sin. The Spirit who dwells in our hearts is the source of true freedom.

Through Christ's sacrifice, the cultic regulations of the Old Testament have been rendered obsolete. As for the juridical norms governing the social and political life of Israel, the apostolic church, inasmuch as it marked the beginning of the reign of God on earth, was no longer held to their observance. This enabled the Christian community to understand the laws and authoritative acts of various peoples. Although lawful and worthy of being obeyed,[68] they could never, inasmuch as they have their origin in such authorities, claim to have a sacred character. In the light of the gospel, many laws and structures seem to bear the mark of sin and prolong its oppressive influence in society.

IV. The New Commandment

55. God's love, poured out into our hearts by the Holy Spirit, involves love of neighbor. Recalling the First Commandment, Jesus immediately adds: "And the second is like it, 'You shall love your neighbor as yourself.' On these two commandments depend all the law and the prophets" (Mt 22:39-40). And St. Paul says that love is the fulfillment of the law.[69]

Love of neighbor knows no limits and includes enemies and persecutors. The perfection which is the image of the Father's perfection and for which the disciple must strive is found in mercy.[70] The parable of the Good Samaritan shows that compassionate love, which puts itself at the service of neighbor, destroys the prejudices which set ethnic or social groups against one another.[71] All the New Testament witnesses to the inexhaustible richness of the sentiments which are included in Christian love of neighbor.[72]

56. Christian love, which seeks no reward and includes everyone, receives its nature from the love of Christ, who gave his life for us: "Even as I have loved you . . . , you also love one another" (Jn 13:34-35).[73] This is the "new commandment" for the disciples.

In the light of this commandment, St. James severely reminds the rich of their duty,[74] and St. John says that a person who possesses the riches of this world but who shuts his heart to his brother in need cannot have the love of God dwelling in him.[75] Fraternal love is the touchstone of love of God: "He who does not love his brother whom he has seen cannot love God whom he has not seen" (1 Jn 4:20). St. Paul strongly emphasizes the link between sharing in the sacrament of the body and blood of Christ and sharing with one's neighbor who is in need.[76]

57. Evangelical love and the vocation to be children of God, to which all are called, have as a consequence the direct and imperative requirement of respect for all human beings in their rights to life and to dignity. There is no gap between love of neighbor and desire for justice. To contrast the two is to distort both love and justice. Indeed, the meaning of mercy completes the meaning of justice by preventing justice from shutting itself up within the circle of revenge.

The evil inequities and oppression of every kind which afflict millions of men and women today openly contradict Christ's Gospel and cannot leave the conscience of any Christian indifferent.

The church, in her docility to the Spirit, goes forward faithfully along paths to authentic liberation. Her members are aware of their failings and their delays in this quest. But a vast number of Christians, from the time of the Apostles onward, have committed their powers and their lives to liberation from every form of oppression and the promotion of human dignity. The experience of the saints and the example of so many works of service to one's neighbor are an incentive and a beacon for the liberating undertakings that are needed today.

V. The Church, People of God
of the New Covenant

58. The people of God of the new covenant is the church of Christ. Her law is the commandment of love. In the hearts of her members the Spirit dwells as in a temple. She is the seed and the beginning of the kingdom of God here below, which will receive its completion at the end of time with the resurrection of the dead and the renewal of the whole of creation.[77]

Thus possessing the pledge of the Spirit,[78] the people of God is led toward the fullness of freedom. The new Jerusalem which we fervently await is rightly called the city of freedom in the highest sense.[79] Then, "God will wipe away every tear from their eyes and death shall be no more, neither shall there be mourning nor crying nor pain any more, for the former things have passed away" (Rv 21:4). Hope is the certain expectation "of new heavens and of a new earth where justice will dwell" (2 Pt 3:13).

59. The transfiguration by the risen Christ of the church at the end of her pilgrimage in no way cancels out the personal destiny of each individual at the end of his or her life. All those found worthy before Christ's tribunal for having, by the grace of God, made good use of their free will are to receive the reward of happiness.[80] They will be made like to God, for they will see him as he is.[81] The divine gift of eternal happiness is the exaltation of the greatest freedom which can be imagined.

60. This hope does not weaken commitment to the progress of the earthly city, but rather gives it meaning and strength. It is of course important to make a careful distinction between earthly progress and the growth of the kingdom, which do not belong to the same order. Nonetheless, this distinction is not a separation; for man's vocation to eternal life does not suppress but confirms his task of using the energies and means which he has received from the Creator for developing his temporal life.[82]

Enlightened by the Lord's Spirit, Christ's church can discern in the signs of the times the ones which advance liberation and those that are deceptive and illusory. She calls man and societies to overcome situations of sin and injustice and to establish the conditions for true freedom. She knows that we shall rediscover all these good things—human dignity, fraternal union and freedom—which are the result of efforts in harmony with God's will, "washed clean of all stain, illumined and transfigured when Christ will hand over to the Father the eternal and universal kingdom,"[83] which is a kingdom of freedom.

The vigilant and active expectation of the coming of the kingdom is also the expectation of a finally perfect justice for the living and the dead, for people of all times and places, a justice which Jesus Christ, installed as supreme judge, will establish.[84] This promise, which surpasses all human possibilities, directly concerns our life in this world. For true justice must include everyone; it must bring the answer to the immense load of suffering borne by all generations. In fact, without the resurrection of the dead and the Lord's judgment, there is no justice in the full sense of the term. The promise of the resurrection is freely made to meet the desire for true justice dwelling in the human heart.

Chapter 4
The Liberating Mission of the Church

61. The church is firmly determined to respond to the anxiety of contemporary man as he endures oppression and yearns for freedom. The political and economic running of society is not a direct part of her mission.[85] But the Lord Jesus has entrusted to her the word of truth which is capable of enlightening consciences. Divine love, which is her life, impels her to a true solidarity with everyone who suffers. If her members remain faithful to the mission, the Holy Spirit, the source of freedom, will dwell in them, and they will bring forth fruits of justice and peace in their families and in the places where they work and live.

I. For the Integral Salvation of the World

62. The Gospel is the power of eternal life, given even now to those who receive it.[86] But by begetting people who are renewed,[87], this power penetrates the human community and its history, thus purifying and giving life to its activities. In this way it is a "root of culture."[88]

The Beatitudes proclaimed by Jesus express the perfection of evangelical love, and they have never ceased to be lived throughout the history of the church by countless baptized individuals and in an eminent manner by the saints.

The Beatitudes, beginning with the first, the one concerning the poor, form a whole which itself must not be separated from the entirety of the Sermon on the Mount.[89] In this sermon Jesus, who is the new Moses, gives a commentary on the Decalogue, the law of the covenant, thus giving it its definitive and fullest meaning. Read and interpreted in their full context, the Beatitudes express the spirit of the kingdom of God which is to come. But, in the light of the definitive destiny of human history thus manifested, there simultaneously appear with a more vivid clarity the foundations of justice in the temporal order.

For the Beatitudes, by teaching trust which relies on God, hope of eternal life, love of justice and mercy which goes as far as pardon and reconciliation, enable us to situate the temporal order in relation to a transcendent order which gives the temporal order its true measure but without taking away its own nature.

In the light of these things, the commitment necessary in temporal tasks of service to neighbor and the human community is both urgently demanded and kept in its right perspective. The Beatitudes prevent us from worshiping earthly goods and from committing the injustices which their unbridled pursuit involves.[90] They also divert us from an unrealistic and ruinous search for a perfect world, "for the form of this world is passing away" (1 Cor 7:31).

63. The church's essential mission, following that of Christ, is a mission of evangelization and salvation.[91] She draws her zeal from the divine love. Evangelization is the proclamation of salvation, which is a gift of God. Through the word of God and the sacraments, man is freed in the first place from the power of sin and the power of the Evil One which oppress him; and he is brought into a communion of love with God. Following her Lord, who "came into the world to save sinners" (1 Tm 1:15), the church desires the salvation of all people.

In this mission, the church teaches the way which man must follow in this world in order to enter the kingdom of God. Her teaching therefore extends to the whole moral order and notably to the justice which must regulate human relations. This is part of the preaching of the gospel.

But the love which impels the church to communicate to all people a sharing in the grace of divine life also causes her, through the effective action of her members, to pursue people's true temporal good, help them in their needs, provide for their education and promote an integral liberation from everything that hinders the development of individuals. The church desires the good of man in all his dimensions, first of all as a member of the city of God and then as a member of the earthly city.

64. Therefore, when the church speaks about the promotion of justice in human societies or when she urges the faithful laity to work in this sphere according to their own vocation, she is not going beyond her mission. She is, however, concerned that this mission should not be absorbed by preoccupations concerning the temporal order or reduced to such preoccupations. Hence she takes great care to maintain clearly and firmly both the unity and the distinction between evangelization and human promotion: unity, because she sees the good of the whole person; distinction, because these two tasks enter in different ways into her mission.

65. It is thus by pursuing her own finality that the church sheds the light of the gospel on earthly realities in order that human beings may be healed of their miseries and raised in dignity. The cohesion of society in accordance with justice and peace is thereby promoted and strengthened.[92] Thus the church is being faithful to her mission when she condemns the forms of deviation, slavery and oppression of which people are victims.

She is being faithful to her mission when she opposes attempts to set up a form of social life from which God is absent, whether by deliberate opposition or by culpable negligence.[93]

She is likewise being faithful to her mission when she exercises her judgment regarding political movements which seek to fight poverty and oppression according to theories or methods of action which are contrary to the Gospel and opposed to man himself.[94]

It is of course true that, with the energy of grace, evangelical morality brings man new perspectives and new duties. But its purpose is to perfect and elevate a moral dimension which already belongs to human nature and with which the church concerns herself in the knowledge that this is a heritage belonging to all people by their very nature.

II. A Love of Preference for the Poor

66. Christ Jesus, although he was rich, became poor in order to make us rich by means of his poverty.[95] St. Paul is speaking here of the mystery of the incarnation of the eternal Son, who came to take on mortal human nature in order to save man from the misery into which sin had plunged him. Furthermore, in the human condition Christ chose a state of poverty and deprivation[96] in order to show in what consists the true wealth which ought to be sought, that of communion of life with God. He taught detachment from earthly riches so that we might desire the riches of heaven.[97] The apostles whom he chose also had to leave all things and share his deprivation.[98]

Christ was foretold by the prophets as the Messiah of the poor;[99] and it was among the latter, the humble, the "poor of Yahweh," who were thirsting for the justice of the kingdom, that he found hearts ready to receive him. But he also wishes to be near to those who, though rich in the goods of this world, were excluded from the community as "publicans and sinners," for he had come to call them to conversion.[100]

It is this sort of poverty, made up of detachment, trust in God, sobriety and a readiness to share, that Jesus declared blessed.

67. But Jesus not only brought the grace and peace of God; he also healed innumerable sick people; he had compassion on the crowd who had nothing to eat and he fed them; with the disciples who followed him he practiced almsgiving.[101] Therefore the Beatitude of poverty which he proclaimed can never signify that Christians are permitted to ignore the poor, who lack what is necessary for human life in this world. This poverty is the result and consequence of people's sin and natural frailty, and it is an evil from which human beings must be freed as completely as possible.

68. In its various forms—material deprivation, unjust oppression, physical and psychological illness, and finally death—human misery is the obvious sign of the natural condition of weakness in which man finds himself since original sin and the sign of his need for salvation. Hence it drew the compassion of Christ the Savior to take it upon himself[102] and to be identified with the least of his brethren (cf. Mt 25:40, 45). Hence also those who are oppressed by poverty are the object of a love of preference on the part of the church, which since her origin and in spite of the failings of many of her members, has not ceased to work for their relief, defense and liberation. She has done this through numberless works of charity which remain always and everywhere indispensable.[103] In addition, through her social doctrine which she strives to apply, she has sought to promote structural changes in society so as to secure conditions of life worthy of the human person.

By detachment from riches, which makes possible sharing and opens the gate of the kingdom,[104] the disciples of Jesus bear witness through love for the poor and the unfortunate to the love of the Father himself manifested in the Savior. This love comes from God and goes to God. The disciples of Christ have always recognized in the gifts placed on the altar a gift offered to God himself.

In loving the poor, the church also witnesses to man's dignity. She clearly affirms that man is worth more for what he is than for what he has. She bears witness to the fact that this dignity cannot be destroyed, whatever the situation of poverty, scorn, rejection or powerlessness to which a human being has been reduced. She shows her solidarity with those who do not count in a society by which they are rejected spiritually and sometimes even physically. She is particularly drawn with maternal affection toward those children who, through human wickedness, will never be brought forth from the womb to the light of day, as also for the elderly, alone and abandoned.

The special option for the poor, far from being a sign of particularism or sectarianism, manifests the universality of the church's being and mission. This option excludes no one.

This is the reason why the church cannot express this option by means of reductive sociological and ideological categories which would make this preference a partisan choice and a source of conflict.

69. The new basic communities or other groups of Christians which have arisen to be witnesses to this evangelical love are a source of great hope for the church. If they really live in unity with the local church and the universal church, they will be a real expression of communion and a means for constructing a still deeper communion.[105] Their fidelity to their mission will depend on how careful they are to educate their members in the fullness of the Christian faith through listening to the word of God, fidelity to the teaching of the magisterium, to the hierarchical order of the church and to the sacramental life. If this condition is fulfilled, their experience, rooted in a commitment to the complete liberation of man, becomes a treasure for the whole church.

70. Similarly, a theological reflection developed from a particular experience can constitute a very positive contribution, inasmuch as it makes possible a highlighting of aspects of the work of God, the richness of which had not yet been fully grasped. But in order that this reflection may be truly a reading of the Scripture and not a projection onto the word of God of a meaning which it does not contain, the theologian will be careful to interpret the experience from which he begins in the light of the experience of the church herself. This experience of the church shines with a singular brightness and in all its purity in the lives of the saints. It pertains to the pastors of the church, in communion with the successor of Peter, to discern its authenticity.

Chapter 5
The Social Doctrine of the Church:
For a Christian Practice of Liberation

71. The salvific dimension of liberation cannot be reduced to the socioethical dimension, which is a consequence of it. By restoring man's true freedom, the radical liberation brought about by Christ assigns to him a task: Christian practice, which is the putting into practice of the great commandment of love. The latter is the supreme principle of Christian social morality, founded upon the gospel and the whole of tradition since apostolic times and the age of the fathers of the church up to and including the recent statements of the magisterium.

The considerable challenges of our time constitute an urgent appeal to put into practice this teaching on how to act.

I. Nature of the Social Doctrine of the Church

72. The church's social teaching is born of the encounter of the gospel message and of its demands, summarized in the supreme commandments of love of God and neighbor in justice,[106] with the problems emanating from the life of society. This social teaching has established itself as a doctrine by using the resources of human wisdom and the sciences. It concerns the ethical aspect of this life. It takes into account the technical aspects of problems but always in order to judge them from the moral point of view.

Being essentially orientated toward action, this teaching develops in accordance with the changing circumstances of history. This is why, together with principles that are always valid, it also involves contingent judgments. Far from constituting a closed system, it remains constantly open to the new questions which continually arise; it requires the contribution of all charisms, experiences and skills.

As an "expert in humanity," the church offers by her social doctrine a set of principles for reflection and criteria for judgment[107] and also directives for action[108] so that the profound changes demanded by situations of poverty and injustice may be brought about, and this in a way which serves the true good of humanity.

73. The supreme commandment of love leads to the full recognition of the dignity of each individual, created in God's image. From this dignity flow natural rights and duties. In the light of the image of God, freedom, which is the essential prerogative of the human person, is manifested in all its depth. Persons are the active and responsible subjects of social life.[109]

Intimately linked to the foundation, which is man's dignity, are the principle of solidarity and the principle of subsidiarity.

By virtue of the first, man with his brothers is obliged to contribute to the common good of society at all its levels.[110] Hence the church's doctrine is opposed to all the forms of social or political individualism.

By virtue of the second, neither the state nor any society must ever substitute itself for the initiative and responsibility of individuals and of intermediate communities at the level on which they can function, nor must they take away the room necessary for their freedom.[111] Hence the church's social doctrine is opposed to all forms of collectivism.

74. These principles are the basis of criteria for making judgments on social situations, structures and systems.

Thus the church does not hesitate to condemn situations of life which are injurious to man's dignity and freedom.

These criteria also make it possible to judge the value of structures. These are the sets of institutions and practices which people find already existing or which they create on the national and international level and which orientate or organize economic, social and political life. Being necessary in themselves, they often tend to become fixed and fossilized as mechanisms relatively independent of the human will, thereby paralyzing or distorting social development and causing injustice. However, they always depend on the responsibility of man, who can alter them, and not upon an alleged determinism of history.

Institutions and laws, when they are in conformity with the natural law and ordered to the common good, are the guarantees of people's freedom and of the promotion of that freedom. One cannot condemn all the constraining aspects of law nor the stability of a lawful state worthy of the name. One can therefore speak of structures marked by sin, but one cannot condemn structures as such.

The criteria for judgment also concern economic, social and political systems. The social doctrine of the church does not propose any particular system; but in the light of other fundamental principles she makes it possible at once to see to what extent existing systems conform or do not conform to the demands of human dignity.

75. The church is, of course, aware of the complexity of the problems confronting society and of the difficulties in finding adequate solutions to them. Nevertheless she considers that the first thing to be done is to appeal to the spiritual and moral capacities of the individual and to the permanent need for inner conversion, if one is to achieve the economic and social changes that will truly be at the service of man.

The priority given to structures and technical organization over the person and the requirements of this dignity is the expression of a materialistic anthropology and is contrary to the construction of a just social order.[112]

On the other hand, the recognized priority of freedom and of conversion of heart in no way eliminates the need for unjust structures to be changed. It is therefore perfectly legitimate that those who suffer oppression on the part of the wealthy or the politically powerful should take action, through morally licit means, in order to secure structures and institutions in which their rights will be truly respected.

It remains true, however, that structures established for people's good are of themselves incapable of securing and guaranteeing that good. The corruption which in certain countries affects the leaders and the state bureaucracy, and which destroys all honest social life is a proof of this. Moral integrity is a necessary condition for the health of society. It is therefore necessary to work simultaneously for the conversion of hearts and for the improvement of structures. For the sin which is at the root of unjust situations is, in a true and immediate sense, a voluntary act which has its source in the freedom of individuals. Only in a derived and secondary sense is it applicable to structures, and only in this sense can one speak of "social sin."[113]

Moreover, in the process of liberation, one cannot abstract from the historical situation of the nation or attack the cultural identity of the people. Consequently, one cannot passively accept, still less actively support, groups which by force or by the manipulation of public opinion take over the state apparatus and unjustly impose on the collectivity an imported ideology contrary to the culture of the people.[114] In this respect, mention should be made of the serious moral and political responsibility of intellectuals.

76. Basic principles and criteria for judgment inspire guidelines for action. Since the common good of human society is at the service of people, the means of action must be in conformity with human dignity and facilitate education for freedom. A safe criterion for judgment and action is this: There can be no true liberation if from the very beginning the rights of freedom are not respected.

Systematic recourse to violence put forward as the necessary path to liberation has to be condemned as a destructive illusion and one that opens the way to new forms of servitude. One must condemn with equal vigor violence exercised by the powerful against the poor, arbitrary action by the police and any form of violence established as a system of government. In these areas one must learn the lessons of tragic experiences which the history of the present century has known and continues to know. Nor can one accept the culpable passivity of the public powers in those democracies where the social situation of a large number of men and women is far from corresponding to the demands of constitutionally guaranteed individual and social rights.

77. When the church encourages the creation and activity of associations such as trade unions which fight for the defense of the rights and legitimate interests of the workers and for social justice, she does not thereby admit that theory that sees in the class struggle the structural dynamism of social life. The action which she sanctions is not the struggle of one class against another in order to eliminate the foe. She does not proceed from a mistaken acceptance of an alleged law of history. This action is rather a noble and reasoned struggle for justice and social solidarity.[115] The Christian will always prefer the path of dialogue and joint action.

Christ has commanded us to love our enemies.[116] Liberation in the spirit of the gospel is therefore incompatible with hatred of others, taken individually or collectively, and this includes hatred of one's enemy.

78. Situations of grave injustice require the courage to make far-reaching reforms and to suppress unjustifiable privileges. But those who discredit the path of reform and favor the myth of revolution not only foster the illusion that the abolition of an evil situation is in itself sufficient to create a more humane society; they also encourage the setting up of totalitarian regimes.[117] The fight against injustice is meaningless unless it is waged with a view to establishing a new social and political order in conformity with the demands of justice. Justice must already mark each stage of the establishment of this new order. There is a morality of means.[118]

79. These principles must be especially applied in the extreme case where there is recourse to armed struggle, which the church's magisterium admits as a last resort to put an end to an obvious and prolonged tyranny which is gravely damaging the fundamental rights of individuals and the common good.[119] Nevertheless, the concrete application of this means cannot be contemplated until there has been a very rigorous analysis of the situation. Indeed, because of the continual development of the technology of violence and the increasingly serious dangers implied in its recourse, that which today is termed "passive resistance" shows a way more conformable to moral principles and having no less prospects for success. One can never approve, whether perpetrated by established power or insurgents, crimes such as reprisals against the general population, torture or methods of terrorism and deliberate provocation aimed at causing deaths during popular demonstrations. Equally unacceptable are detestable smear campaigns capable of destroying a person psychologically or morally.

80. It is not for the pastors of the church to intervene directly in the political construction and organization of social life. This task forms part of the vocation of the laity acting on their own initiative with their fellow citizens.[120] They must fulfill this task conscious of the fact that the purpose of the church is to spread the kingdom of Christ so that all men may be saved and that through them the world may be effectively ordered to Christ.[121] The work of salvation is thus seen to be indissolubly linked to the task of improving and raising the conditions of human life in this world.

The distinction between the supernatural order of salvation and the temporal order of human life must be seen in the context of God's singular plan to recapitulate all things in Christ. Hence in each of these spheres the lay person, who is at one and the same time a member of the church and a citizen of his country, must allow himself to be constantly guided by his Christian conscience.[122]

Social action, which can involve a number of concrete means, will always be exercised for the common good and in conformity with the gospel message and the teaching of the church. It must be ensured that the variety of options does not harm a sense of collaboration, or lead to a paralysis of efforts or produce confusion among the Christian people.

The orientation received from the social doctrine of the church should stimulate an acquisition of the essential technical and scientific skills. The social doctrine of the church will also stimulate the seeking of moral formation of character and a deepening of the spiritual life. While it offers principles and wise counsel, this doctrine does not dispense from education in the political prudence needed for guiding and running human affairs.

II. Evangelical Requirements for an In-Depth Transformation

81. Christians working to bring about that "civilization of love" which will include the entire ethical and social heritage of the Gospel are today faced with an unprecedented challenge. This task calls for renewed reflection on what constitutes the relationship between the supreme commandment of love and the social order considered in all its complexity.

The immediate aim of this in-depth reflection is to work out and set in motion ambitious programs aimed at the socioeconomic liberation of millions of men and women caught in an intolerable situation of economic, social and political oppression.

This action must begin with an immense effort at education: education for the civilization of work, education for solidarity, access to culture for all.

82. The life of Jesus of Nazareth, a real "Gospel of work," offers us the living example and principle of the radical cultural transformation which is essential for solving the grave problems which must be faced by the age in which we live. He, who though he was God became like us in all things, devoted the greater part of his earthly life to manual labor.[123] The culture which our age awaits will be marked by the full recognition of the dignity of human work, which appears in all its nobility and fruitfulness in the light of the mysteries of creation and redemption.[124] Recognized as a form of the person, work becomes a source of creative meaning and effort.

83. Thus the solution of most of the serious problems related to poverty is to be found in the promotion of a true civilization of work. In a sense, work is the key to the whole social question.[125]

It is therefore in the domain of work that priority must be given to the action of liberation in freedom. Because the relationship between the human person and work is radical and vital, the forms and models according to which this relationship is regulated will exercise a positive influence for the solution of a whole series of social and political problems facing each people. Just work relationships will be a necessary precondition for a system of political community capable of favoring the integral development of every individual.

If the system of labor relations put into effect by those directly involved, the workers and employers, with the essential support of the public powers, succeeds in bringing into existence a civilization of work, then there will take place a profound and peaceful revolution in people's outlooks and in institutional and political structures.

84. A work culture such as this will necessarily presuppose and put into effect a certain number of essential values. It will acknowledge that the person of the worker is the principle, subject and purpose of work. It will affirm the priority of work over capital and the fact that material goods are meant for all. It will be animated by a sense of solidarity involving not only rights to be defended but also the duties to be performed. It will involve participation aimed at promoting the national and international common good and not just defending individual or corporate interests. It will assimilate the methods of confrontation and of frank and vigorous dialogue.

As a result, the political authorities will become more capable of acting with respect for the legitimate freedoms of individuals, families and subsidiary groups; and they will thus create the conditions necessary for man to be able to achieve his authentic and integral welfare, including his spiritual goal.[126]

85. A culture which recognizes the eminent dignity of the worker will emphasize the subjective dimension of work.[127]

The value of any human work does not depend on the kind of work done; it is based on the fact that the one who does it is a person.[128] There we have an ethical criterion whose implications cannot be overlooked.

Thus every person has a right to work, and this right must be recognized in a practical way by an effective commitment to resolving the tragic problem of unemployment. The fact that unemployment keeps large sectors of the population, and notably the young, in a situation of marginalization is intolerable. For this reason the creation of jobs is a primary social task facing individuals and private enterprise, as well as the state. As a general rule, in this as in other matters the state has a subsidiary function. But often it can be called upon to intervene directly, as in the case of international agreements between different states. Such agreements must respect the rights of immigrants and their families.[129]

86. Wages, which cannot be considered as a mere commodity, must enable the worker and his family to have access to a truly human standard of living in the material, social, cultural and spiritual orders. It is the dignity of the person which constitutes the criterion for judging work, not the other way round. Whatever the type of work, the worker must be able to perform it as an expression of his personality. There follows from this the necessity of a participation which, over and above a sharing in the fruits of work, should involve a truly communitarian dimension at the level of projects, undertakings and responsibilities.[130]

87. The priority of work over capital places an obligation in justice upon employers to consider the welfare of the workers before the increase of profits. They have a moral obligation not to keep capital unproductive and in making investments to think first of the common good. The latter requires a prior effort to consolidate jobs or create new ones in the production of goods that are really useful.

The right to private property is inconceivable without responsibilities to the common good. It is subordinated to the higher principle which states that goods are meant for all.[131]

88. This teaching must inspire reforms before it is too late. Access for everyone to the goods needed for a human, personal and family life worthy of the name is a primary demand of social justice. It requires application in the sphere of industrial work and in a particular way in the area of agricultural work.[132] Indeed, rural peoples, especially in the Third World, make up the vast majority of the poor.[133]

Promotion of Solidarity

89. Solidarity is a direct requirement of human and supernatural brotherhood. The serious socioeconomic problems which occur today cannot be solved unless new fronts of solidarity are created: solidarity of the poor among themselves, solidarity with the poor to which the rich are called, solidarity among the workers and with the workers. Institutions and social organizations at different levels, as well as the state, must share in a general movement of solidarity. When the church appeals for such solidarity, she is aware that she herself is concerned in a quite special way.

90. The principle that goods are meant for all, together with the principle of human and supernatural brotherhood, express the responsibilities of the richer countries toward the poorer ones. These responsibilities include solidarity in aiding the developing countries, social justice through a revision in correct terms of commercial relationships between North and South, the promotion of a more human world for all, a world in which each individual can give and receive, and in which the progress of some will no longer be an obstacle to the development of others nor a pretext for their enslavement.[134]

91. International solidarity is a necessity of the moral order. It is essential not only in cases of extreme urgency but also for aiding true development. This is a shared task, which requires a concerted and constant effort to find concrete technical solutions and also to create a new mentality among our contemporaries. World peace depends on this to a great extent.[135]

IV. Cultural and Educational Tasks

92. The unjust inequalities in the possession and use of material goods are accompanied and aggravated by similarly unjust inequalities in the opportunity for culture, which is the specific mode of a truly human existence to which one gains access through the development of one's intellectual capacities, moral virtues, abilities to relate with other human beings and talents for creating things which are useful and beautiful. From this flows the necessity of promoting and spreading education, to which every individual has an inalienable right. The first condition for this is the elimination of illiteracy.[136]

93. The right of each person to culture is only assured if cultural freedom is respected. Too often culture is debased by ideology, and education is turned into an instrument at the service of political or economic power. It is not within the competence of the public authorities to determine culture. Their function is to promote and protect the cultural life of everyone, including that of minorities.[137]

94. The task of educating belongs fundamentally and primarily to the family. The function of the state is subsidiary: Its role is to guarantee, protect, promote and supplement. Whenever the state lays claim to an educational monopoly, it oversteps its rights and offends justice. It is parents who have the right to choose the school to which they send their children and the right to set up and support educational centers in accordance with their own beliefs. The state cannot, without injustice, merely tolerate so-called private schools. Such schools render a public service and therefore have a right to financial assistance.[138]

95. The education which gives access to culture is also education in the responsible exercise of freedom. That is why there can only be authentic development in a social and political system which respects freedoms and fosters them through the participation of everyone. This participation can take different forms; it is necessary in order to guarantee a proper pluralism in institutions and in social initiatives. It ensures, notably by the real separation between the powers of the state, the exercise of human rights, also protecting them against possible abuses on the part of the public powers. No one can be excluded from this participation in social and political life for reasons of sex, race, color, social condition, language or religion.[139] Keeping people on the margins of cultural, social and political life constitutes in many nations one of the most glaring injustices of our time.

When the political authorities regulate the exercise of freedoms, they cannot use the pretext of the demands of public order and security in order to curtail those freedoms systematically. Nor can the alleged principle of national security, or a narrowly economic outlook or a totalitarian concept of social life prevail over the value of freedom and its rights.[140]

96. Faith inspires criteria of judgment, determining values, lines of thought and patterns of living which are valid for the whole human community.[141] Hence the church, sensitive to the anxieties of our age, indicates the lines of a culture in which work would be recognized in its full human dimension and in which all would find opportunities for personal self-fulfillment. The church does this by virtue of her missionary outreach for the integral salvation of the world, with respect for the identity of each people and nation.

The church, which is a communion which unites diversity and unity through its presence in the whole world, takes from every culture the positive elements which she finds there. But inculturation is not simply an outward adaptation; it is an intimate transformation of authentic cultural values by their integration into Christianity and the planting of Christianity in the different human cultures.[142] Separation between the Gospel and culture is a tragedy of which the problems mentioned are a sad illustration. A generous effort to evangelize cultures is therefore necessary. These cultures will be given fresh life by their encounter with the Gospel. But this encounter presupposes that the Gospel is truly proclaimed.[143] Enlightened by the Second Vatican Council, the church wishes to devote all her energies to this task, so as to evoke an immense liberating effort.

Conclusion

97. "Blessed is she who believed" (Lk 1:45). At Elizabeth's greeting, the heart of the mother of God would burst into the song of the Magnificat.

It tells us that it is by faith and in faith like that of Mary that the people of God express in words and translate into life the mysterious plan of salvation with its liberating effects upon individual and social existence. It is really in the light of faith that one comes to understand how salvation history is the history of liberation from evil in its most radical form and of the introduction of humanity into the true freedom of the children of God. Mary is totally dependent on her Son and completely directed toward him by the impulse of her faith; and, at his side, she is the most perfect image of freedom and of the liberation of humanity and of the universe. It is to her as mother and model that the church must look in order to understand in its completeness the meaning of her own mission.

It is altogether remarkable that the sense of faith found in the poor leads not only to an acute perception of the mystery of the redeeming cross but also to a love and unshakable trust in the mother of the Son of God, who is venerated in so many shrines.

98. Pastors and all those who, as priests, laity or men and women religious, often work under very difficult conditions for evangelization and integral human advancement should be filled with hope when they think of the amazing resources of holiness contained in the living faith of the people of God. These riches of the *sensus fidei* must be given the chance to come to full flowering and bear abundant fruit. To help the faith of the poor to express itself clearly and to be translated into life through a profound meditation on the plan of salvation as it unfolds itself in the Virgin of the Magnificat—this is a noble ecclesial task which awaits the theologian.

Thus a theology of freedom and liberation which faithfully echoes Mary's Magnificat preserved in the church's memory is something needed by the times in which we are living. But it would be criminal to take the energies of popular piety and misdirect them toward a purely earthly plan of liberation, which would very soon be revealed as nothing more than an illusion and a cause of new forms of slavery. Those who in this way surrender to the ideologies of the world and to the alleged necessity of violence are no longer being faithful to hope, to hope's boldness and courage, as they are extolled in the hymn to the God of mercy which the Virgin teaches us.

99. The *sensus fidei* grasps the very core of the liberation accomplished by the Redeemer. It is from the most radical evil, from sin and the power of death, that he has delivered us in order to restore freedom to itself and to show it the right path. This path is marked out by the supreme commandment, which is the commandment of love.

Liberation in its primary meaning, which is salvific, thus extends into a liberating task, as an ethical requirement. Here is to be found the social doctrine of the church, which illustrates Christian practice on the level of society.

The Christian is called to act according to the truth[144] and thus to work for the establishment of that "civilization of love" of which Pope Paul VI spoke.[145] The present document, without claiming to be complete, has indicated some of the directions in which it is urgently necessary to undertake in-depth reforms. The primary task, which is a condition for the success of all the others, is an educational one. The love which guides commitment must henceforth bring into being new forms of solidarity. To the accomplishment of these tasks urgently facing the Christian conscience, all people of good will are called.

It is the truth of the mystery of salvation at work today in order to lead redeemed humanity toward the perfection of the kingdom which gives true meaning to the necessary efforts for liberation in the economic, social and political orders and which keeps them from falling into new forms of slavery.

100. It is true that before the immensity and the complexity of the task, which can require the gift of self even to a heroic degree, many are tempted to discouragement, skepticism or the recklessness of despair. A formidable challenge is made to hope, both theological and human. The loving Virgin of the Magnificat, who enfolds the church and humanity in her prayer, is the firm support of hope. For in her we contemplate the victory of divine love which no obstacle can hold back, and we discover to what sublime freedom God raises up the lowly. Along the path which she shows us, the faith which works through love must go forward with great resolve.[146]

During an audience granted to the undersigned prefect, His Holiness Pope John Paul II approved this instruction, adopted it in an ordinary session of the Congregation for the Doctrine of the Faith, and ordered it to be published.

Given at Rome, from the congregation, March 22, 1986, the solemnity of the annunciation of our Lord.

Cardinal Joseph Ratzinger, *prefect*
Archbishop Alberto Bovone, *secretary*

Notes to Appendix

1. Congregation for the Doctrine of the Faith, *Instruction on Certain Aspects of the Theology of Liberation (Libertatis Nuntius)*, Introduction: AAS 76 (1984), pp. 876-877.

2. Cf. *Gaudium et Spes* and *Dignitatis Humanae* of Vatican Council II; the encyclicals *Mater et Magistra, Pacem in Terris, Populorum Progressio, Redemptor Hominis* and *Laborem Exercens;* the apostolic exhortations *Evangelii Nuntiandi* and *Reconciliatio et Paenitentia;* the apostolic letter *Octogesima Adveniens*. Pope John Paul II dealt with this theme in his opening address to the Third General Conference of the

Latin American Episcopate at Puebla: AAS 71 (1979), pp. 187-205. He has returned to it on numerous other occasions. The theme has also been dealt with at the Synod of Bishops in 1971 and 1974. The Latin American episcopal conferences have made it the immediate object of their reflections. It has also attracted the attention of other episcopal conferences, as for example the French: *Libération des hommes et salut en Jesus-Christ,* 1975.

3. Paul VI, apostolic letter *Octogesima Adveniens,* 1-4: AAS 63 (1971), pp. 401-404.

4. Cf. Jn 4:42; 1 Jn 4:14.

5. Cf. Mt 28:18-20; Mk 16:15.

6. *Dignitatis Humanae,* 10.

7. Paul VI, apostolic exhortation *Evangelii Nuntiandi,* 78-80: AAS 68 (1976), pp. 70-75; *Dignitatis Humanae,* 3; John Paul II, encyclical *Redemptor Hominis,* 12: AAS 71 (1979), pp. 278-281.

8. Cf. *Libertatis Nuntius,* XI, 10.

9. Cf. John Paul II, *Redemptor Hominis,* 17; discourse of 10 March 1984, to the Fifth Conference of Jurists: *L'Osservatore Romano,* 11 March 1984, p. 8.

10. Cf. *Libertatis Nuntius,* XI, 5; John Paul II, opening address at Puebla.

11. Cf. *Gaudium et Spes,* 36.

12. Cf. ibid.

13. Cf. ibid., 41.

14. Cf. Mt 11:25; Lk 10:21.

15. Cf. *Evangelii Nuntiandi,* 48.

16. Cf. *Libertatis Nuntius,* VII, 9; VIII, 1-9.

17. Cf. Gn 1:26.

18. *Redemptor Hominis,* 21.

19. Cf. Rom 6:6; 7:23.

20. Cf. Gn 2:18-23, "It is not good that man should be alone. . . . This is flesh of my flesh and bone of my bones": In these words of Scripture, which refer directly to the relationship between man and woman, one can discern a more universal meaning. Cf. Lv 19:18.

21. Cf. John XXIII, encyclical *Pacem in Terris,* 5-15: AAS 55 (1963), pp. 259-265; John Paul II, letter to Dr. Kurt Waldheim, secretary general of the United Nations, on the 30th anniversary of the Universal Declaration on Human Rights: AAS 71 (1979), p. 122; the pope's speech to the United Nations, 9: AAS 71 (1979), p. 1149.

22. Cf. St. Augustine, *Ad Macedonium,* II, 7-17 (PL 33, 669-673); CSEL 44, 437-447).

23. Cf. Gn 1:27-28.

24. Cf. *Redemptor Hominis,* 15.

25. Cf. *Gaudium et Spes,* 13.1.

26. Cf. John Paul II, *Reconciliatio et Paenitentia,* 13: AAS 77 (1985), pp. 208-211.

27. Cf. Gn 3:16-19; Rom 5:12; 7:14-24; Paul VI, *Sollemnis Professio Fidei,* 30 June 1968, 16: AAS 60 (1968), p. 439.

28. Cf. Rom 1:18-32.

29. Cf. Jer 5:23; 7:24; 17:9; 18:12.

30. Cf. St. Augustine, *De Civitate Dei*, XIV, 28 (PL 41, 435; CSEL 40-2, 56-57; CCL 14-2, 451-452).

31. Cf. *Libertatis Nuntius*, Introduction.

32. Cf. Is 41:14; Jer 50:34. *Goel:* This word implies the idea of a bond of kinship between the one who frees and the one who is freed. Cf. Lv 25:25; 47-49; Ru 3:12; 4:1. *Padah* means "to obtain for oneself." Cf. Ex 13:13; Dt 9:26; 15:15; Ps 130:7-8.

33. Cf. Gn 12:1-3.

34. Cf. *Libertatis Nuntius*, IV, 3.

35. Cf. Dt 6:5.

36. Cf. Lv 19:18.

37. Cf. Dt 1:16-17; 16:18-20; Jer 22:3-15; 23:5; Ps 33:5; 72:1, 99:4.

38. Cf. Ex 22:20-23; Dt 24:10-22.

39. Cf. Jer 31:31-34; Ez 36:25-27.

40. Is 11:1-5; Ps 72:4, 12-14; *Libertatis Nuntius*, IV, 6.

41. Cf. Ex 23:9; Dt 24:17-22.

42. Cf. Pss 25, 31, 35, 55; *Libertatis Nuntius*, IV, 5.

43. Cf. Jer 11:20; 20:12.

44. Cf. Ps 73:26-28.

45. Cf. Pss 16, 62, 84.

46. Cf. Zep 3:12-20; *Libertatis Nuntius*, IV, 5.

47. Cf. Lk 1:46-55.

48. Cf. Paul VI, apostolic exhortation *Marialis Cultus*, 37: AAS 66 (1974), pp. 148-149.

49. Cf. Acts 2:39; Rom 10:12; 15:7-12; Eph 2:14-18.

50. Cf. Mk 1:15.

51. Cf. Is 61:9.

52. Cf. 2 Cor 8:9.

53. Cf. Mt 25:31-46; Acts 9:4-5.

54. Cf. *Libertatis Nuntius*, IV, 9.

55. Cf. opening address at Puebla, I, 5.

56. Cf. Rom 5:10; 2 Cor 5:18-20.

57 Cf. Jn 14:27.

58. Cf. Mt 5:9; Rom 12:18; Heb 12:14.

59. Cf. 1 Cor 15:26.

60. Cf. Jn 12:31; Heb 2:14-15.

61. Cf. Eph 6:11-17.

62. Cf. Rom 8:37-39.

63. Cf. Rom 8:2.

64. Cf. 1 Tm 1:8.

65. Cf. Rom 13:8-10.

66. Cf. Rom 13:1-7.

67. Cf. Rom 8:2-4.

68. Cf. Rom 13:1.

69. Cf. Rom 13:8-10; Gal 5:13-14.

70. Cf. Mt 5:43-48; Lk 6:27-28.

71. Cf. Lk 10:25-37.

72. Cf. for example 1 Thes 2:7-12; Phil 2:1-4; Gal 2:12-20; 1 Cor 13:4-7; 2 Jn 12; 3 Jn 14; Jn 11:1-5, 35-36; Mk 6:34; Mt 9:36; 18:21 ff.

73. Cf. Jn 15:12-13; 1 Jn 3:16.

74. Cf. Jas 5:1-4.

75. Cf. 1 Jn 3:17.

76. Cf. 1 Cor 11:17-34; *Libertatis Nuntius,* IV, 11. St. Paul himself organizes a collection for the "poor among the saints at Jerusalem" (Rom 15:26).

77. Cf. Rom 8:11-21.

78. Cf. 2 Cor 1:22.

79. Cf. Gal 4:26.

80. Cf. 1 Cor 13:12; 2 Cor 5:10.

81. Cf. Jn 3:2.

82. *Gaudium et Spes,* 39.2.

83. Cf. ibid., 39.3.

84. Cf. Mt 24:29-44, 46; Acts 10:42; 2 Cor 5:10.

85. Cf. *Gaudium et Spes,* 42.2.

86. Cf. Jn 17:3.

87. Cf. Rom 6:4; 2 Cor 5:17; Col 3:9-11.

88. Cf. *Evangelii Nuntiandi,* 18 and 20.

89. Cf. Mt 5:3.

90. Cf. *Gaudium et Spes,* 37.

91. Cf. *Lumen Gentium,* 17; *Ad Gentes,* 1; *Evangelii Nuntiandi,* 14.

92. *Gaudium et Spes,* 40.3.

93. Cf. *Reconciliatio et Paenitentia,* 14.

94. Cf. *Libertatis Nuntius,* XI, 10.

95. Cf. 2 Cor 8:9.

96. Cf. Lk 2:7; 9:58.

97. Mt 6:19-20, 24-34; 19:21.

98. Cf. Lk 5:11, 28; Mt 19:27.

99. Cf. Is 11:4; 61:1; Lk 4:18.

100. Cf. Lk 19: 1-10; Mk 2:13-17.

101. Cf. Mt 8:6; 14:13-21; Jn 13:29.

102. Cf. Mt 8:17.

103. Cf. *Populorum Progressio,* 12 and 46; document of the Third General Conference of the Latin American Episcopate at Puebla, 476.

104. Cf. Acts 2:44-45.

105. Cf. Second extraordinary synod, Final Report, II, C, 6: *L'Osservatore Romano,* 10 Dec. 1985, p. 7; *Evangelii Nuntiandi,* 58.

106. Cf. Mt 22:37-40; Rom 13:8-10.

107. Cf. *Octogesima Adveniens,* 4; Opening Address at Puebla, III, 7.

108. Cf. *Mater et Magistra,* 235: AAS 53 (1961), p. 461.

109. Cf. *Gaudium et Spes,* 25.

110. Cf. *Mater et Magistra,* 132-133.

111. Cf. Pius XI, encyclical *Quadragesimo Anno*, 79-80: AAS 23 (1931), p. 203; *Mater et Magistra*, 138; *Pacem in Terris*, 74.

112. Cf. *Evangelii Nuntiandi*, 18; *Libertatis Nuntius*, XI, 9.

113. Cf. *Reconciliatio et Paenitentia*, 16.

114. Cf. *Octogesima Adveniens*, 25.

115. Cf. John Paul II, encyclical *Laborem Exercens*, 20: AAS 73 (1981), pp. 629-632; *Libertatis Nuntius*, VII, 8; VIII, 5-9; XI, 11-14.

116. Cf. Mt 5:44; Lk 6:27-28, 35.

117. Cf. *Libertatis Nuntius*, XI, 10.

118. Cf. Puebla Document, 533-534. Cf. John Paul II, homily at Drogheda, 30 Sept. 1979: AAS 71 (1979), pp. 1076-1085.

119. *Populorum Progressio*, 31. Cf. Pius XI, encyclical *Nos es muy conocida:* AAS 29 (1937), pp. 208-209.

120. Cf. *Gaudium et Spes*, 76.3; *Apostolicam Actuositatem*, 7.

121. Cf. ibid., 20.

122. Cf. ibid., 5.

123. Cf. *Laborem Exercens*, 6.

124. Cf. ibid, chapter 5.

125. Cf. ibid., 3; address at Loreto, 10 May 1985: AAS 77 (1985), 967-969.

126. Cf. *Octogesima Adveniens*, 46.

127. Cf. *Laborem Exercens*, 6.

128. Cf. ibid.

129. Cf. John Paul II, apostolic exhortation *Familiaris Consortio* 46: AAS 74 (1982), pp. 137-139; *Laborem Exercens*, 23. Cf. Holy See, Charter of Rights of the Family, art. 12, *L'Osservatore Romano*, 25 Nov. 1983.

130. Cf. *Gaudium et Spes*, 68; *Laborem Exercens*, 15; discourse of 3 July 1980: *L'Osservatore Romano*, 5 July 1980, pp. 1-2.

131. Cf. *Gaudium et Spes*, 69; *Laborem Exercens*, 12 and 14.

132. Cf. *Quadragesimo Anno*, 72; *Laborem Exercens*, 19.

133. Cf. document of the Second General Conference of the Latin American Episcopate at Medellín, Justice, I, 9; Puebla Document 31, 35, 1245.

134. Cf. *Mater et Magistra*, 163; *Populorum Progressio*, 51; John Paul II, discourse to the Diplomatic Corps of 1 Jan. 1986: *L'Osservatore Romano*, 12 Jan. 1986, pp. 4-5.

135. Cf. *Populorum Progressio*, 55.

136. Cf. *Gaudium et Spes*, 60; John Paul II, discourse to UNESCO of 2 June 1980, 8: AAS 72 (1980), pp. 739-740.

137. Cf. *Gaudium et Spes*, 59.

138. Cf. *Gravissimum Educationis*, 3 and 6; Pius XI, encyclical *Divini Illius Magistri*, 28, 38 and 66: AAS 22 (1930), pp. 59, 63 and 68. Cf. Holy See, Charter of Rights of the Family, art. 5.

139. Cf. *Gaudium et Spes*, 29; *Pacem in Terris*, 73-74 and 79.

140. Cf. *Dignitatis Humanae*, 7; *Gaudium et Spes*, 75. Puebla document, 311-314; 317-318; 548.

141. Cf. *Evangelii Nuntiandi*, 19.

142. Cf. Second extraordinary synod, Final Report II, D, 4.

143. Cf. *Evangelii Nuntiandi,* 20.

144. Cf. Jn 3:21.

145. Cf. Paul VI, general audience of 31 Dec. 1975: *L'Osservatore Romano,* 1 Jan. 1976, p. 1. John Paul II took up this idea again in the discourse to the Meeting for Friendship between People of 29 Aug. 1982: *L'Osservatore Romano,* 30-31 Aug. 1982. The Latin American bishops also alluded to this idea in the Message to the Peoples of Latin America, 8, and in the Puebla document, 1188 and 1192.

146. Cf. Gal 5:6.

Chapter Notes

Prologue

1. John L. McKenzie in Quentin Quesnell, *The Gospel of Christian Freedom* (New York: Herder and Herder, 1969), viii.
2. Ibid., viii-ix.
3. U.S. Bishops' Pastoral Message and Letter, "Economic Justice for All: Catholic Social Teaching and the U.S. Economy," *Origins: NC Documentary Service* 16 (November 27, 1986): 408-455.
4. Ibid., no. 252, 436.
5. Ibid., no. 254, 436.
6. Ibid., no. 258, 436.
7. Richard Hofstadter, *Anti-intellectualism in American Life* (New York: Knopf, 1963), 416.

Chapter 1

1. Walter M. Abbott, S.J., *The Documents of Vatican II* (New York: America Press, 1966), 673. I would disagree with Murray on this point, since an equally intense argument on freedom may be found in St. Paul, especially in his letters to the Galatians and to the Corinthians. Cf. Quentin Quesnell, *The Gospel of Christian Freedom* (New York: Herder and Herder, 1969).
2. Ibid., 674. Murray gave his own view of the future argument, which strikes me as somewhat dour: "The issues are many—the dignity of the Christian, the foundations of Christian freedom, its object or content, its limits and their criterion, the measure of its responsible use, its relation to the legitimate use of authority and to the saving counsels of prudence, the perils that lurk in it, and the forms of corruption to which it is prone."
3. Richard J. Regan, *Conflict and Consensus: Religious Freedom and the Second Vatican Council* (New York: Macmillan, 1967), 155.
4. Donald E. Pelotte, *John Courtney Murray: Theologian in Conflict* (New York: Paulist Press, 1975), 105. For another detailed view of Murray's thought, see J. Leon Hooper, *The Ethics of Discourse: The Social Philosophy of John Courtney Murray* (Washington, D.C.: Georgetown University Press, 1986).
5. Ibid., 187.

6. John Courtney Murray, ed., *Freedom and Man* (New York: P.J. Kenedy, 1965), 12.

7. John Courtney Murray, "Freedom in the Age of Renewal," *American Benedictine Review* 18,3 (September 1967): 319.

8. Ibid., 320.

9. Ibid

10. Ibid, 322.

11. Ibid.

12. Ibid., 323.

13. Charles E. Curran, *Directions in Catholic Social Ethics* (Notre Dame, Ind.: University of Notre Dame Press, 1985), 45.

14. Ibid., 47 and 43. Curran notes that this shift in methodology is apparent above all in the four chapters of Part I of *Gaudium et Spes*. In the overall context of this book, he relates the change to liberation theology as follows: "One of the best illustrations of this change has been the liberation theology which arose in Latin America in the light of the conciliar development and as a response to the distinctive characteristics of Latin American life. Liberation theology strongly insists that not only must the gospel message of redemption and freedom affect souls and the spiritual dimension of human existence but the gospel also is a call to liberation from oppression and injustice in all the spheres of human existence, including the political, the social, the cultural, and the economic" (48-49).

15. Murray, "Freedom in the Age of Renewal," 324.

16. John Courtney Murray, *The Problem of Religious Freedom* (Westminster, Md.: Newman Press, 1965), 100.

17. Ibid., 82.

18. Ibid.

19. Murray, "Freedom in the Age of Renewal," 320.

20. Murray, *Freedom and Man*, 15.

21. Ibid., 13.

22. David Hollenbach, "Public Theology in America: Some Questions for Catholicism after John Courtney Murray," *Theological Studies* 37 (June 1976): 300.

23. Curran, *Directions in Catholic Social Ethics,* 67.

24. Charles E. Curran, *American Catholic Social Ethics: Twentieth Century Approaches* (Notre Dame, Ind.: University of Notre Dame Press, 1982), 232.

25. Ibid., 226.

26. Ibid., 232. Curran's further comments in this area are, to say the least, thought-provoking: "The danger of Murray is to forget the sinful and to accept the existing reality as an expression of the natural which is not infected by sin. From a philosophical perspective the American Jesuit puts great stress on reason, order, and harmony. However, human problems are rooted not only in the intelligence but also in the will. It is not enough merely to know what is the right thing to do. His overly intellectual approach, together with his failure to stress grace, helps to explain the failure to stress the need for a change of heart on the part of all if there is to be true justice and peace in our world. Likewise, his highly rational approach does not give enough importance to the realities of power and conflict in all their ramifications."

27. Ibid., 231.

28. Pelotte, *Theologian in Conflict,* 187.
29. One observation of Pelotte in this area, however, remains very apropos. After noting that Murray's vindication at the Second Vatican Council came only after the solid and enthusiastic support of the American bishops, he asserts: "His experience points to the need for hierarchical sensitivity to the importance of intellectual freedom in scholarly research. Excellence is needed for the emergence of new ideas, new techniques, and new answers in response to both old and new questions. The Church is thus in need of scholarly masters with intellects stimulated by an atmosphere of faith and trust, and free to range widely in their theological task" (ibid., 188).
30. Ibid., 190.
31. Abbott, *The Documents of Vatican II,* 674. In another text, Murray expresses this even more candidly: "Its achievement was simply to bring the Church abreast of the developments that have occurred in the secular world. The fact is the right to religious freedom has already been accepted and affirmed by the common consciousness of mankind" (Pelotte, *Theologian in Conflict,* 100).
32. John Courtney Murray, "Freedom, Authority, Community," *America* (December 3, 1966): 734-41.
33. Ibid., 734.
34. Ibid., 736.
35. Ibid., 737.
36. Ibid., 740.
37. Ibid., 741.
38. Ibid., 740.

Chapter 2

1. Karl Rahner, "Towards a Fundamental Theological Understanding of Vatican II," *Theological Studies* 40 (December 1979): 716-27.
2. Ibid., 722.
3. Ibid., 717.
4. Alfred T. Hennelly, S.J., "Today's New Task: Geotheology," *America* (18 January 1975): 27-29. This was developed at greater length in "The Challenge of Juan Luis Segundo," *Theological Studies* 38 (March 1977): 125-35 and in "Who Does Theology in the Americas?" *America* (20 September 1975): 137-39.
5. Walter Buhlmann, *The Coming of the Third Church: An Analysis of the Present and Future of the Church* (Maryknoll, N.Y.: Orbis Books, 1976), 4. The Italian edition of this book, entitled *La Terza Chiesa alle porte,* was published in 1974.
6. *La Voz de los Sin Voz: La Palabra Viva de Monseñor Romero* (San Salvador: UCA Editores, 1980).
7. Sergio Torres and Virginia Fabella, eds. (Maryknoll, N.Y.: Orbis Books, 1978). The conference which this book describes took place at Dar es Salaam, Tanzania, 5-12 August 1976.
8. Virginia Fabella and Sergio Torres, eds. (Maryknoll, N.Y.: Orbis Books, 1983). This conference took place at New Delhi, India, 17-29 August 1981, and represented the fifth meeting of the Ecumenical Association of Third World Theologians (EATWOT).

9. Quoted in *The New York Times* (12 July 1987), A4.

10. Segundo has explained the reasons for his position in "Les Deux Théologies de la Libération en Amérique Latine," *Études* 361/3 (September 1984): 149-61.

11. William K. Tabb, ed., *Churches in Struggle: Liberation Theologies and Social Change in North America* (New York: Monthly Review Press, 1986), xv.

12. Good examples of Metz's work are to be found in: *Faith in History and Society* (New York: Seabury Press, 1980) and *The Emergent Church* (New York: Crossroad, 1981). In stressing the originality of the Latin Americans, I do not mean to denigrate Metz, whom I consider to be the most creative among contemporary European theologians. An interesting recent interpretation of Metz, Moltmann, Gutiérrez, and Míguez Bonino may be found in Rebecca S. Chopp, *The Praxis of Suffering: An Interpretation of Liberation and Political Theologies* (Maryknoll, N.Y.: Orbis Books, 1986). Chopp concludes after a careful survey of both theologies: "Liberation theology, in sum, both continues and radically departs from modern theology. As a continuation, liberation theology represents a radical engagement of Christianity with the world, with the intent to represent human freedom and God's gratuitous activity in the questions and issues of the day. As a radically new paradigm and departure from modern theology, liberation theology reflects and guides a Christianity that is identified with those who suffer, that represents a freedom of transformation, and that proclaims a God whose love frees us for justice and faith" (153). This appears to be in agreement with my views later on in this chapter.

13. Conor Cruise O'Brien, "God and Man in Nicaragua," *The Atlantic Monthly* (August 1986): 57.

14. The undated publication of Patmos Verlag also noted in large type that "Ab Frühjahr 1987 erscheint die lange erwartete, auf insgesamt 53 Bände angelegte BIBLIOTHEK THEOLOGIE DER BEFREIUNG das grosse Basiswerk lateinamerikanischer Theologie."

15. All quotes in the text are from Gregory Baum, "Liberation Theology and Marxism," *The Ecumenist* (January-February 1987): 22. Baum's concluding answer to the relationship mentioned in the title of the above article is quite interesting: "We conclude from this brief discussion that liberation theology has engaged in critical dialogue with Marxism, that it has enriched, through the dialogue, the understanding of biblical categories and Christian doctrine, but that its reliance on Marxism is only in the area of social analysis, and even there this reliance is tangential" (ibid., 26). Another appropriate description of liberation theology has been provided in a valuable general introduction to liberation theology by Phillip Berryman, *Liberation Theology: The Essential Facts about the Revolutionary Movement in Latin America and Beyond* (New York: Pantheon Books, 1987): "1) An interpretation of Christian faith out of the suffering, struggle, and hope of the poor; 2) A theological critique of society and its ideological underpinnings; 3) A critique of the practice of the church and of Christians" (205).

16. Enrique Dussel, "Sobre la Historia de la Teología en América Latina," in *Liberación y cautiverio: Debates en torno al método de la teología en América latina* (Mexico City: Comité Organizador, 1976), 19-68. Dussel is sometimes considered a

liberation theologian, as in the work of Michael Novak, *Will It Liberate? Questions about Liberation Theology* (New York: Paulist, 1986), 106-25. But his work is too rhetorical and simplistic to merit this designation. His real contribution to Latin American thought is through his work as a historian; see, for example, his *A History of the Church in Latin America: Colonialism to Liberation* (Grand Rapids, Mich.: Eerdmans, 1981) and *El Episcopado Latinamericano y la Liberación de los Pobres (1504-1620)* (Mexico City: Centro de Reflexión Teológica, 1979).

17. Dussell, "Sobre la Historia," 35. Dussell includes on pp. 35-37 samples of de Las Casas' fierce condemnation and I will cite several of these. The Dominican preacher referred to "the Conquest" by Spain as "tantos escándalos e infamias de nuestra santa fe, tantos robas, tantas injusticias, tantos estragos, tantas matanzas, tantos cautiverios, tantas usurpaciones de estado y señorios ajenos, y, finalmente tan universales asolaciones y despoblaciones. . . . " Calling this "pecado y gravisima injusticia," de las Casas does not hesitate to conclude regarding a just war by the Indians: "[porque] las gentes naturales de todas las partes cualquiera de ellas donde habemos entrado en las Indias tienen derecho adquirido de hacernos guerra justísima y raernos de ha haz de la tierra, y este derecho les durará hasta el día del Juicio."

18. An excellent historical and theological study on these communities has recently been published by Marcello de C. Azevedo, *Basic Ecclesial Communities in Brazil: The Challenge of a New Way of Being Church* (Washington, D.C.: Georgetown University Press, 1987).

19. Juan Luis Segundo, *El hombre de hoy ante Jesús de Nazaret: I. Fe e ideologia; II/1. Historia y actualidad: Sinópticos y Pablo; II/2. Las cristologias en la espiritualidad* (Madrid: Ediciones Cristiandad, 1982). The English translation is being published in five volumes under the general title *Jesus of Nazareth Yesterday and Today* (Maryknoll, N.Y.: Orbis Books, 1984-).

20. Juan Luis Segundo, *Etapas precristianos de la fe: Evolución de la idea de Dios en el Antiguo Testamento* (Montevideo: Cursos de Complementación Cristiana, 1962). The lectures presented in this volume were first given in 1959.

21. Segundo, *The Shift within Latin American Theology* (Toronto: Regis College Press, 1982), 2.

22. Ibid., 3. Segundo includes at this point a comment regarding ideology-criticism which sheds some light on the hotly debated issue of the relation between liberation theology and Marxist thought: "It was not, of course, necessary to be a Marxist to make such a common sense discovery, but it is also true that many Christian students at the university were led by their Marxist fellows to this realization and to be concerned with this fact."

23. *The Liberation of Theology* (Maryknoll, N.Y.: Orbis Books, 1976), 40.

24. Roger Haight, *An Alternative Vision: An Interpretation of Liberation Theology* (New York: Paulist Press, 1985), 15-24. Haight's approach is systematic and synchronic; for a historical and diachronic view, see Roberto Olivares Maqueo, *Liberación y Teología: Génesis y Crecimiento de una Reflexión (1966-1976)* (Mexico City: Centro de Reflexión Teológica, 1977).

25. This American characteristic is analyzed and criticized in an excellent recent study by Robert Bellah et al., *Habits of the Heart: Individualism and Commitment in American Life* (Berkeley: University of California Press, 1985).

26. General use of this term is usually attributed to the influential work of Peter Berger and Thomas Luckman, *The Social Construction of Reality: A Treatise in the Sociology of Knowledge* (Garden City, N.Y.: Doubleday Anchor, 1967).

27. Richard Hofstadter, *The Paranoid Style in American Politics and Other Essays* (New York: Alfred Knopf, 1965), 3-40.

28. Arthur F. McGovern, *Marxism: An American Christian Perspective* (Maryknoll, N.Y.: Orbis Books, 1980). See especially his comments on liberation theology's relation to Marxism in pp. 172-203.

29. Sobrino used this example in a conversation during a visit he made to the Woodstock Theological Center, Washington, D.C., in 1982.

30. The best recent example of such a spirituality of liberation theology is the book by Gustavo Gutiérrez, *We Drink from Our Own Wells: The Spiritual Journey of a People* (Maryknoll, N.Y.: Orbis Books, 1984). But note the books published a decade before this by Segundo Galilea: *Contemplación y apostolado* (Bogotá: Indo-American Press, 1972) and *Espiritualidad de la liberación* (Santiago: ISPAJ, 1973).

31. Ignacio Ellacuria, *Freedom Made Flesh: The Mission of Christ and His Church* (Maryknoll, N.Y.: Orbis Books, 1976), 148.

32. Ibid., 146.

33. The text I am referring to here is the English translation issued by *Origins: NC Documentary Service* 15 (17 April 1986): 713-27.

34. Suggestions on what this document should mean for a U.S. theology of liberation, as well as an analysis of the rest of the Instruction, may be found in my article "The Red-Hot Issue: Liberation Theology," *America* (24 May 1986): 425-28.

35. The pope's address, entitled "Giant Brazil at a Crossroads," was published in *Origins: NC Documentary Service* 15 (3 April 1986): 681-85. The quotes referred to in the text are from p. 684. Pope John Paul also noted that "my hopes and prayers—and I am sure that they are also those of everyone—are that out of the reflection of these days—dispassionate, fraternal—may come a more lively awareness of the positive elements of a legitimate 'theology of liberation'." From the next document it appears that his prayer was answered.

36. My quotes are from the "Pope's Letter to Brazilian Episcopal Conference" in *L'Osservatore Romano* (28 April 1986): 6 and 7.

Chapter 3

1. Juan Luis Segundo, *The Liberation of Theology* (Maryknoll, N.Y.: Orbis Books, 1976), 39-40.

2. Gustavo Gutiérrez, *A Theology of Liberation: History, Politics and Salvation* (Maryknoll, N.Y.: Orbis, 1973).

3. Ibid., 3. In this respect, Peter Hebblethwaite presents the view of Pierre Jossua, a professor at Le Saulchoir, who held that theology was not a specialized activity confined to those who possess scientific competence, "but simply the activity of any true Christian who reflects on his faith and is qualified by the fact that he belongs to the People of God through baptism." Jossua is reported to have gone so far as to say that the idea of a professional theologian, a specialist in God, is

blasphemous. The citation is from *The Runaway Church: Post-Conciliar Growth or Decline* (New York: Seabury, 1975), 110.
4. Gutiérrez, *A Theology of Liberation*, 5.
5. Ibid., 6.
6. Ibid. It is important to note that while he calls his method "new," Gutiérrez insists that it "has its roots in the first centuries of the Church's life," a clear example being Augustine's *City of God.*
7. Ibid., 11. On the previous page, Gutiérrez has an interesting supporting quotation from the distinguished Dutch theologian Edward Schillebeeckx: "And this, it seems to me, has been the greatest transformation which has taken place in the Christian conception of existence. It is evident that thought is also necessary for action. But the Church has for centuries devoted her attention to formulating truths and meanwhile did almost nothing to better the world. In other words, the Church focused on orthodoxy and left orthopraxis in the hands of nonmembers and nonbelievers." The only reference given for this text is Schillebeeckx's article "La Teología," in *Los católicos holandeses* (Bilbao: Desclée de Brouwer, 1970).
8. Gutiérrez, *A Theology of Liberation*, 13.
9. Ibid., 15. For further exemplifications of Gutiérrez's method, see his other books, *Cristianismo y tercer mundo* (Madrid: ZYX, 1973) and *Praxis de liberación y fe cristiana* (Madrid: ZYX, 1974), and the article "Evangelio y praxis de liberación," in *Fe cristiana y cambio social en América Latina: Encuentro de El Escorial, 1972* (Salamanca: Sígueme, 1973), 231-45.
10. Juan Luis Segundo, *The Liberation of Theology* (Maryknoll, N.Y.: Orbis, 1976). Perhaps the best early example of the method may be found in *Concepción cristiana del hombre* (Montevideo: Mimeográfica "Luz," 1964), where he utilizes existentialist and Marxist insights for a reinterpretation of Christian anthropology.
11. *The Liberation of Theology*, 8.
12. Ibid.
13. Ibid., 9.
14. Ibid., 13. A key element in Segundo's quarrel with academic theology is that it "may well be unaware of its unconscious partiality, but the very fact that it poses as something impartial is a sign of its conservative partiality from the very start" (ibid.).
15. Ibid., 28. The reference given is to Cone's *A Black Theology of Liberation* (Philadelphia: Lippincott, 1970), 22.
16. Ibid. Segundo describes this technique more in detail: "In other words, the oppressor constructs an ideological edifice in which the *cause* of the oppressed people's suffering is not even mentioned, much less studied. In this way law, philosophy, and religion join with the mechanism of oppression and become its witting or unwitting accomplices."
17. For a good survey, see T. Howland Sanks and Brian H. Smith, "Liberation Ecclesiology: Praxis, Theory, Praxis," *Theological Studies* 38 (1977): 3-38.
18. Jon Sobrino, "El conocimiento teológico en la teología europea y latinoamericana," *Liberación y cautiverio*, 177-207. The author's caution on this division should be kept in mind throughout, namely, "al hablar de teología 'europea' y 'latinoamericana' estamos dando una definición nominal de dos diversos modos de

concebir el quehacer teológico. Evidentemente no se puede encasillar todo lo que se hace en Europa y en América Latina en esa división" (205). Sobrino is comparing basic tendencies or directions in "progressive" European theology with those of the Latin American "theology of liberation."

19. *Cristología desde América Latina: Esbozo a partir del seguimiento del Jesús Histórico* (Mexico City: Ediciones CRT, 1976). A further clarification of method with specific regard to Christology may be found in pp. 38-43 of this work, "Sobre una cristología latinoamericana." In my opinion, this radical and very original book has not received the attention of specialists in Christology that it deserves. And those interested in spirituality cannot afford to overlook his analysis of the *Spiritual Exercises* of Ignatius Loyola in a final chapter, "El Cristo de los ejercicios espirituales de san Ignacio" (321-46). It may be noted that Sobrino has already complied with the important observation made by David Tracy: "The problem of the contemporary systematic theologian . . . is actually to do systematic theology" (*Blessed Rage for Order: The New Pluralism in Theology* (New York: Seabury, 1975), 238.

20. Sobrino, "El conocimiento teológico," 206.

21. Ibid.

22. Ibid., 192. Charles Davis underlines the same important point in discussing Marx's understanding of praxis: "The common characteristic constituting human activities as *praxis* is their power to transform reality and society and make them more human. Only those activities contributing to the humanization of man are *praxis* in the strict sense" ("Theology and Praxis," *Cross Currents* 23 [1973]: 158).

23. "El conocimiento teológico," 193. Again, a full development and analysis of this idea may be found in Sobrino's Christology, e.g., in "El Jesús histórico como punto de partida de la cristologia" (pp. 9-22). Note that several Western theologians have objected to the term "orthopraxis" and have suggested instead "Christopraxis" or "Christopraxy." See Frederick Herzog in his introduction to Hugo Assmann's *Theology for a Nomad Church* (Maryknoll, N.Y.: Orbis, 1976), 18, and Gerald O'Collins, *The Case against Dogma* (New York: Paulist, 1975), 99.

24. Sobrino refers approvingly to Jürgen Moltmann's influential book, *The Crucified God: The Cross of Christ as the Foundation and Criticism of Christian Theology* (New York: Harper & Row, 1974), noting that the book "marca el momento más importante de la incorporación de la ruptura epistemológica en el conocimiento teológico europeo" ("El conocimiento teológico," 201). Elsewhere, however, he expresses his basic disagreement with Moltmann, as well as with other progressive Europeans such as Metz and Schillebeeckx: "La crítica fundamental desde la teología de la liberación ha sido que esa teología de la praxis sigue siendo abstracta, es decir, pensada más que 'hecha'" (ibid., 194, n. 23). For a sharp rejoinder of Moltmann to his Latin American critics, see his "An Open Letter to José Miguez Bonino," *Christiantiy and Crisis* 36 (1976): 57-63.

25. Sobrino, "El conocimiento teológico," 196.

26. Ibid., 201.

27. Ibid., 202.

28. In the *Concilium* 96 volume, Leonardo Boff stresses this same important point (pp. 90-91). Boff also adopts a dialectical position with regard to various mod-

els of liberation; for he asserts that the Christian "must embrace them with great zeal, because they constitute the Kingdom which is present in the ambiguities of history, and on the other hand, must die to them because they are not the whole liberation or the whole Kingdom" (ibid., 90).

29. Sobrino, "El conocimiento teológico," 207.
30. Cf. n. 22 above.
31. Davis, "Theology and Praxis," 167.
32. Ibid.
33. Matthew Lamb, "The Theory-Praxis Relationship in Contemporary Christian Theologies," Catholic Theological Society of America, *Proceedings of the Thirty-First Annual Convention* (New York: Manhattan College, 1976), 149-78.
34. Ibid., 178.
35. Ibid., 171-72.
36. Ibid., 175.
37. Ibid., 178.
38. David Tracy, *Blessed Rage*, 237-58.
39. Ibid., 240.
40. Ibid., 245-46.
41. An excellent example of such a critique is found in Sobrino's Christology in the chapter "El Jesús histórico y el Cristo de la fe: Tensión entre fe y religión" (221-55).
42. Tracy, *Blessed Rage*, 28.
43 Avery Dulles, "Method in Fundamental Theology," 316. See also the review of Tracy's book by Charles Davis, where he observes: "If actual experience in its social and cultural diversity becomes the point of reference, then theology's concern with *praxis* cannot be left to the last chapter. To see the task of constructing present meaning in fundamental and systematic theology and the task of reconstructing past meaning in historical theology as both preceding the concern with the future in practical theology is to miss the implications of man's becoming in history and the mediation of truth through history" (*Commonweal* 103 [1976]: 152).
44. Tracy, *Blessed Rage*, 240.
45. Also, I am unable to find in Tracy's work any evidence of the "epistemological break" emphasized by Sobrino. Once again, Dulles highlights the key issue: "The method of correlation, as Tracy describes it, seems to be a one-way process, in which the Christian positions are shown to be consonant with the secular vision of life. I doubt whether anyone is likely to become a Christian simply in order to have his secular faith elucidated or expressed by better symbols. Heretofore Christianity has been thought to be capable of offering a new message and of correcting and transforming any vision of reality attainable apart from Christianity itself" ("Method," 310).
46. Baum, *Religion and Alienation*, 194.
47. Ibid., 197.
48. Ibid., 220.
49. Ibid. Baum was a participant in a week-long conference with Latin American theologians and social scientists in August, 1975. He has presented an account of the conference and an elaboration of his own views on different social

analyses in "The Christian Left at Detroit," *Ecumenist* 13 (1975): 81-100. I presented my views on the conference in "Who Does Theology in the Americas?" *America* 133 (1975): 37-39.

50. Leonardo Boff refers to the whole of Latin American culture, including religion, as a "realidad espejo" and not a "fuente," in *Liberación y cautiverio*, 136-37.

51. Regarding this problematic, Matthew Lamb quotes the interesting observation of Bernard Lonergan that "it is only after the age of innocence has passed that praxis is accorded serious academic attention" (Lamb, "The Theory-Praxis Relationship," 172).

52. The incident is related by Juan Carlos Scannone in *Fe cristiana*, 356. Monika Hellwig has suggested a perspective similar to mine: "Liberation theology has been taken by some as a new attempt at political ethics, and therefore as a branch of applied theology. The liberation theologians do not accept this, but claim to be working with a perspective, or focus, or framework for the asking of all theological questions" ("Liberation Theology: An Emerging School," *Scottish Journal of Theology* 30 [1976]: 142).

53. Joseph P. Fitzpatrick, "Justice as a Problem of Culture," *Studies in the International Apostolate of Jesuits* 5 (December 1976): 28. Fitzpatrick goes on to note that "this problem became aggravated in the last century and the early part of this century because we tended with our theological and philosophical systems to identify many of our cultural definitions as the natural law" (p. 29). Rosemary Ruether has also pointed out that "for Christians, the contribution of Latin America is unique because it is the only region in the world where a predominantly Christian people are aligned with the revolutionary development of the Third World" (*Liberation Theology: Human Hope Confronts Christian History and American Power* [New York: Paulist, 1972], 176).

54. The article appears in *The Faith That Does Justice: Examining the Christian Sources for Social Change*, ed. John C. Haughey (New York: Paulist, 1977), 10-46. Another good example of sympathetic dialogue, from a Protestant perspective, may be found in John C. Bennett's *The Radical Imperative: From Theology to Social Ethics* (Philadelphia: Westminster, 1975), 131-41.

55. E.g., Dulles observes that "the liberationist stress on external activity and social involvement runs the risk of minimizing the dimension of interiority in the life of faith," and that "in the liberation theologians I have read, there is no adequate study of the psychological complexity of the act of faith" ("The Meaning of Faith," 39-40).

56. Gregory Baum, "The Impact of Sociology on Catholic Theology," Catholic Theological Society of America, *Proceedings of the Thirtieth Annual Convention* (New York: Manhattan College, 1975), 23. A classic in introducing theologians to this area is *The Social Construction of Reality: A Treatise in the Sociology of Knowledge* (New York: Doubleday, 1966), by Peter L. Berger and Thomas Luckman.

57. For example, one could wish to contribute to a sincere but in fact overly privatized spiritual theology. This would clearly be amenable to those who profit from an unjust system or practice. Bluntly put, it would keep the natives from getting restless about such matters and suit the interests of those who are profiting.

58. Edward Schillebeeckx, "Critical Theories and Christian Political Commitment," in *Political Commitment and Christian Community* (*Concilium* 84; New York: Herder and Herder, 1974), 50. He notes that the reverse is equally true, that "Christianity has also become incredible to those who, against all Christian reason, persist in maintaining their established positions in society" (ibid.).

59. The urgency of the task is seen graphically by a perusal of *The Gospel of Peace and Justice: Catholic Social Teaching since Pope John* (Maryknoll, N.Y.: Orbis, 1976), compiled by Joseph Gremillion.

60. Pierre Teilhard de Chardin, "Introduction à la vie chrétienne," 2; cited in Robert L. Faricy, *Teilhard de Chardin's Theology of the Christian in the World* (New York: Sheed and Ward, 1967), 80.

61. Dietrich Bonhoeffer, *Letters and Papers from Prison* (New York: Macmillan, 1967), 161.

Chapter 4

1. An excellent example of the spirited debate concerning the question of criticism among liberation theologians may be found in Hugo Assmann, "Os ardís do amor em busca de sua eficácia," *Perspectiva Teológica* 15 (1983): 223-59. In this article, Assmann takes Juan Luis Segundo to task for a "critica mordaz e irônica" of liberation theologians such as Gustavo Gutiérrez and Jon Sobrino. Segundo promptly replied and defended his position vigorously in "Nota sobre ironias e tristezas," *Perspectiva Teológica* 15 (1983): 385-400.

2. Scannone used this description during a visit he made to Georgetown University, Washington, D.C., in 1983. In my view, his major contribution to the field has been in achieving clarity and logical rigor, but not in original ideas.

3. Juan Carlos Scannone, "La Teología de la Liberación: Caracterización, Corrientes, Etapas," *Separata de Medellín* 9 (June, 1983): 259-88. Other works of Scannone in this area include: "Volksreligiosität, Volksweisheit und Philosophie in Lateinamerika," *Theologische Quartalscrift* 164 (Heft 3, 1984): 203-14; "Theology, Popular Culture, and Discernment," in Rosino Gibellini, ed., *Frontiers of Theology in Latin America* (Maryknoll, N.Y.: Orbis Books, 1979), 213-39. Part 3, "Corrientes y momentos dentro de la Teología de la Liberación," extends from p. 271 to p. 287.

4. The only representative of this approach named by Scannone is Bishop E. Pironio in his *Escritos pastorales* (Madrid, 1973), 272.

5. Scannone, "La Teología," 271-72. For a good example of a critical dialogue with Marxism, see Juan Luis Segundo, *Faith and Ideologies* (Maryknoll, N.Y.: Orbis Books, 1984), especially "Problematic Aspects of Marxist Thought," 176-247. The author refers to Assmann's book, *Teología desde la praxis de liberación* (Salamanca: Sigueme, 1973). This appeared in English as *Theology for a Nomad Church* (Maryknoll, N.Y.: Orbis Books, 1976). For the Latin American socialist movement, cf. John Eagleson, ed., *Christians and Socialism: Documentation of the Christians for Socialism Movement in Latin America* (Maryknoll, N.Y.: Orbis Books, 1975).

6. Scannone, "La Teología," 273.

7. Cristián Johansson, "Tendencias teológicas en Latinoamérica," *Teología y Vida* 27 (1986): 73-80.

8. Ibid., 74.

9. Indeed, he cites only one article: Ignacio Ellacuría, "Los pobres: Lugar teológico en América Latina," *Diakonía* 21 (April, 1982): 41-57.

10. Johansson, ibid., 76-77. The quotation is from J.C. Scannone, "La relación teoría-praxis en la teología de la liberación," *Christus* 42 (June 1977): 14.

11. Johansson, 77-79. The works cited are: Bonaventure Kloppenburg, "La necessidad del pluralismo eclesial," *Communio* 2 (1983): 44-55; Jon Sobrino, "Unidad y conflicto dentro de la Iglesia," *Fe y solidaridad* (January 1979): 1-23; and Gustavo Gutiérrez, "Teología y ciencias sociales," *Páginas* (September 1984): 4-15.

12. Juan Luis Segundo, "Les deux théologies de la libération en Amérique latine," *Études* 361/3 (September 1984): 121. The English version was published as "The Shift within Latin American Theology" (Toronto: Regis College Press, 1983). All further references are to the English version of the article. Segundo has since published a chapter entitled "Dos teologías de liberación," in *Teología Abierta: III Reflexiones Críticas* (Madrid: Ediciones Cristiandad,1984), 128-59. However, in this chapter he is more concerned with popular religion, and that is not helpful here for my purposes.

13. "Shift," 2.

14. Ibid., 4.

15. Ibid., 8.

16. Leonardo Boff, "Teologia a Escuta do Povo," *Revista Eclesiástica Brasileira* 41 (March 1981): 65.

17. Leonardo Boff, *Eclesiogénese* (Petrópolis: Vozes, 1977); Gustavo Gutiérrez, *La Fuerza Histórica de los Pobres: Selección de Trabajos* (Lima: CEP, 1979). Enrique Dussell also popularized the expression, *the discipleship of the poor.*

18. "Shift," 11.

19. Ibid., 4-5.

20. Ibid., 12.

21. Ibid., 6.

22. Ibid., 18. The book of Sobrino referred to is *Resurrección de la Verdadera Iglesia: Los Pobres, Lugar Teológico de la Eclesiología* (Santander: Sal Terrae, 1981), 21-53.

23. Sobrino, *Resurrección,* 163. Here I have translated Sobrino's text directly from the Spanish version of Segundo's article, "El cambio dentro de la teología Latinoamericana (Dos Etapas)," *Cuadernos de Teología,* 20.

24. Segundo, "Shift," 18.

25. Segundo, "Shift," 14. Probably Segundo is thinking of Boff's books, *Ecclesiogenesis: The Base Communities Reinvent the Church* (Maryknoll, N.Y.: Orbis Books, 1986) and *Church: Charism and Power* (New York: Crossroad, 1985).

26. See chapter 8, "The Vatican and Liberation Theology."

27. See Segundo, *The Liberation of Theology,* chapter 1; and Alfred Hennelly, *Theologies in Conflict,* chapter 6.

28. Segundo, "Perspectivas para uma Teologia Latino-americana," *Perspectiva Teológica* 9 (January-June, 1977): 11.

29. Ibid., 12.

30. Ibid., 15.

31. Ibid., 18.

32. Ibid., 23.

33. Ibid.

34. Ibid.

35. Ibid., 25.

36. Ibid.

37. Monika Hellwig, "Good News to the Poor: Do They Understand It Better?" in James Hug, ed., *Tracing the Spirit: Communities, Social Action, and Theological Reflection* (New York: Paulist Press, 1983), 122-48.

38. Ibid., 145.

Chapter 5

1. For this information, I am dependent on Denis Collins, *Paulo Freire: His Life, Works and Thought* (New York: Paulist Press, 1977), 3-39. See also César Jérez and Juan Hernández-Pico, "Cultural Action for Freedom," in *LADOC Keyhole Series 1* (Washington, D.C.: U.S. Catholic Conference): 29-30.

2. James A. Farmer, Jr., "Adult Education for Transiting," in Stanley Grabowski, ed., *Paulo Freire: A Revolutionary Dilemma for the Adult Educator* (Syracuse, N.Y.: Syracuse University Publications in Continuing Education, 1972), 1. The eyewitness is identified only as an ex-priest who had worked with Freire in South America and contributed this report in a course on adult education at UCLA.

3. Freire, *Pedagogy of the Oppressed* (New York: Seabury Press, 1973), 58.

4. Ibid., 70-71.

5. Paulo Freire, "Cultural Freedom in Latin America," in Louis M. Colonnese, ed., *Human Rights and the Liberation of Man in the Americas* (Notre Dame: University of Notre Dame Press, 1970), 171.

6. Paulo Freire, "Cultural Action and Conscientization," *Harvard Educational Review* 40 (3, 1970): 474.

7. Phillip Berryman, "Popular Catholicism in Latin America," *Cross Currents* 21 (Summer 1971): 298-99.

8. César Jérez and Juan Hernández Pico, "Cultural Action for Freedom," 30.

9. Second General Conference of Latin American Bishops, *The Church in the Present-Day Transformation of Latin America in the Light of the Council: II Conclusions* (Washington, D.C.: U.S. Catholic Conference, 1973), 48 ("Justice," #16-17). The bishops also note the importance of the mass media in this respect, insisting that these are "a necessary and proper instrument for social education and for 'concientización' ordered to changing the structures and the observance of justice" (ibid., 51).

10. Ibid., 62 ("Peace," #18).

11. Ibid., 80-81 ("Education," #3).

12. Gustavo Gutiérrez, *A Theology of Liberation: History, Politics and Salvation* (Maryknoll, N.Y.: Orbis Books, 1973), 91.

13. Ibid., 214. Gutiérrez continues: "This kind of person, whose actions are directed toward a new society yet to be built, is in Latin America more of a motivating ideal than a reality already realized and generalized. But things are moving in this direction. A profound aspiration for the creation of a new man underlies the process of liberation which the continent is undergoing."

14. Ibid., 232-39. The following is a summary of his main ideas: "Utopia necessarily means a denunciation of the existing order. Its deficiencies are to a large extent the reason for the emergence of a utopia. The repudiation of a dehumanizing situation is an unavoidable aspect of utopia. . . . But utopia is also an annunciation, an annunciation of what is not yet, but will be; it is the forecast of a different order of things, a new society. It is the field of creative imagination which proposes the alternative values to those rejected. The denunciation is to a large extent made with regard to the annunciation" (p. 233).

15. Ibid., 92.

16. Juan Luis Segundo, *Our Idea of God* (Maryknoll, N.Y.: Orbis Books, 1974), 174. Note also the explicit link that Segundo envisions between conscientization and evangelization: "An evangelization committed to man's liberation is deeply tied up with the new form of literacy-training: i.e., one incorporated within a process of consciousness-raising. This new form of literacy-training, as a process of liberation, possesses an educational technique in the service of man that is completely similar to those of the evangelization process. *We should not even think of two different processes, but of one single movement for the gradual liberation of man within which evangelization is effected*" (174-75; my italics).

17. Juan Luis Segundo, *The Sacraments Today* (Maryknoll, N.Y.: Orbis Books, 1970), 104. Another text points out more clearly the similarities between Freire's "pedagogy of liberation" and that of the sacraments: "At the very wellspring of Christianity, the sacraments too are a communitarian pedagogy of liberation. So we should not be surprised to find that both pedagogies, to a large extent, formulate the same criticism on the negative side and on the positive side are grounded on the same foundations and constructed by the same methods. Here we shall take over statements from Paulo Freire, simply replacing such terms as *literacy-training, education* and *culture* with the corresponding terms in our discussion: i.e. *sacraments, grace, the Christian task,* etc." (p. 101). See my further discussion of this in *Theologies in Conflict,* 96-98.

18. Quoted in César Jérez and Juan Hernández-Pico, "Cultural Action for Freedom," 30. The authors believe that "this is about as much as Freire has explained his deepest faith." I hope what I am presenting here is evidence that they are wrong, and that Freire has actually explained many other aspects of his Christian faith.

19. Paulo Freire, "Conscientizing as a Way of Liberating," 8.

20. Freire, "The Educating Role of the Churches in Latin America," 16.

21. Freire, "The Third World and Theology," 14. In this same text is an intriguing reference to Freire's role as a theologian: "I am not a theologian but merely an onlooker intrigued by theology, which has indelibly marked what my pedagogy seems to be developing into."

22. Freire, "The Educating Role of the Churches," 27.

23. Freire, "Letter to a Young Theology Student," 12.

24. Freire, "The Third World and Theology," 13.

25. Freire, "The Educational Role of the Churches in Latin America," 15. Note that both the "innocent" and the "astute" are united in their failure to face the social reality: "Those who want the Church and its educational work to be neutral are either totally 'innocent' in their understanding of the Church and of history, or they are 'astute' and are just concealing their real views. Both groups, as a matter of fact, by wanting the Church to adopt such an impossible neutrality toward history, toward political activity, are themselves taking a political stand—in favor of the dominating classes and against the dominated classes."

26. Ibid., 20.

27. Ibid., 23-24.

28. Ibid., 26.

29. Freire, "The Adult Literacy Process as Cultural Action for Freedom," *Harvard Educational Review* 40 (2, 1970): 210. Just before this, Freire attacks a caricature of the marginalized that is quite familiar to us in the First World: "There are many people who consider slum dwellers marginal, intrinsically wicked and inferior. To such people we recommend the profitable experience of discussing the slum situation with slum dwellers themselves. As some of these critics are often simply mistaken, it is possible they may rectify their mythical clichés and assume a more scientific attitude. They may avoid saying that the illiteracy, alcoholism and crime of the slums, that its sickness, infant mortality, learning deficiencies, and poor hygiene reveal the 'inferior nature' of its inhabitants. They may even end up realizing that if intrinsic evil exists it is part of the structures, and that it is the structures that need to be transformed" (ibid., 219).

30. Paulo Freire, "Cultural Action and Conscientization," *Harvard Educational Review* 40 (3, 1970): 468. Note that Freire stresses that "after the revolutionary reality is inaugurated, conscientization continues to be indispensable. Further, it is a force countering the bureaucracy, which threatens to deaden the revolutionary vision and dominate the people in the very name of their freedom. Finally conscientization is a defense against another threat, that of the potential mythification of the technology which the new society requires to transform its backward infrastructure" (ibid., 473).

31. Gustavo Gutiérrez, *A Theology of Liberation: History, Politics and Salvation* (Maryknoll, N.Y.: Orbis Books, 1973).

32. Ibid., 36. Developmentalism, Gutiérrez says in another context, proved ineffective and even counterproductive in accomplishing real change because "the poor countries are becoming ever more clearly aware that their underdevelopment is only the by-product of the kind of relationship which exists between the rich and the poor countries. Moreover, they are realizing that their own development will come about only with a struggle to break the domination of the rich countries" (ibid., 26).

33. Ibid., 36 and 32; italics are the author's. Once again, Gutiérrez refers to the similarity of this view with that of the French Jesuit Pierre Teilhard de Chardin: "Teilhard de Chardin has remarked that man has taken hold of the reins of evolution. History, contrary to essentialist and static thinking, is not the development of

potentialities preexistent in man; it is rather the conquest of new, qualitatively different ways of being a man in order to achieve an ever more total and complete fulfillment of the individual in solidarity with all mankind."
    34. Ibid., 37.

Chapter 6

1. Clodovis Boff, "BECs e Práticas de Libertação," *Revista Eclesiástica Brasileira* 40 (December 1980): 625. Boff and his better known brother, Leonardo, have published a book together called *Salvation and Liberation* (Maryknoll, N.Y.: Orbis Books, 1984).
    2. Books focusing on base communities in Brazil, which has by far the largest number of them, include: A. Barreiro, *Communidades Eclesiales de Base e Evangelização dos Pobres* (São Paulo: Edições Loyola, 1977); C. Boff, *Comunidade Eclesial/ Comunidade Politica* (Petrópolis: Editora Vozes, 1979); R. Caramura de Barros, *Communidade Eclesial de Base: Uma Opção Pastoral Decisiva* (Petrópolis: Editora Vozes, 1967); and P. Demo, *Comunidade: Igreja na Base* (São Paulo: Edições Paulinas, 1974).
    3. Scott Mainwaring, *The Catholic Church and Politics in Brazil 1916-1985* (Stanford: Stanford University Press, 1986), 109. Mainwaring also adds that "the base communities generally sprang from grass-roots pastoral agents. The hierarchy issued documents calling for creation of CEBs, but local-level priests and nuns committed to the ideals of community and greater lay participation actually started them. In São Paulo, according to Archbishop Paulo Evaristo Arns, 'The base communities came from the base. All I did was support the pastoral agents who had already started something new'."
    4. Marcello de C. Azevedo, S.J., *Basic Ecclesial Communities in Brazil: The Challenge of a New Way of Being Church* (Washington, D.C.: Georgetown University Press, 1987), 39.
    5. *The Church in the Present-Day Transformation of Latin America II: Conclusions*, 2nd ed. (Washington: Division for Latin America, U.S.C.C., n.d.), 201.
    6. For the Puebla documents, along with analyses and commentaries, cf. John Eagleson and Philip Scharper, eds., *Puebla and Beyond* (Maryknoll, N.Y.: Orbis Books, 1979). A fine history and analysis of the Puebla conference has been provided by Frei Betto, *17 días de la Iglesia Latino-americana: Diario de Puebla* (Mexico: CRT, 1979).
    7. José Marins, "Basic Ecclesial Community," *UISG Bulletin* (no. 55, 1981): 35. A student of the BECs in Brazil, Thomas E. Bruneau, reaches similar conclusions: "It must be recognized that CEBs are not all of one piece; they vary tremendously from one country or even from one diocese to another . . . and what is being presented here is a general statement reflecting the higher or more defined level of the CEBs": "Basic Christian Communities in Latin America: Their Nature and Significance (especially in Brazil)," in Daniel H. Levine, ed., *Churches and Politics in Latin America* (Beverly Hills, Calif.: Sage Publications, 1979), 226. Also helpful is Thomas C. Bruneau, *Religiosity and Politicization in Brazil* (São Paulo: Edições Loyola, 1979) and *The Church in Brazil: The Politics of Religion* (Austin: Uni-

versity of Texas Press, 1982). Very concrete descriptions and evaluations of how BECs actually function in different national contexts may be found in *LADOC: Basic Christian Communities* (United States Catholic Conference, Washington, D.C.: Latin America Documentation, 1976).

8. Daniel H. Levine, ed., *Religion and Political Conflict in Latin America* (Chapel Hill: University of North Carolina Press, 1986), 247-48. Levine ends his book with a clear summary of the fears on the part of church leaders which will hinder the future development of the popular church: "Those who control the central institutions of Latin American Catholicism (mostly bishops) have many fears relevant to our considerations. They may be placed in rank order. First, they fear being drawn into potentially dangerous political confrontations through the activities of popular groups identified in some way with the church. This is not a major concern, but rather an inconvenience to be avoided if possible. Second, they fear that the growing salience of class-based groups and demands in the church may dilute its spiritual and religious mission, turning it into just another ephemeral pressure group. Third, they fear the consequences of defining a religiously legitimate space for such groups, which would endanger established understandings of authority and undercut the central role of bishops and clergy. Finally, the bishops fear that redefinition of the church's base in class terms effectively precludes appealing to all social groups and bringing all social classes a message of salvation. These fears are understandable. They grow out of the bishops' role as leaders of a large, heterogeneous institution and rest on their concept of the church's core structure and social mission" (250).

9. Gottfried Deelen, "The Church on Its Way to the People: Basic Christian Communities in Brazil," *Pro Mundi Vita Bulletin* 81 (April 1980): 5; cf. also J.B. Libânio, "Experiences with the Base Ecclesial Communities in Brazil," *Missiology: An International Review* (July 1980): 319-38.

10. Carlos Mesters, "The Use of the Bible in Christian Communities of the Common People," in Sergio Torres and John Eagleson, eds., *The Challenge of Basic Christian Communities* (Maryknoll, N.Y.: Orbis Books, 1981), 197-210.

11. Ibid., 199.

12. Ibid., 204-210.

13. Gustavo Gutiérrez, *A Theology of Liberation: History, Politics and Salvation* (Maryknoll, N.Y.: Orbis Books, 1972), 11.

14. Juan Luis Segundo, *The Liberation of Theology* (Maryknoll, N.Y.: Orbis Books, 1976), 7-38. For a discussion of the hermeneutic circle, cf. Alfred T. Hennelly, *Theologies in Conflict: The Challenge of Juan Luis Segundo* (Maryknoll, N.Y.: Orbis Books, 1979), 107-22.

15. Azevedo, *Basic Ecclesial Communities*, 80-81.

16. Ibid., 90. Italics are the author's.

17. Felix A. Pastor, "Evangelização e comunidade de base," in *O reino e a história: Problemas teóricos de uma teologia da praxis* (São Paulo: Ed. Loyola, 1982), 73-74.

18. Azevedo, *Basic Ecclesial Communities*, 83.

19. Ibid., 95. Italics are the author's.

20. Ibid., 96.

21. Ibid., 138.

22. Ibid., 157.

23. Tony Clarke, "Communities for Justice," *The Ecumenist* 19 (January-February 1981): 19.

24. Enrique Dussell, *History and the Theology of Liberation* (Maryknoll, N.Y.: Orbis Books, 1976), 171.

25. Joe Holland and Peter Henriot, *Social Analysis: Linking Faith and Justice* (Washington, D.C.: Center of Concern, 1980), 38.

26. Libânio, "Experiences," 324.

27. *Developing Basic Christian Communities—A Handbook* (National Federation of Priests' Councils, 1979), 1.

28. Ibid., 4.

29. Ibid., 25.

30. Ibid., 46.

31. Ibid., 49-50.

32. Ibid., 59.

33. As a possible pastoral aid in meeting this challenge, I include here the address of the task force that is collecting and distributing information on BCCs in the U.S.: BCC Task Force, NFPC, 1307 South Wabash Avenue, Chicago, IL 60605. A very helpful analysis of BECs has been provided by Kate Pravera in "The United States: Realities and Responses," *Christianity and Crisis* (21 September 1981): 251-55. On the theological level, Avery Dulles has analyzed the model of church for the 1980s as "a community of disciples" in "Imaging the Church for the 1980's," *The Catholic Mind* (November 1981): 9-26. In my judgment, that is exactly what the many BECs around the world are attempting to initiate and to foster.

Chapter 7

1. *Pacem in Terris: Peace on Earth*, in Joseph Gremillion, ed., *The Gospel of Peace and Justice* (Maryknoll, N.Y.: Orbis Books, 1976), no. 9, p. 203.

2. Ibid., no. 10.

3. Juan Luis Segundo, "Derechos humanos, evangelización e ideología," *Christus* 43 (November 1978): 33-34. He also charges that the churches in the rich nations "continue to preach a strange universal good news, without conversion" (ibid., 34).

4. Ignacio Ellacuría, "La Iglesia de los pobres, sacramento histórico de liberación," *Estudios Centroamericanos* (October/November 1977): 717.

5. *Puebla and Beyond: Documentation and Commentary*, John Eagleson and Philip Scharper, eds. (Maryknoll, N.Y.: Orbis Books, 1979), 264. For the Spanish version, see *Puebla: La evangelización en el presente y en el futuro de América Latina* (Bogotá: CELAM, 1979).

6. *Puebla and Beyond*, 267.

7. Segundo Galilea, "The Church in Latin America and the Struggle for Human Rights," *Concilium 124: The Church and the Rights of Man* (New York: Seabury, 1979): 100.

8. Ibid., 101.

9. Ibid., 102.

10. Cf. Adolfo Pérez Esquivel, *Christ in a Poncho: Testimonials of the Nonviolent Struggles in Latin America,* ed. Charles Antoine (Maryknoll, N.Y.: Orbis Books, 1983). This book merely sketches the life of Pérez; I am not aware of any more definitive work.

11. Segundo Galilea, "Human Rights in the Church," 104-05.

12. Hollenbach, *Claims in Conflict,* 204-07.

13. For a good summary of this history, see Jean-Marie Aubert, "Les droits de l'homme interpellent les Églises," *Le Supplément* 141 (May 1982): 149-78. Aubert believes that a clear recognition of church violations of human rights is the best bulwark against repeating such violations in the present and future. Especially useful in this regard is his section entitled "L'Église contre les droits de l'homme?", 154-67.

14. John Langan, "Human Rights in Roman Catholicism," *Journal of Ecumenical Studies* (Summer 1982): 32. See also Bernard Plongeron, "Anathema or Dialogue? Christian Reactions to Declarations of the Rights of Man in the United States and Europe in the Eighteenth Century," *Concilium 124: The Church and the Rights of Man* (New York: Seabury, 1979): 39-48.

15. *Pilgrim of Peace: The Homilies and Addresses of His Holiness Pope John Paul II on the Occasion of His Visit to the United States of America* (Washington, D.C.: U.S. Catholic Conference, 1979), 20.

16. Langan, "Human Rights in Roman Catholicism," 39.

17. Leonardo Boff, *Church: Charism and Power* (New York: Crossroad, 1985), 32. Boff also clearly asserts that "the purpose of this reflection is to foster a greater and more effective authenticity in the commitment of the local churches to human rights; the contradiction in terms of theory and practice is not found within these churches themselves but in their collision with authority" (p. 33).

18. Ibid., 33-36. See also Aubert, "Droits de l'homme," especially the section "Regarder la vérité en face," 149-54; and James Coriden, "Human Rights in the Church: A Matter of Credibility and Authenticity," in *Concilium 124:* 67-76.

19. Note that Boff asserts that "the majority of those in authority in the Church are men of good faith, clear conscience, impeccable personal character"; he then concludes that "the problem lies on a deeper level, on the structure that to a great degree is independent of persons" (p. 39).

20. Ibid., 40.

21. Ibid. Boff goes on to assert that "the Roman and feudal style of power in the Church today, however, constitutes one of the principal sources of conflict with the rising consciousness of human rights" (ibid.). He also believes that "the Second Vatican Council recognized the historicity of the forms of power within the Church and elaborated a theological understanding of authority that was less monarchical and more congenial, in itself paving the way for new structures of participation in ecclesial life" (ibid., 41).

22. Norbert Greinacher, "A Community Free of Rule," in *Concilium 63: Democratization of the Church* (New York: Herder and Herder, 1971): 107.

23. See, for example, Rudolf Pesch, "The New Testament Foundations of a Democratic Form of Life in the Church," *Concilium 63:* 48-59; Karl Lehmann, "On

the Dogmatic Justification for a Process of Democratization in the Church," ibid., 60-86; Charles Wackenheim, "The Theological Meaning of the Rights of Man," ibid., 49-56; and Stephan Pfurtner, "Human Rights in Christian Ethics," ibid., 57-66.

24. Boff, *Church*, 42 and 46.

25. Pedro A. de Achutegui, S.J., ed., *John Paul II in the Philippines: Addresses and Homilies* (Manila: Cardinal Bea Institute, 1981), 5. Italics are in the text.

26. Ibid. Obviously, the fact that the church, too, is a "social organization" that exists for the service of man is a clear teaching of the New Testament.

27. Ibid., 44. Note that Boff (despite his own experiences with the Vatican) remains optimistic: "We must recognize that in the past few years, especially after Vatican II, extremely important steps have been taken. Just as the church previously took on Roman and feudal structures, it is now taking on structures found in today's civil societies that are more compatible with our growing sense of human rights. This is the often argued 'democratization of the church'" (ibid.).

28. See Leonardo Boff, *Ecclesiogenesis: The Base Communities Reinvent the Church* (Maryknoll, N.Y.: Orbis Books, 1986).

29. Boff, *Charism and Power*, 46.

30. Sydney Callahan, "Association for the Rights of Catholics in the Church," *America* (July 19-26, 1986): 22-23. An excellent synthetic statement of this argument has also been advanced by Rosemary Ruether: "Historically, it is evident that the church evolved from a congregational to a hierarchical structure primarily by growing up in and imitating the imperial bureaucracy of the Roman Empire. It further forged this structure by taking on feudal and then absolutist elements in medieval and early modern Europe. The political form of the church is a historical construct influenced by the political systems about it, not a divine given. Theologically, one should at least be able to ask whether a democratic polity would not be a more adequate expression of a community of salvation than one modeled after Roman imperialism, medieval feudalism and Renaissance absolutism" ("Criticisms and Challenges of Catholicism Today," *America* [March 1, 1986]: 152).

Chapter 8

1. The text used here is from *Origins: NC Documentary Service* 15 (17 April 1986): 713-28. In this article, I make no reference to the previous document, entitled "Instruction on Certain Aspects of the 'Theology of Liberation'," since I believe the theology of that document is seriously flawed. A convincing demonstration of this may be found in the book of Juan Luis Segundo, *Theology and the Church* (New York: Seabury, 1985). In a review of Segundo's book, I summarized his achievement as follows: "In brief, there are two major movements in contemporary Catholic thought which his book is aimed at opposing: the negative evaluation of the Second Vatican Council and a similar negative evaluation of the entire postconciliar period. The book, then, rather than being seen as a mere commentary on a curial instruction, will retain enduring value as a formidable bulwark against these subterranean but powerful movements. Or, as Segundo puts it with his usual succinctness, 'This book will have achieved its purpose if it convinces the reader that the implementa-

tion of the Council has not gone too far; that, on the contrary, it has been blocked midway in its journey'." (*Theological Studies* 47 [September 1986]: 533).

2. For the text of the encyclical and an excellent commentary, see Gregory Baum, *The Priority of Labor* (New York: Paulist Press, 1982).

3. *The Challenge of Peace: God's Promise and Our Response.* Pastoral Statement of the National Conference of Catholic Bishops (Boston: St. Paul Editions, 1983); *Economic Justice for All: Catholic Social Teaching and the U.S. Economy.* U.S. Bishops' Pastoral Message and Letter (*Origins* 16 [17 November 1986]: 408-55).

4. Pablo Richard, "El Vaticano, El Papa y La Teología de la Liberación Latino-Americana," *Misiones Extranjeras* 95 (September-October 1986): 344. Richard's article is a clear and balanced evaluation of the strengths and weaknesses of the instruction.

5. Quoted by Denis E. Hurley, "What Can the Church Do to Overcome Apartheid?" in *Concilium 124: The Church and the Rights of Man* (New York: Seabury, 1979): 118.

Epilogue

1. John Paul II, "Sollicitudo Rei Socialis," *Origins: NC Documentary Service* 17 (3 March 1988): 641-60. Although it was released on 19 Feb. 1988, the encyclical is dated 30 Dec. 1987. This is due to the fact that the letter was commemorating the twentieth anniversary of Paul VI's *The Progress of Peoples,* published in 1967. The citation is from no. 13.

2. Quoted in William K. Tabb, ed., *Churches in Struggle: Liberation Theologies and Social Change in North America* (New York: Monthly Review Press, 1986), 289.

3. William K. Tabb, "The Shoulds and the Excluded Whys: The U.S. Catholic Bishops Look at the Economy," in *Churches in Struggle,* 278-90. The citations are from 278-79.

Index

encyclical letters, 106-7, 129-30
Enlightenment, 42, 110
"epistemological break," 43, 183
"eschatological reserve," 51
ethical standards for human rights, 99
Eurocentric Church, 24, 109
Europe, 21, 26, 45, 57, 110, 181-82
evangelization, 73-74, 154-55, 162,
   166, 188
"evil empire," 124
exile, 77-78
experience and thinking, 43
"expert in humanity" (the church),
   158

faith, faith seeking intellectum, 116;
   Latin America and Europe, 45;
   liberation process, 140
faith-conversion, 49
"false consciousness," 62
family role, 165
"Family that Prays Together Stays
   Together," 75
Farmer, James A. Jr., 187
fatalism, 69
feudal structures, 101, 102, 193, 194
Fitzpatrick, Joseph P., 50, 184
Fourth World, 125
Freedom and Man (Murray), 12
freedom: apprentices in the uses of
   freedom, 2; freedom and human
   society, 143-44; freedom and
   liberation, 34; freedom of thought,
   139; human freedom and dominion
   over nature, 144; human rights as
   bulwark of freedom, 95-104; J. C.
   Murray, 7-18, 175; man's vocation
   to freedom, 141-44; method for
   liberating theology, 37-52; practice
   of freedom, 4; sources for a
   theology of freedom, 53-66; state of
   freedom in the world today, 135-41;
   Vatican and liberation theology,
   105-17; wars of independence, 27
Freire, Paulo, 5, 28, 31, 67-80, 81, 189
French Revolution, 110

fundamental charism of the Latin
   American Church, 33

Galilea, Segundo, 97-99
Gaudium et Spes. see *Pastoral
   Constitution on the Church*.
geographical anachronism, 45
geopolitics, 124, 132
geospirituality, 128-29
"geotheology," 22
Gera, Lucio, 55
Germany, 20, 25
God: freedom and liberation, 142;
   God and human suffering, 44; God
   as alienation, 138; sin and
   oppression, 145-46; Yahweh as
   liberator, 108, 111, 147.
   See also Holy Spirit; Jesus Christ.
Goel (bond of kinship), 170
good and evil, 62, 142, 146, 150
government, *Sollicitudo Rei Socialis*,
   125
grace, structures of sin and grace,
   119-32
Gramsci, Antonio, 26
grassroots church, 5, 81-94
Greek thought, 44
Greinacher, Norbert, 102
Gutiérrez, Gustavo, 22, 24, 29, 35,
   38-39, 55, 58, 60, 73, 79-80, 85, 181,
   188, 189

Haight, Roger, 30-31, 179
Hebblethwaite, Peter, 180
Hegel, Georg W. F., 39
Hellwig, Monika, 65, 184
Hennelly, Alfred T., 1-3, 191
Henriot, Peter, 91, 94
"hermeneutic circle," 39, 40, 62-63,
   85
"hermeneutical place," 56, 61
hermeneutical privilege of the poor,
   64-65
Hernández-Pico, Juan, 72, 188
hierarchy, Church, 111-12, 131
Hispanics in U.S., 90, 92